Law and Responsible Supply Chain Management

Corporate social responsibility (CSR) has for long been on the agenda in the business world and recently, it has also become a political agenda in the European Union. Focusing on international supply chains and their control based on studies of law in several European jurisdictions, this book aims to advance the discussion on the application and enforcement of CSR. Drawing parallels to US and Canadian law, the book explores to what extent private law tools can be used as an enforcement device and it ultimately asks if what we are witnessing is the formation of a new area of law, employing the interplay of contract and tort – a law of "production liability", as a corollary of the concept of "product liability".

Vibe Ulfbeck is a professor of private law at the Law Faculty at the University of Copenhagen.

Alexandra Andhov (JUDr., LL.M., S.J.D.) is an assistant professor of corporate law at the University of Copenhagen, Faculty of Law.

Kateřina Mitkidis is an associate professor at the Department of Law, Aarhus University.

Routledge Research in Corporate Law

Available titles in this series include:

Legal Approaches and Corporate Social Responsibility
Towards a Llewellyn's Law-Jobs Approach
Adaeze Okoye

Disqualification of Company Directors
A Comparative Analysis of the Law in the UK, Australia, South Africa, the US and Germany
Edited by Jean Jacques du Plessis and Jeanne Nel de Koker

Beyond Shareholder Wealth Maximisation
Towards a More Suitable Corporate Objective for Chinese Companies
Min Yan

Corporate Law and Financial Instability
Andreas Kokkinis

Behavioural Risks in Corporate Governance
Regulatory Intervention as a Risk Management Mechanism
Ngozi Vivian Okoye

Indonesian Company Law
Soonpeel Edgar Chang

Regulation and Inequality at Work
Isolation and Inequality Beyond the Regulation of Labour
Vanisha Sukdeo

Regulation and the Credit Rating Agencies
Restraining Ancillary Services
Daniel Cash

Law and Responsible Supply Chain Management
Contract and Tort Interplay and Overlap
Vibe Ulfbeck, Alexandra Andhov and Katerina Mitkidis

Law and Responsible Supply Chain Management

Contract and Tort Interplay and Overlap

Edited by
Vibe Ulfbeck, Alexandra Andhov and
Kateřina Mitkidis

Routledge
Taylor & Francis Group
LONDON AND NEW YORK

First published 2019
by Routledge
2 Park Square, Milton Park, Abingdon, Oxon OX14 4RN

and by Routledge
605 Third Avenue, New York, NY 10017

First issued in paperback 2021

Routledge is an imprint of the Taylor & Francis Group, an informa business

Publisher's Note
The publisher has gone to great lengths to ensure the quality of this reprint but points out that some imperfections in the original copies may be apparent.

British Library Cataloguing in Publication Data
A catalogue record for this book is available from the British Library

Library of Congress Cataloging-in-Publication Data
A catalog record has been requested for this book

Typeset in Galliard
by Taylor & Francis Books

ISBN 13: 978-1-03-224155-5 (pbk)
ISBN 13: 978-1-138-61840-4 (hbk)

DOI: 10.4324/9780429461231

Contents

List of tables

List of contributors

Alexandra Andhov (JUDr., LL.M., S.J.D.) is assistant professor of corporate law at the University of Copenhagen, Faculty of Law. Alexandra holds an S.J.D. in International Business Law from the Central European University (2015) and an LL.M in International Business Law. She has been a visiting researcher at Cornell Law School (2014) and Oxford Law School (2013). Before joining the University of Copenhagen, she was a research fellow at the Center for Integrity in Business and Government at the CEU Business School (2012–2015) and she worked with CMS Cameron McKenna in Budapest on their litigation and white-collar crime team. Alexandra's main areas of research are corporate law, corporate social responsibility and capital market law. On these topics, she has published articles in numerous European and US law journals and reviews.

Andreas Ehlers is associate professor of tort law at the University of Copenhagen, Faculty of Law. He obtained his master's degree from the University of Copenhagen in 2004 and subsequently worked for the law firm Kromann Reumert. In 2006, he was awarded the Sir Gerrard Brennan Scholarship at the University of Queensland (Australia), where he obtained an LL.M. degree in 2007. In 2011, Andreas published his PhD thesis on the doctrine of adequacy in torts. In 2017, Andreas published an LL.D. thesis on causation and personal injury. Moreover, Andreas has published several articles on tort law and related issues in Danish and foreign law journals.

Ole Hansen is a professor of private law at the Law Faculty at the University of Copenhagen. He is a co-founder and a member of the research centre the Centre for Enterprise Liability (CEVIA). His area of research is general contract law with a special emphasis on long term contracts and the interplay between public law and private law and legal aspects of private governance. His doctorate work was on construction law contracts and he is currently heading a research project on the digitalization of construction law.

Kasey McCall-Smith is a lecturer in public international law and the director of the LLM in Human Rights at the University of Edinburgh Law School. Her research and publications examine reservations rules in the law of treaties and, in particular, the way in which human rights obligations and treaty body outputs are implemented and interpreted in national legal systems. Most recently these lines of enquiry have focused on the incorporation of human rights treaties, US detention operations in Guantanamo Bay and modern slavery in global supply chains. She is currently the executive chair of the Association of Human Rights Institutes.

Kateřina Mitkidis is an associate professor at the Department of Law, Aarhus University. Kateřina's research focuses on the practice of using private law tools to advance public interests, especially in the CSR and environmental regulation areas. She has published a book on this topic, titled *Sustainability Clauses in International Business Contracts*, focusing on the interplay between sustainability goals and international contract law (Eleven International Publishing, 2015). Kateřina is also interested in the ways law and legal tools are designed and used to steer behaviour in socially and environmentally sound and responsible directions. She was a visiting scholar at Duke University (2016) and Vanderbilt University (2012). Before joining academia, Kateřina worked as legal trainee for Baker & McKenzie, Prague office, and as a junior lawyer in Hájek & Zrzavecký, Czech Republic.

Andreas Rühmkorf is a Lecturer in Commercial Law at the University of Sheffield, UK. Andreas has a PhD from the same institution and he is also admitted to the bar in Germany (*Rechtsanwalt*). His research interests are the legal regulation of CSR in global supply chains, focusing on the developing laws in this area in the home states of transnational corporations as well as company law and corporate governance. Andreas is the author of the monograph *Corporate Social Responsibility, Private Law and Global Supply Chains* (Edward Elgar Publishing, 2015). Andreas has authored several articles and book chapters about CSR in global supply chains.

Jaakko Salminen (LL.D., LL.M., M.A.) has focused on researching the role of law in enabling, structuring and governing global value chains. Focusing on a trifecta of comparative private governance, private law and transnational regulation, Jaakko's interests range from the theories, typologies and practices of governance through contract to debating the amount of liability companies should have over the environmental and labour contingencies of their transnational production chains and through which legal means. Jaakko has lectured extensively in particular at the University of Turku Faculty of Law, presented his research at numerous international conferences and participated in several externally funded research projects. In 2017, he received his doctorate for the manuscript *From National Product Liability Regimes towards Transnational Production Liability: Conceptualizing the Relationship of Law and Global Production*.

Vibe Ulfbeck is a professor of private law at the Law Faculty at the University of Copenhagen. She has an LL.M from the University of Cambridge, UK, and her doctorate work was on the topic of privity of contract, for which she received the Jorck's Prize for excellent research. She is head of the research centre the Centre for Enterprise Liability (CEVIA), of which she was one of the founders. She specializes in contract law and tort law with a special interest in private governance issues and the interplay between private law and public law. She is the author of several publications in both national and international law journals and she has been a visiting scholar at various places, including UC Berkeley, the University of San Diego (USD) and the European University Institute (EUI), Florence. Before joining academia, Vibe Ulfbeck was employed in the Danish justice department.

Louise A. Vytopil (MSc, PhD) is a senior counsel business conduct, responsible for the business partner programme at Royal FrieslandCampina N.V. After completing a bachelor's degree in Liberal Arts from University College Utrecht (2002, cum laude), she gained an MSc in Religion in Contemporary Society from the London School of Economics (2003). She then studied law at Utrecht University and practiced as a corporate lawyer. Between 2010 and 2015, she wrote a PhD dissertation titled *Contractual Control in the Supply Chain: On Corporate Social Responsibility, Codes of Conduct, Contracts and (Avoiding) Liability*, defended at Utrecht University in 2015. She is affiliated with Utrecht University as an honorary assistant professor, lecturing in – inter alia – international and European corporate law and CSR. She publishes regularly with respect to CSR, supply chains and transparency obligations and legislation for multinational corporations.

Preface

This book is the result of research that has been ongoing in CEVIA (Centre for Enterprise Liability) at the Law Faculty of the University of Copenhagen, Denmark over the past years. The work has been carried out in collaboration with external and international partners and the idea for the book grew out of the international conference "To pursue or not to pursue CSR", organized by CEVIA (University of Copenhagen), INTRAlaw (University of Aarhus) and the Horizon 2020 project, SMART (University of Oslo), and held in the autumn 2016. We would like to thank everyone who contributed to this conference with papers, comments and inspiring discussions.

The book is a contribution to the CEVIA project Private-Public Enterprise Liability, funded by the Danish Council for Independent Research, and to the SMART project.

Vibe Ulfbeck
Alexandra Andhov
Kateřina Mitkidis

1 Introduction

Vibe Ulfbeck, Alexandra Andhov and Kateřina Mitkidis

1 The concept of the supply chain and supply chain management

Increasing global interconnectedness, often subsumed under the term “‘globalization”, has led to the fragmentation of production processes. It has become feasible and economically advantageous for companies, bigger or smaller, to outsource some or most of their activities, often to Asian or South American regions.[1] However, often suppliers from these regions outsource parts of the production to further supply chain tiers. Production thus unfolds through intricate supply chains, crossing physical and jurisdictional boundaries of states and continents. Supply chains are the heart and the venous system of companies and societies. They represent a series of business transactions that starts with raw material and ends with the sale of the finished product or service.[2] During the last two decades, the coordination of these chains has been described with the term “supply chain management”.[3] While the concept of supply chain management is not formally defined,[4] one of the most cited definitions reads,

1 For example, Walmart, one of the largest global retailers, clearly stipulates that it has ‘thousands of businesses around the world that proudly call themselves Walmart supplier’; see Walmart, ‘Becoming a Supplier’ available online at: <https://corporate.walmart.com/suppliers> accessed 30 August 2018.

2 The OECD illustrates the complexity and multi-layered nature of supply chain when defining a mineral supply chain in the following way: ‘The process of bringing a raw mineral to the consumer market involves multiple actors and generally includes the extraction, transport, handling, trading, processing, smelting, refining and alloying, manufacturing and sale of end product. The term supply chain refers to the system of all the activities, organisations, actors, technology, information, resources and services involved in moving the mineral from the extraction site downstream to its incorporation in the final product for end consumers’; see OECD, *OECD Due Diligence Guidance for Responsible Supply Chains of Minerals from Conflict-Affected and High-Risk Areas* (2nd edn, OECD Publishing 2013), available online at: <www.oecd.org/corporate/mne/GuidanceEdition2.pdf> accessed 30 August 2018.

3 M C Cooper, D M Lambert, & J D Pagh, ‘Supply Chain Management: More Than a New Name for Logistics’ (1997) 8(1) The International Journal of Logistics Management 1–14.

4 J Mentzer et al., ‘Defining Supply Chain Management’ (2001) 22(2) Journal of Business Logistics 22.

> The management of upstream and downstream relationships with suppliers and customers in order to deliver superior customer value at less cost to the supply chain as a whole.[5]

Supply chains bring many advantages to companies (cost reduction, gaining access to production facilities, streamlining and increasing efficiency), to societies (employment, economic development) and to consumers (lower prices, wider product choices, increased competitiveness among companies).[6] However, supply chains also bring a series of challenges for the wellbeing of the global population, the quality of the environment, the protection of employees and the ability to reasonably use states' natural resources and raw materials. For example, it has been shown that supply chain activities contribute to global warming and the depletion of natural, non-renewable resources.[7] Ultimately, supply chains represent a foundation, but also a hazard, for economic growth and improving the standard of living and, thus, due considerations must be given to its proper regulation and organization for the benefit of all involved parties.

At the inception, supply chain management was concerned with the flow of material.[8] However, increasingly the understanding of supply chain management has broadened out to consider not only flow of material but also services, finances, information and marketing,[9] as well as the indirectly connected aspects of production, such as the impact of production processes on the environment and local communities. The indirect – social and environmental – effects have come to the

5 M Christopher, *Logistics & Supply Chain Management* (5th edn, FT Press 2016) 3.
6 On the effect of supply chains, see generally R D Klassen & D C Whybark, 'Environmental Management in Operations: The Selection of Environmental Technologies' (1999) 30(3) Decision Sciences 601–631; C R Carter, 'Purchasing Social Responsibility and Firm Performance: The Key Mediating Roles of Organizational Learning and Supplier Performance' (2005) 35(3/4) International Journal of Physical Distribution and Logistics Management 177–194; A V Roth et al., 'Unraveling the Food Supply Chain: Strategic Insights from China and the 2007 Recalls' (2008) 44(1) Journal of Supply Chain Management: A Global Review of Purchasing and Supply 22–39; G T M Hult et al., 'Supply Chain Orientation and Balanced Scorecard Performance' (2008) 20(4) Journal of Managerial Issues 526–544.
7 See generally R D Klassen & A Vereecke, 'Social Issues in Supply Chains: Capabilities Link Responsibility, Risk (Opportunity), and Performance' (2012) 140(1) International Journal of Production Economics 103–115; A Jadhav, S Orr, & M Malik, 'The Role of Supply Chain Orientation in Achieving Supply Chain Sustainability' International Journal of Production Economics (in press); B Sundarakani et al., 'Modeling Carbon Footprints Across the Supply Chain'(2010) 128(1) International Journal of Production Economics 43–50.
8 S C Graham, 'Integrating the Supply Chains' (1989) 8(8) International Journal of Physical Distribution and Materials Management 3–8. 'The objective of managing the supply chain is to synchronize the requirements of the customer with the flow of materials from suppliers in order to effect a balance between what are often seen as conflicting goals of high customer service, low inventory management, and low unit cost.'
9 J T Mentzer et al., 'Defining Supply Chain Management' (2001) 22(2) Journal of Business Logistics 4.

centre of attention especially when suppliers are based in developing economies, in which the rule of law is not as strong or possibly even absent and the governments do not pay necessary attention to protecting labour rights, human rights or the environment. A new concept of sustainable supply chain management has developed.[10]

2 The concept of CSR and sustainability

Since Milton Friedman, in 1962 in his *Capitalism and Freedom*, limited the responsibility of businesses purely to 'increase company's profits',[11] the literature on CSR has grown exponentially. With the rise of the economic power of multinational corporations, the search to find a balanced solution for the social, human rights and environmental challenges posed by them has been on the minds of international and regional organizations since the mid-1970s. The period between 1975 and 1980 saw the unveiling of three major individual initiatives relating to the social regulation of multinational corporations. First were the OECD Guidelines in 1976,[12] followed by the 1977 International Labour Organization Tripartite Declaration Concerning Multinational Enterprises and Social Policy (ILO Tripartite Declaration)[13] and the Draft UN Code of Conduct on Transnational Corporations (Draft UN Code).[14]

10 On green supply chain management, see S K Srivastava, 'Green Supply-Chain Management: A State-of-the-Art Literature Review' (2007) 9(1) International Journal of Management Reviews 54–55.

11 M Friedman, 'The Social Responsibility of Business Is to Increase its Profits' (1963) The New York Times Magazine.

12 In 1976, the OECD Guidelines were originally adopted as part of the Declaration on International Investment and Multinational Enterprises, stipulating obligations of multinational corporations as well as of individual states. The OECD Guidelines were subsequently revised six times. Current version was adopted in 2011. Available online at: <www.oecd.org/corporate/mne/oecdguidelinesformultinationalenterprises.htm> accessed 30 August 2018.

13 In the 1960s and 1970, the ILO was concerned about the activities of multinational corporations and labour-related and social policy issues were among those concerns to which the activities of MNEs gave rise. As a consequence of debate in this regard, the ILO Governing Body adopted the Tripartite Declaration of Principles concerning Multinational Enterprises and Social Policy. The most recent revision of the ILO Tripartite Declaration took place in January 2000. Available online at: <www.ilo.org/empent/Publications/WCMS_101234/lang–en/index.htm> accessed 30 August 2018.

14 The UN established the United Nations Centre on Transnational Corporations in November 1975. The purpose of the Centre was to develop a framework that would define the rights and responsibilities of multinational corporations and host-country governments, namely if operating in developing countries – the Draft UN Code. A specially appointed inter-governmental working group (the UNCTC group) began work on the code in January 1977. The Draft UN Code included numerous cross-references to the International Code of Conduct on the Transfer of Technology (negotiated by UNCTAD) as well as the ILO Tripartite Declaration. There were multiple version of the Draft UN Code. However, the negotiations were ultimately abandoned in 1992. The 1983 version is available online at: <http://investmentpoli

After this initial and important work, by the 1990s the enthusiasm for human, environmental and labour rights issues had waned. As with any policy considerations, these were changed for some others. However, what remained was the common understanding of the importance of CSR in global business operations. The UNCTC group,[15] despite fierce disagreements leading to the Draft UN Code's remaining only a draft, was able to agree on what they understood as "CSR".[16] The concept comprised (1) human rights, (2) environmental and (3) consumer protection obligations.[17] It is important to remember that this was only the 1990s, when the majority of the EU consumer protection regulation was not yet in place.

Currently, the regulatory environment works with various CSR definitions, although one could say that these are close to one another. The EU understands CSR as the responsibility of companies for their impact on society.[18] The concept of CSR is often used in parallel to or even interchangeably with the concept of sustainability. Sustainable development has been introduced as a goal to strive for within international environmental law, later expanding into other areas as well.[19] Currently sustainability is widely understood as defined by the Brundtland Commission in 1987: 'Sustainable development is development that meets the needs of the present without compromising the ability of future generations to meet their own needs.'[20] The principle of sustainable development speaks to all parts of society and it could be argued that it should lead action at all international, states, companies and individual levels.[21]

cyhub.unctad.org/Download/TreatyFile/2891> accessed 30 August 2018. For more on the Draft UN Code, see K P Sauvant, 'The Negotiations of the United Nations Code of Conduct on Transnational Corporations: Experience and Lessons Learned' (2015) 16(1) The Journal of World Investment and Trade 11–87.

15 Ibid.

16 J Zerk, 'Towards an International Law of CSR?' In *Multinationals and Corporate Social Responsibility: Limitations and Opportunities in International Law* (Cambridge University Press 2006) 245–248.

17 UNCTC, 'Transnational Corporations, Services and the Uruguay Round' UN Doc. ST/CTC/103 (UN 1990) 175 and 177.

18 Communication from the Commission to the European Parliament, the Council, the European Economic and Social Committee and the Committee of the Regions: A renewed EU strategy 2011–14 for Corporate Social Responsibility, COM/2011/0681 final.

19 D Ebner & R J Baumgartner 'The Relationship Between Sustainable Development and Corporate Social Responsibility' Corporate Responsibility Research Conference 4–5 September 2006, Dublin, 2, available at <http://citeseerx.ist.psu.edu/viewdoc/download?doi=10.1.1.485.5912&rep=rep1&type=pdf> accessed 21 August 2018.

20 UN, *Report of the World Commission on Environment and Development: Our Common Future* (20 March 1987) transmitted to the General Assembly as an Annex to document A/42/427 – 'Development and International Cooperation: Environment'.

21 For example, Article 3(3) of the Treaty on European Union (Consolidated Version of the Treaty on European Union (TEU) [2012] OJ C 326/13) reads as follows: '...It shall work for the sustainable development of Europe based on balanced economic growth and price stability, a highly competitive social market economy, aiming at full employment and social progress, and a high level of protection and improvement of the quality of the environment...'

While neither of the terms – "CSR" or "sustainability" – has a universal legal definition, we may detect a common theme of balancing human rights, environmental, social and economic interests. Nowadays, CSR thus refers to the pursuance of societal goals by corporations, such as social and environmental well-being and respect for human rights as agreed by the UN in 1990, but has increasingly covered other areas such as the fight against corruption or gender equality. It is primarily company-driven, although increasingly more regulation is adopted by states on national and supranational levels to ensure greater social and human rights protection, environmentally sound management and the elimination of corruption practices. These "new" regulations aim to inspire and indirectly steer companies' responsible behaviour rather than impose specific business conduct with respect to business, social and environmental impacts. An example is one of the most recent acts, the Modern Slavery Act 2015 (MSA), adopted by the British Parliament on March 26, 2015.[22] The MSA has been also called "Transparency in Supply Chains", which suggests the principal aim of this recent legislation is to oblige companies to disclose the steps they have taken in the last financial year to ensure their business and supply chains are free from modern slavery and human trafficking.[23] Hence, what we observe is that new regulations and legislations are adopted in order to target diverse aspects of CSR and to support the sustainability efforts of national governments and international communities.

3 The concept of sustainable supply chains

Combining supply chains and sustainability/CSR amounts to sustainable supply chains. Yet, what does "sustainable supply chain" mean exactly?

Walmart, one of the largest global retailers, sells its goods to nearly 270 million customers, who visit more than '11,700 stores under 65 banners in 28 countries and e-commerce websites', while employing approximately 2.3 million associates worldwide.[24] Given the economic position of companies like these, they usually have some kind of control over their supply chains. On this basis one could argue that these companies, which are sometimes called "chain leaders", should not only enjoy the benefits of complex supply chains, but also be responsible for the behaviour within them to the extent of their control and power.

In line with this, one of the most recent business and human rights initiatives emanating from the UN, the 2011 Guiding Principles (Guiding Principles),[25]

22 The MSA came into force on 31 July 2015, available online at: <www.legislation.gov.uk/ukpga/2015/30/contents/enacted> accessed 30 August 2018.

23 Section 54 of the MSA obliges the multinational corporations (those of at least £36 million in worldwide revenue) to publish a *transparency statement.*

24 Walmart, 'Our Story' available online at: <https://corporate.walmart.com/our-story> accessed 30 August 2018.

25 Human Rights Council, 'Guiding Principles on Business and Human Rights: Implementing the United Nations' "Protect, Respect and Remedy" Framework: Report of the Special Representative of the Secretary-General on the issue of Human Rights and Transnational Corporations and Other Business Enterprises', A/HRC/17/31 (21

stipulates that a company's responsibility with regard to human rights applies not only to the company's 'own activities' but also to those impacts that are 'directly linked to their operations, products or services by their business relationships, even if they have not contributed to those impacts.'[26] The Commentary to the Guiding Principles clarifies that business relationships include 'business partners, entities, in its value chain, and any other non-state or state entity directly linked to its business operations, products or services.'[27] The Guiding Principles thus clearly foresee that companies' responsibility to respect human rights goes beyond the bounds of the company itself and its direct subsidiaries.

As a consequence, the proper organization of supply chains is an area of increasing strategic importance for every business, due to the many unforeseeable and potentially unrecognized legal risks and liabilities related to it, including daunting reputational loss and ultimately the loss of customers.[28] Hence, multinational corporations as chain leaders, particularly those with well-known brands, have come under increasing public pressure to show that they are responsible, that they care for the workers in their supply chains and consider protection of the environment in all affected countries – in other words, to show that they function as sustainable supply chains. Consequently, companies have started to implement CSR-related provisions and instruments into their supply chain contracts and to develop codes of conduct and other corporate policies as tools for implementing CSR throughout their supply chains. In addition, an increasing number of companies, especially large multinational corporations, have implemented environmental annual reports and sustainability strategies.

4 The aim of this book

The phenomenon of the supply chain has received considerable academic interest in recent years, covering predominantly issues of logistics, logistics management, operations management, transactional cost economics, supply chain economics, product design, marketing, distribution channels and warehousing, to name a few. For the rising interest in the organization of supply chains, researchers from many disciplines with different research approaches and knowledge have found a common interest. This group of various researchers has been joined recently by legal researchers, who have been analyzing legal aspects and legal risks of supply chains.[29]

March 2011). Available online at: <www.ohchr.org/Documents/Publications/GuidingPrinciplesBusinessHR_EN.pdf> accessed 30 August 2018.

26 Ibid., Principle 13.

27 Ibid.

28 Q Wang, J Dou, & S Jia, 'A Meta-Analytic Review of Corporate Social Responsibility and Corporate Financial Performance: The Moderating Effect of Contextual Factors' (2016) 55(8) Business & Society 1083.

29 See generally: A L Stoler, 'Transnational Corporations and the Global Supply Chain' in A Stoler, J Redden, & L Jackson (eds), *Trade and Poverty Reduction in the Asia-Pacific Region: Case Studies and Lessons from Low-income Communities* (Cambridge

The aim of this publication is to contribute to the growing research and literature on supply chains and the law, and to advance the discussion on the operations and enforcement of CSR in international supply chains. However, whereas much research so far has focused on CSR principles as developed at the international and regional level, this publication focuses on private law issues related to sustainable supply chain management. The reason for this is that international law tools and soft law instruments suffer from the weakness that they are not directly binding on companies and not enforceable upon companies by courts of law. Private law, in contrast, offers tools such as contract and tort law that can – in principle – form the basis of enforcement in courts of law. The book explores to what extent these private law tools can be used as an enforcement device with regard to responsible supply chain management. In this respect, it focuses on the liability of both the chain leader and the supplier and it examines both contract law and tort law avenues to liability.

5 Methodology

The book focuses on European private law. The reason for this is that, although supply chain activities often take place in the developing world, the legal systems in these places of the world are, for historical reasons going back to colonial times, often based on European law, including English law, French law and German law. Thus, although rules on private international law may lead to the result that a case must be decided in accordance with the law in a country in the developing world, the relevant legal system will often be based on a European legal tradition.

The book takes a "European private law approach". Thus, some of the chapters focus primarily on one legal system that has been chosen as an example. However, other chapters do not provide a fully jurisdictionally focused or legal comparative analysis. Rather they attempt to capture general private law rules and principles that are common in various European jurisdictions to draw up a picture of a general development. This method could be called a "semi-abstract" method in that it sits itself in between a very abstract approach that can be carried out entirely detached from actual legal systems and a very detailed approach that can only be carried out by focusing on a specific national legal system. This "semi-abstract" method can in part be based on the numerous comparative studies that have by now been carried out in different areas of private law identifying common trends and principles and on work done with the goal of trying to identify or suggest common European principles of private law, such as the Draft Common Frame of

University Press 2009); J Nolan, 'Human Rights and Global Corporate Supply Chains' in S Deva & D Bilchitz (eds), *Building a Tray on Business and Human Rights: Context and Contours* (Cambridge University Press 2017) 238–265; D Kaufmann, A Kraay, & M Mastruzzi, 'The Worldwide Governance Indicators: Methodology and Analytical Issues' (2011) 3(2) Hague Journal on the Rule of Law 220–246, or M Miller, 'Corporate Codes of Conduct and Working Conditions in the Global Supply Chain' in J Martin & K Bravo (eds), *The Business and Human Rights Landscape: Moving Forward, Looking Back* (Cambridge University Press 2015) 432–467.

Reference (DCFR), the Principles of European Tort Law (PETL) and the Principles of European Contract Law (PECL). In the book, case law and legal concepts originating in other jurisdictions, in particular in the US, are used to enlighten the discussion where relevant.

Already now, a number of studies have been carried out on the topic of the relationship between private law and CSR. For instance, Mitkidis, in her work *Sustainability Clauses in International Business Contracts*, has presented a contractual analysis of the use of sustainability clauses in the light of "international contract law".[30] Similarly, Beckers, in her work *Enforcing Corporate Social Responsibility Codes: On Global Self-Regulation and National Law*, has carried out an analysis of codes of conduct from the perspectives of contract law, tort law and unfair commercial practices law in both German law and English law.[31] Furthermore, Vytopil, in the monograph *Contractual Control in the Supply Chain. On Corporate Social Responsibility, Codes of Conduct, Contracts and (Avoiding) Liability*, has analyzed codes of conduct in both contract law and tort law perspectives in Dutch law, UK law and Californian law.[32] Finally, Rühmkorf, in the monograph *Corporate Social Responsibility, Private Law and Global Supply Chains*, has analyzed CSR issues in the context of UK contract law.[33] This volume builds on these works in looking into contract law and tort law in the light of the latest developments in case law. It then goes one step further by identifying some new themes that have not previously been dealt with, namely the question of interplay and overlap between contract and tort with regard to supply chain liability issues. Moreover, the interplay between the legal regimes gives rise to some liability dilemmas that are also dealt with in the book. One of them concerns the liability of the chain leader and the problem that, on one hand, the chain leader is encouraged in a variety of ways to take contractual control with the supply chain, whilst taking contractual control, on the other hand, may lead to tortious liability towards third parties. Another liability dilemma concerns the liability of the supplier and the tension between the societal push to impose CSR obligations on the supplier to create benefits for external third parties, and, at the same time, the need to protect the supplier as the weaker party in the internal relation vis à vis the chain leader. In observing the overlap between contracts and torts, the book ultimately asks if what we are witnessing is the formation of a new area of enterprise liability law in the shape of a "production liability", as a corollary of the concept of "product liability".

30 K Peterkova Mitkidis, *Sustainability Clauses in International Business Contracts* (Eleven International Publishing 2015).*Sustainability clauses in international business contracts* (Eleven International Publishing 2015).

31 A Beckers, *Enforcing Corporate Social Responsibility Codes: On Global Self-Regulation and National Law* (Hart Publishing 2015).

32 A L Vytopil, *Contractual Control in the Supply Chain. On Corporate Social Responsibility, Codes of Conduct, Contracts and (Avoiding) Liability* (Eleven International Publishing 2015).

33 A Rühmkorf, *Corporate Social Responsibility, Private Law and Global Supply Chains* (Edward Elgar 2015).

Facing the abundance of definitions of CSR and sustainability concepts, the contributors to this volume adopt their own definition of the concept to the extent necessary in order to allow for the readers' understanding of the legal analysis.

6 Chapters and the red thread

The book starts with an introductory chapter (Chapter 1) that reflects on the concept of CSR in supply chains. The Introduction represents the starting point for all the readers who are not necessarily fully familiar with the notion of CSR and the notion of sustainable supply chains. The introduction also discloses the delimitation of the book and the understanding of major concepts used throughout the book. Subsequently, the book is built on three pillars.

Part I analyzes contract law and CSR. The purpose of Chapter 2 is to introduce and assess the phenomenon of incorporation of public international CSR soft law standards into codes of conduct that are meant to govern, *inter alia*, the relationship between the chain leader and the supplier. The chapter starts with a review of terms and conditions of 30 FTSE 100 companies' supplier codes, revealing a direct reference to international CSR tools. Based on this observation, the chapter continues to critically assess the business practice of directly incorporating international soft law standards into codes of conduct from both a public international law and a private law perspective. Chapter 3 builds on Chapter 2 and asks the consequent question, which is under which circumstances CSR obligations found, *inter alia*, in codes of conduct may become part of the contract and enforceable by means of contract law and to what extent there may be a need to protect the supplier as the weaker party against enforcement. Following this chapter, Chapter 4 focuses on the critical issue of the doctrine of privity of contract. Even though the use of CSR clauses has become a widespread practice, CSR contractual clauses are often disconnected from the contract's subject matter. They primarily protect the interests of third parties, such as suppliers' employees, inhabitants of the contract performance location, other businesses or simply the public in general. This naturally leads to asking whether these third parties are legally empowered to enforce such contractual provisions. The chapter analyzes this question in order to assess whether there is a realistic possibility for succeeding in enforcement by third parties.

Following the contract law part, Part II focuses on tort law and responsible supply chains. Chapter 5 starts where Part I ends, focusing on the rights of third parties and assessing the potential for both direct and vicarious liability of the chain leader for the acts and omissions of contractual partners–suppliers. Across the globe, particularly in developing countries, disasters have occurred due to factories' not having taken sufficient safety measures to protect their employees and the environment. In many cases, the applicable law allows for injured parties to recover against the immediate tortfeasor (the supplier). However, such remedy is often only theoretical. In practice, there are several obstacles to successful enforcement. For this reason, the harmed party may wish to explore the possibility of suing other interested parties. This chapter focuses on the question of whether the chain leader may be held liable in tort law for the supplier's workers' injuries and environmental harm caused by a supplier. Chapter 6 moves a step further, towards the position of consumers. It examines the extent to which new transparency requirements may pave the way for tort law claims raised by consumers on the basis of the notion of false advertisement. This chapter examines under which circumstances a company can be held liable vis-à-vis a consumer on the basis of the European Union's Unfair Commercial Practices Directive and under which circumstances corporate CSR statements could give rise to such liability.

In Part III, this book concludes the legal inquiry into CSR enforcement by focusing on the interplay and overlap between tort and contract. This approach is largely lacking in the existing literature. The analyses in Part III of the book rely on the analyses undertaken in Parts I and II of contract law and tort law. Chapter 7 analyzes different ways in which contract law and tort law interact in a supply chain setting. The focus is on situations in which actions brought under tort law may trigger contractual reactions and vice versa. Notably, the chapter reflects on the consequences of the application of the criterion of contractual "control" as a central element in the tort liability standard applicable with regard to the chain leader's liability. Chapter 8 ultimately shows that there might be lessons to be learned from the development of product liability with a view to establishing a new concept of "production liability". Current product liability regimes can be seen as a "marriage" of contract and tort that overcomes the deficiencies inherent in causes of action under both liability regimes. This chapter illustrates the possibility and justification for a similar marriage of contract and tort in developing supply chain liability.

Bibliography

Beckers A, *Enforcing Corporate Social Responsibility Codes: On Global Self-Regulation and National Law* (Hart Publishing 2015).

Carter C R, 'Purchasing Social Responsibility and Firm Performance: The Key Mediating Roles of Organizational Learning and Supplier Performance' (2005) 35(3/4) *International Journal of Physical Distribution and Logistics Management* 177–194.

Christopher M, *Logistics & Supply Chain Management* (5th edn, FT Press 2016) 3.

Cooper M C, Lambert D M, & Pagh J D, 'Supply Chain Management: More Than a New Name for Logistics' (1997) 8(1) *The International Journal of Logistics Management* 1–14.

Ebner D & Baumgartner R J, 'The Relationship Between Sustainable Development and Corporate Social Responsibility' Corporate Responsibility Research Conference4–5 September 2006, Dublin, 2, available at <http://citeseerx.ist.psu.edu/viewdoc/download?doi=10.1.1.485.5912&rep=rep1&type=pdf> accessed 21 August 2018.

Friedman M, 'The Social Responsibility of Business is to Increase its Profits' (1963) *The New York Times*, September 13, 1970: 32–33.

Graham S C, 'Integrating the Supply Chains' (1989) 8(8) *International Journal of Physical Distribution and Materials Management* 3–8.

Hult G T M *et al.*, 'Supply Chain Orientation and Balanced Scorecard Performance' (2008) 20(4) *Journal of Managerial Issues* 526–544.

Jadhav A, Orr S, & Malik M, 'The Role of Supply Chain Orientation in Achieving Supply Chain Sustainability' (in press) *International Journal of Production Economics.*

Kaufmann D, Kraay A, & Mastruzzi M, 'The Worldwide Governance Indicators: Methodology and Analytical Issues' (2011) 3(2) *Hague Journal on the Rule of Law* 220–246.

Klassen R D & Vereecke A, 'Social Issues in Supply Chains: Capabilities Link Responsibility, Risk (Opportunity), and Performance' (2012) 140(1) *International Journal of Production Economics.*

Klassen R D & Whybark D C, 'Environmental Management in Operations: The Selection of Environmental Technologies' (1999) 30(3) *Decision Sciences* 601–631.

Mentzer J et al. 'Defining Supply Chain Management' (2001) 22(2) *Journal of Business Logistics* 22.

Miller M, 'Corporate Codes of Conduct and Working Conditions in the Global Supply Chain' in Martin J & Bravo K (eds), *The Business and Human Rights Landscape: Moving Forward, Looking Back* (Cambridge University Press 2015).

Nolan J, 'Human Rights and Global Corporate Supply Chains' in Deva S & Bilchitz D (eds), *Building a Tray on Business and Human Rights: Context and Contours* (Cambridge University Press 2017).

Peterkova Mitkidis K, *Sustainability Clauses in International Business Contracts* (Eleven International Publishing 2015).

Roth A V *et al.*, 'Unraveling the Food Supply Chain: Strategic Insights from China and the 2007 Recalls' (2008) 44(1) *Journal of Supply Chain Management: A Global Review of Purchasing and Supply* 22–39.

Rühmkorf A, *Corporate Social Responsibility, Private Law and Global Supply Chains* (Edward Elgar 2015)

Sauvant K P, 'The Negotiations of the United Nations Code of Conduct on Transnational Corporations: Experience and Lessons Learned' (2015) 16(1) *The Journal of World Investment and Trade* 11–87.

Srivastava S K, 'Green Supply-Chain Management: A State-of-the-Art Literature Review' (2007) 9(1) *International Journal of Management Reviews* 54–55.

Stoler A L, 'Transnational Corporations and the Global Supply Chain' in Stoler A, Redden J, & Jackson L (eds), *Trade and Poverty Reduction in the Asia-Pacific Region: Case Studies and Lessons from Low-income Communities* (Cambridge University Press 2009).

Sundarakani B *et al.*, 'Modeling Carbon Footprints Across the Supply Chain' (2010) 128 (1) *International Journal of Production Economics* 43–50.

Vytopil A L, *Contractual Control in the Supply Chain: On Corporate Social Responsibility, Codes of Conduct, Contracts and (Avoiding) Liability* (Eleven International Publishing 2015).

Wang Q, Dou J, & Jia S, 'A Meta-Analytic Review of Corporate Social Responsibility and Corporate Financial Performance: The Moderating Effect of Contextual Factors' (2016) 55(8) *Business & Society* 1083.

Zerk J, 'Towards an International Law of CSR?' in *Multinationals and Corporate Social Responsibility: Limitations and Opportunities in International Law* (Cambridge University Press 2006) 245–248.

Part I

CONTRACT LAW

2 From international law to national law

The opportunities and limits of contractual CSR supply chain governance

Kasey McCall-Smith and Andreas Rühmkorf

1 Introduction

Transnational Corporations (TNCs) with global supply chains regularly incorporate a supplier code of conduct into their relations with their suppliers.[1] These codes stipulate Corporate Social Responsibility (CSR) obligations. Whilst there are different methods of incorporating supplier codes of conduct into the supply chain, a common method is through contracts, which is the focus of this chapter. Hard and soft international law instruments such as International Labour Organization (ILO) conventions and the UN Global Compact often feature in documents such as the supplier codes of conduct.

This chapter explores the potential gap-bridging role of contract law as a means of giving force to international CSR standards, through the imposition of CSR obligations on companies in other countries through supply chain contracts. Therefore the discussion considers the ways in which CSR standards can become an enforceable part of a contract. It will assess the opportunities and limitations that the use of and reference to international law instruments in supply contracts provides for the promotion of CSR in global supply chains. The chapter focuses on English law, the frequent law of choice in international sales contracts, even where neither of the contracting parties is UK-based.[2]

The chapter is divided into three parts. The first is the data analysis of the practice of using contract law as an instrument for imposing international standards on suppliers. Supplier codes of conduct and, where available, terms and conditions of purchase of 30 FTSE100 companies are examined. This analysis reveals the international law standards most commonly referenced by TNCs vis-à-vis their suppliers. We examine how these standards are used in supplier contracts, i.e. are the international standards simply mentioned in the supplier code of

1 Details of data analysis on file with the authors. S S Thorsen & S Jeppensen, 'Changing Course – A Study into Responsible Supply Chain Management' (2011) Global CSR and Copenhagen Business School for the Danish Ministry 9.

2 See E McKendrick, *Contract Law* (8th edn, Palgrave Macmillan 2009) 10.

conduct by general or specific reference or are they expressly incorporated into supply chain contracts?

The second part then critically assesses the business practice of incorporating international standards into supply contracts from both a public international law and a contract law perspective. It explores the opportunities and the limitations that this linkage provides for the promotion of CSR in global supply chains. Issues that this practice raises from an international law perspective are, *inter alia*, the barriers to applicability in international law as well as the respective use of hard and soft law instruments. From a contract law perspective, the linkage of international and national law concerns issues such as drafting, incorporation, enforcement and the privity of contract doctrine.

Thirdly, the chapter assesses the implications of this international law–national contract law interaction in the context of CSR in global supply chains. This assessment includes the hybridised regulatory system that is created and the important role of legislation on CSR in global supply chains in the home-states of TNCs (such as transparency laws) as well as adequate enforcement mechanisms.

In terms of its terminology, the chapter refers to both the supply chain management of TNCs and to supply chain contracts. Supply chain management is the planning and management of all activities involved in sourcing and procurement and all logistics management activities. It also includes coordination and collaboration with partners, particularly suppliers.[3] The literature on supply chain management thus usually focuses on issues such as purchasing, cost and quality of the goods.[4] The inclusion of CSR policies in supply chain management by companies is referred to as responsible supply chain management.[5] To that end, companies usually develop a supplier code of conduct, which they incorporate into their relationships with their suppliers in different ways and to varying legal effects.[6] One way of including the supplier code of conduct in the relationship with the supplier company is through contracts, since contract law provides the framework for the purchasing of goods.[7]

This chapter contributes to the existing literature that analyses the use of CSR in supply chain contracts by focusing on the use of international law standards, which is an issue that has, so far, only played a minor role in the academic literature. There is significant literature on the incorporation of CSR in supply chain

3 See for an introduction into supply chain management S Chopra & P Meindl, *Supply Chain Management: Strategy, Planning, and Operation* (5th edn, Pearson Education 2013).
4 R M Monczka et al., *Purchasing & Supply Chain Management* (South-Western 2010).
5 See: M van Opijnen & J Oldenziel, *Responsible Supply Chain Management: Potential Success Factors and Challenges for Addressing Prevailing Human Rights and other CSR Issues in Supply Chains of EU-based Companies* (CREM and SOMO for the European Commission 2011).
6 A Millington, 'Responsibility in the Supply Chain' in A Crane et al. (eds), *The Oxford Handbook of Corporate Social Responsibility* (Oxford University Press 2008) 365.
7 Ibid., 358.

contracts, which primarily consists of doctrinal, socio-legal and empirical studies of the use of CSR in such buyer-supplier contracts.[8]

2 The use of international law standards in global supply chains

In this section, the findings of data analysis of how listed, UK-based TNCs incorporate international law standards on CSR into their supply chain management are presented. The analysis covers supplier codes of conduct and, where available, terms and conditions of purchase of 30 FTSE100 companies.

The methodology employed involved the selection of 30 FTSE100 companies with an international supplier base and international operations. We examined TNCs' supplier codes of conduct, standard terms and conditions of purchase or any other additional information on the TNCs' use of international CSR standards. Given their size and public standing, FTSE100 companies were selected due to the amount of publicly available information on their websites. Table 2.1 shows a preponderance of the secondary and tertiary economic sectors among the companies selected due to the decreasing size of the primary economic sector in developed countries.

The documentary sources analysed by the authors 'provide a rich source of data'[9] though the analysis inevitably is influenced by the nature of the documents. As such, the key inquiry was the content and wording of the documents in terms of international CSR standards. For example, we were interested to understand how contract law may or may not give legal force to international CSR standards; therefore, stringency was a criterion against which the wording of the documents was examined.

This approach has limitations and advantages. A limitation is that the companies were selected expressly due to their international operations, not randomly chosen. Also, whilst all companies published their supplier codes of conduct online, few publicised their standard terms and conditions of purchase. We focused on documents in the public domain, as transparency is a cornerstone of effective CSR.[10] It

8 See, for example, K Peterkova Mitkidis, *Sustainability Clauses in International Business Contracts* (Eleven International Publishing 2015); L Vytopil, *Contractual Control in the Supply Chain: On Corporate Social Responsibility, Codes of Conduct, Contracts and (Avoiding) Liability* (Eleven International Publishing 2015); A Beckers, *Enforcing Corporate Social Responsibility Codes: On Global Self-Regulation and National Private Law* (Hart Publishing 2015); F Cafaggi, 'Regulation through Contracts: Supply-Chain Contracting and Sustainability Standards' (2016) 12(3) European Review of Contract Law 1; D McBarnet & M Kurkchiyan, 'Corporate Social Responsibility through Contractual Control? Global Supply Chains and "Other Regulation"' in D McBarnet, A Voiculescu, & T Campbell (eds), *The New Corporate Accountability: Corporate Social Responsibility and the Law* (Cambridge University Press 2007) 59.

9 L Webley, 'Qualitative Approaches to Empirical Legal Research' in P Cane & H Kritzer (eds), *The Oxford Handbook of Empirical Legal Research* (Oxford University Press 2010) 938.

10 UN Office of the High Commissioner for Human Rights, *The Corporate Responsibility to Respect Human Rights: An Interpretive Guide* (UN Doc HR/PUB/12/02 2012) 25.

Table 2.1 Sectors and business areas of the 30 companies

Primary	*Secondary*	*Tertiary*
Mining Anglo American, BHP Billiton, Randgold, Rio Tinto	*Retail and consumer goods* Diaego, Marks & Spencer, Next, Reckitt Benckiser, Unilever, Tesco, Burberry, British American Tobacco, Imperial Brands, Sainsbury's	*Hotels* Intercontinental Hotels
-	*Defence, automobiles, automotive/aerospace components* GKN, BAE Systems, Rolls Royce	*Outsourcing and communications* Bunzl, British Telecom Group, Vodafone
	Pharmaceuticals and medical equipment Astra Zeneca, GlaxoSmithKline, Hikma Pharmaceuticals, Smith & Nephew	*Inspection and product testing* Intertek
	Chemicals Johnson Matthey	
	Energy industry and petroleum Centrica, Royal Dutch Shell, BP	

Table 2.2 Frequency of incorporation/reference to international CSR standards

International CSR standard	*Frequency of use*
Universal Declaration of Human Rights	19x
International Labour Organisation conventions/labour standards	19x
UN Global Compact	17x
Ethical Trading Initiative Base Code	6x
The UN Guiding Principles on Business and Human Rights	5x
OECD Guidelines for Multinational Enterprises	4x

is therefore possible that companies use international CSR standards in ways that are not visible from an outside perspective.

The advantage of documentary analysis is that it allowed us access to a larger set of companies than would have been possible through an in-depth study of a few companies. This provided greater insight on the actual use of international CSR standards by leading UK-listed companies. Thus examining these documents enabled detection of similarities and differences from a larger sample and greater insight into not only how often international standards are used, but also how they are used, such as through direct incorporation into a supplier code of conduct. Effectively, documents were examined to determine how they used international CSR standards, such as whether the supplier code is based on a particular international standard, the results of which are shown in Table 2.2. Furthermore, doctrinal legal assessment of the documents underpins the following analysis about the wording and enforceability of these documents.

Table 2.1 shows the economic sector and business areas of the companies examined representing a cross-industry study, including pharmaceuticals, retail, fashion, mining, oil and gas and telecommunication. The focus is the information they publish about CSR in their supply chain, particularly their supplier code of conduct, and what these documents say about international CSR standards. Both CSR and/or sustainability sections of each website were examined, as it appears that in business practice these terms are increasingly used interchangeably.[11] CSR/sustainability reports were not examined, as our analysis focused on the ways TNCs use international CSR standards vis-à-vis their suppliers and these reports contain little information that adds to the aim of the analysis.

Our understanding of CSR is based on two definitions: First, the definition adopted by the European Commission in its 2011 Communication on CSR, in which it defines CSR as 'the responsibility of enterprises for their impacts on society'.[12] Whilst this definition shows that CSR can be both mandatory and voluntary, it does not say much about its content. We therefore also adopt the following definition from Campbell and Vick:

> At a minimum the term implies an obligation on the part of large companies to pursue objectives advancing the interests of all groups affected by their activities – not just shareholders but also employees, consumers, suppliers, creditors and local communities. These interests are not just economic, but also include environmental, human rights and 'quality of life' concerns. The obligation to be socially responsible is usually conceived of as being over and above the minimum requirement imposed on companies by formal legal rules, although this is not invariably the case.[13]

Table 2.2 presents the frequency with which different international CSR standards are used in the supply chain documents of the 30 companies assessed. Where the documents, such as the supplier code of conduct, refer to more than one international standard, each standard mentioned was counted. The issue of

11 The Institute for Human Rights and Business (IHRB) uses the terms interchangeably; see S S Thorsen, 'Are Current Approaches to Responsible Supply Chain Management Working?' (12 August 2010) Institute for Human Rights and Business <www.ihrb.org/focus-areas/commodities/commentary-current-approaches-responsible-supply-chain-management-working> accessed 25 May 2018; R Strand, RE Freeman, & K Hockerts, 'Corporate Social Responsibility and Sustainability in Scandinavia: An Overview' (2015) 127(1) Journal of Business Ethics 1, 2.

12 European Commission, 'Communication from the Commission to the European Parliament, the Council, the European Economic and Social Committee and the Committee of the Regions: A Renewed EU Strategy 2011–14 for Corporate Social Responsibility' COM (2011) 681 final, para. 3.1.

13 K Campbell & D Vick, 'Disclosure Law and the Market for Corporate Social Responsibility' in D McBarnet et al. (eds), *The New Corporate Accountability* (Cambridge University Press 2007) 242.

referencing more than one standard (combination of different standards) is addressed following Table 2.2.

This analysis revealed the following findings. First, the supply chain documents analysed demonstrate a widespread reference to international CSR standards. Twenty-nine of the 30 companies analysed refer to or incorporate different international CSR standards into their supplier codes of conduct.[14] Second, Table 2.2 conveys that the most widely referenced international documents are the United Nations Universal Declaration of Human Rights (UDHR), the conventions and labour standards set out by the International Labour Organisation (ILO) and the UN Global Compact. Third, we find that many TNCs state that the provisions in their supplier code of conduct are based on international CSR standards, which are, in turn, labelled as 'reference points'.[15] By this the companies suggest that their supplier codes are based on one or more of the international standards in Table 2.2. For example, this can mean that there are provisions, such as on forced and child labour, that are based on the principles found in the international standards to which the code makes reference. Fourth, the documents assessed address a range of CSR issues, from labour standards (e.g. working hours, prohibition of child and forced labour) to environmental issues and bribery. The frequent reference to variable international CSR standards indicates an interaction between public international law and national contract law in global supply chains. The remainder of this chapter assesses this interaction.

3 International law perspectives

Global supply chains raise many issues in international law due to their transnational nature and the human capital that is part and parcel of all supply chains. Not only is the role of individuals in the supply chain a primary consideration, but the positive and negative influences of suppliers on the local population and environment in which they operate are also a concern. Thus, from an international legal perspective, there is a clear opportunity to contribute to the social and economic development of the local community through entrenchment of human rights, the rule of law, poverty alleviation and sustainable development, reflecting the broad range of international agreements covering these topics.[16] However, due to poor implementation and enforcement of states' international obligations or the absence of national law, international standards for the protection of individual's rights and the environment are often ignored by supply chain contributors in

14 The only company that does not refer to any international standard is BAE Systems. See for example BAE's Supplier Code of Conduct 'Supplier Principles: Guidance for Responsible Business 2016'.

15 See for example Vodafone, *Code of Ethical Purchasing, Version 2.0*, References.

16 See for example ILO *Resolution Concerning Decent Work in Global Supply Chains*, 'Conclusions' (105th Session, Geneva 8 July 2016), para. 1–2; Traidcraft/CORE, 'Above the Law? Time to Hold Irresponsible Companies to Account' (November 2015) <www.traidcraft.co.uk/media.ashx/above-the-law-nov-15-final.pdf> accessed 23 May 2018.

order to maximise the economic value of their input. This pits economic value against societal values and is the tension that responsible supply chain management must navigate. As the last three decades of business and human rights discourse have revealed, while the international community continues to establish legal standards of human rights protection, the only actors from which it may demand compliance are states.

In the increasingly globalised world, international law is, however, slowly adapting to evolving actors on the international legal plane. While sovereignty and the supremacy of the state remain guiding principles, international law and practice have engendered a gradual increase in legal personality for individuals, international organisations and TNCs.[17] These three categories of international actors relate uniquely to the consideration of global supply chains and their management. This section considers how international law struggles to ensure responsibly managed supply chains and the role of variable forms of international law relied upon in the context of protecting against supply chain mismanagement. It begins with a brief overview of international legal actors and how international law endows each with limited rights and duties. It then proceeds to examine a number of international laws designed to improve the relationship between corporate activity and individual human rights holders through global supply chain management. Finally, the relationship between international law and contract law in protecting against irresponsible supply chain management will be introduced.

3.1 Addressing actors in global supply chains

The inability of public international law to regulate global supply chains stems from its very nature as a body of law designed to govern relations between states. Admittedly, this definition is no longer strictly applicable,[18] yet the adjudicatory mechanisms of international law remain, strictly speaking, open to states or, in the realm of human rights, open to individuals in claims against states. Accessing justice against a transnational corporation directly at the international level is not currently an option and therefore other legal approaches, including actions in tort and contract law at the national level, are inevitably necessary to construct an accountability framework. International human rights courts, such as the European Court of Human Rights and the Inter-American Court of Human Rights have permitted a minor circumnavigation of this situation in limited circumstances where a state facilitated or was complicit in permitting a corporation to act in a way that impeded the rights of individuals. These cases have generally been framed as environmental harms resulting in a breach of human rights similar to private law

17 The present authors have elaborated this elsewhere, K McCall-Smith & A Rühmkorf, 'Reconciling Human Rights and Supply Chain Management through Corporate Social Responsibility' in V R Abou-Nigm, K McCall-Smith, & D French (eds), *Linkages and Boundaries in Private and Public International Law* (Hart Publishing 2018) 147–173.

18 R Higgins, *Problems & Process: International Law and How to Use It* (Clarendon Press 1995) 12.

tort claims or nuisance claims for conduct occurring within – or, in the case of the Inter-American Court of Human Rights, across – states' borders.[19]

This line of opinion is limited and does not expressly respond to the core problems of supply chain management, which typically involves breaches of human rights, environmental laws, anti-corruption laws and/or labour protections in a foreign state where the supplier is located. When the harm takes place in a foreign state, a further impediment arises in that the principle of non-extraterritoriality prevents application of home-state laws outside its jurisdiction against nationals of the foreign host-state. In extremely limited situations, this impediment may be overcome, such as through the Alien Tort Statute in the US, which permits tort claims by foreign victims against foreign perpetrators committing violations of the law of nations on foreign soil – the 'foreign-cubed' claim.[20] While viewed as a law of great potential by human rights lawyers, most general international lawyers view foreign-cubed claims as a challenge to the principle of extraterritoriality or question the ability of individuals to raise breaches of international agreements in a national court.[21]

Still, it has been acknowledged that allowing a state to commit human rights violations on the territory of another state would be "unconscionable"; therefore it seems logical to assume that permitting a corporate actor to breach home-state laws in the territory of another state would also be viewed as such.[22] While logical, the legal extrapolation of such a position in terms of corporate actors is not straightforward due to the failure of international law to accommodate corporate actors in the accountability processes, save in extremely limited exercises of diplomatic protection or in the aforementioned cases where the state serves as the surrogate for the corporate environmental harm perpetrator.

Recently, a further advance was made when the Inter-American Court of Human Rights took a view on transboundary environmental harm that breached human rights obligations across borders. But again, in this instance the state was

19 For example, *Taşkin v. Turkey* [2006] 42 EHRR 50; *Öneryildiz v. Turkey* [2004] 41 EHRR 20; *Lopez Ostra v. Spain* [1994] 20 EHRR 277; Inter-American Court of Human Rights (IACtHR), Advisory Opinion OC-23/17 on Environment and Human Rights, 7 February 2018.

20 'Foreign cubed' refers to a foreign defendant committing a human rights violation against a foreign person in a foreign country; see S M Grant & D Zilka, 'The Rise of Foreign Investors in Federal Securities Class Actions' (2004) Securities Litigation & Enforcement Institute PLI Corp. Law & Practice, Course Handbook Ser. No. B-1442 91, 96 as cited in M Steinitz, 'The Case for an International Court of Civil Justice' (2014) 37 Stanford Law Review Online 75, 78, n 20. See discussion in McCall-Smith & Rühmkorf (n 18) 154–155.

21 S D Murphy 'Does International Law Obligate States to Open Their National Courts to Persons for the Invocation of Treaty Norms That Protect or Benefit Persons?' in D Sloss (ed), *The Role of Domestic Courts in Treaty Enforcement* (Cambridge University Press 2009).

22 Human Rights Committee, *Communication No R.12/52, López Burgos v. Uruguay*, UN Doc A/36/40 (1981) 176. See J Cerone, 'Regional Human Rights Law Beyond Regional Frontiers: The Inter-American Commission on Human Rights and US Activities in Iraq' (2005) 9(32) ASIL Insights 32.

the perpetrator of the harm, rather than a corporate actor, and the individual harmed was deemed to be under the perpetrating state's authority, responsibility or control for purposes of jurisdiction.[23] The case is interesting, as the extra-territorial application of the human rights treaty in question tracks an argument not dissimilar to that required to overcome the jurisdictional barriers to corporate accountability for human rights abuse in global supply chains. Namely, that the home-state obligations are binding outside its own territorial jurisdiction, which requires a legal fiction to be created to overcome the jurisdictional impediment. In the Inter-American case, this was done by crafting a limited agency relationship between the perpetrating state and the victim, despite the victim otherwise having no tie to the perpetrating state. However, the focus on the state as the responsible perpetrator due to its act or omission maintains the heretofore existing legal hurdle in that corporations cannot directly be held accountable in the international system.

Recognising the 'continuous evolution in international law' in the *Barcelona Traction* case, the 'considerable influence on international relations' was highlighted by the International Court of Justice (ICJ) as a reason necessitating that states give greater consideration to the growing body 'of rules governing the creation and operation of corporate entities' – entities that hold their own rights and responsibilities as legal actors.[24] The logic of *Barcelona Traction* resonates in the twenty-first century struggle with supply chain governance in light of the previously described difficulty in holding corporations accountable at the international level. Notably, the idea that the volume of rules governing corporations would increase is a starting point for this discussion. The nature of these rules in terms of operation is represented by two distinct areas of law: domestic legal regulations and international law. Simultaneously, there is an increasing cadre of treaties demanding that the state protect individuals against harm from third parties.[25] In general, the various rules can be viewed as preventative. The key difficulty is that parallel rules responding to violations of the preventative standards in terms of access to justice at the international level have not increased in any meaningful way and remain limited at the domestic level. Until there is a marked shift at the international level, one way of addressing the inequality between rule and redress in the public international law field is contract law, since individual claims against corporations operating in a foreign state have difficulty getting to trial.[26] Whereas

23 IACtHR, *Advisory Opinion OC-23/17.*

24 *Barcelona Traction* case (*Belgium v. Spain*) [1970] ICJ Reports 3, para. 39.

25 For example: International Covenant on Civil and Political Rights, 999 UNTS 171, 16 December 1966; International Covenant on Economic, Social and Cultural Rights, 993 UNTS 3, 16 December 1966; Convention on the Elimination of all forms of Discrimination Against Women, 1249 UNTS 13, 18 December 1979; Convention on the Rights of the Child, 1577 UNTS 3, 20 November 1989.

26 J Zerk, 'Corporate Liability for Gross Human Rights Abuses: Towards a Fairer and More Effective System of Domestic Law Remedies. A Report Prepared for the Office of the UN High Commissioner for Human Rights' (2012) Office of the High Commissioner for Human Rights 44, 94; P Zumbansen, 'Defining the Space of Transnational Law: Legal Theory, Global Governance, and Legal Pluralism' (2012) 21(2)

tort law focuses on the harmed individual(s), a breach of contract claim under these circumstances can have an impact for the breaching supplier in the chain. This can be the case if the buyer procures a remedy for a breach of its CSR policy, including termination of the contract. Whilst, at least in the UK, there is no case law related to a violation of a CSR policy by a supplier yet, this does not mean that the use of contract law as an instrument of imposing CSR duties on suppliers would be futile. First, the existence of a remedy for a breach of a contractual term that incorporates a CSR policy into the buyer-supplier contract alone means that there is redress available, even if buyer companies choose not to use it, though enforcement will be variable and contingent on the nature of the clause and the law of the jurisdiction. Second, the fact that a CSR policy is contractual might lead the buyers to use their right to terminate a contract in case it is breached, but it might also lead to them not renewing the contract. As previous studies have shown, individual criminal and tort actions against corporations for abuse by suppliers or subsidiaries further down the supply chain are notoriously difficult.[27] The following section sets out a number of international laws and standards that are non-justiciable at the international level and then introduces key advances in "hardening" these soft principles through contracts.

3.2 Relevant law

Because existing international treaties are unable to directly regulate corporate actors due to their limited international legal personality, soft law regimes have developed as a means of guiding states and businesses in their interactions with one another and their activity that directly impacts human rights. These soft regimes integrate elements of hard international law through explicit incorporation or direct reference, which serves to reinforce the obligations previously taken up by states.[28] Though soft law is often criticised as a weak form of governance or simply "not law" due to its non-binding nature, it is undoubtedly the most prolific in terms of both form and governance in many areas of international law.[29] Not only is it much easier to agree due to the lack of prescribed formalities, the ability to capitalise on a multi-stakeholder approach that includes issue-specific experts aids in ensuring that soft laws can provide a greater depth than that which is

Transnational Law & Contemporary Problems 305, 305; Traidcraft/CORE, 'Above the Law?' 8.

27 Zerk (n 27) Appendix 2. See discussion in A Chander, 'Unshackling Foreign Corporations: Kiobel's Unexpected Legacy' (2013) 107(4) American Journal of International Law 829; Traidcraft/CORE, 'Above the Law?'; Murphy has examined the issue of enforcing international obligations, including human rights, in domestic courts more generally; see Murphy (n 22) 94 et seq.

28 C Rodríguez-Garavito, 'Business and Human Rights: Beyond the End of the Beginning' in C Rodríguez-Garavito (ed), *Business and Human Rights: Beyond the End of the Beginning* (Cambridge University Press 2017) 14.

29 A Boyle & C Chinkin, *The Making of International Law* (Oxford University Press 2007) 212–213; J d'Aspremont, *Formalism and the Sources of International Law* (Oxford University Press 2011) 128–129.

generally agreed by diplomats in a negotiating forum – an issue of key importance in the examination of global supply chains due to the fast-paced nature of these operations.

Varying forms of international law offer key opportunities to guide responsible global supply chain management and fill the gaps otherwise left by the international legal framework of human rights treaties. This chapter now considers the most-referenced international standards, identified in Section 2, and why they seem to have the greatest pull in the corporate sector. The most widely referenced international documents are the UDHR, ILO standards and the UN Global Compact. However, as will be explained, the UN Guiding Principles on Business and Human Rights: Implementing the UN 'Protect, Respect and Remedy' Framework (UNGPs) must also be considered, as this is the fastest-growing point of reference across the overarching CSR regimes and in business practice (discussed in the following sections).[30]

3.2.1 The UDHR

Adopted 70 years ago, the UDHR is the genesis of all human rights treaties and though it is not a binding instrument, many of its norms are binding through either customary international law or having been codified in a treaty. Most of the abuses suffered as a result of poor supply chain management are directly addressed in the UDHR, including non-discrimination, the prohibition against torture, the right to life, the prohibition against slavery, the right to effective remedy, freedom of opinion and expression, freedom of association, etc. That two-thirds of the TNCs examined in our survey sample (Section 2) refer to the UDHR is unsurprising, as it is the most widely available human rights document in the world and the umbrella for the modern human rights system and is consistently referenced by all UN organs. The frequency with which the document is referred to in both international and national governance structures facilitates the ease with which corporations have professed their commitment to its principles. In line with traditional international law, it expressly refers to the UN Member States and their pledge to observe and promote the UDHR standards of achievement with no mention of corporate actors.

3.2.2 ILO conventions and policies

The ILO has facilitated the adoption of around 200 conventions and protocols addressing a wide range of labour issues, including those endemic to poor supply chain management, such as child labour, modern slavery, collective bargaining and

30 UN Guiding Principles on Business and Human Rights, UN Doc A/HRC/17/31 (21 March 2011) annex (UNGPs). See Rodríguez-Garavito (n 29); A Sanders, 'The Impact of the "Ruggie Framework" and the United Nations Guiding Principles on Business and Human Rights on Transnational Human Rights Litigation' in J Martin & K E Bravo, *The Business and Human Rights Landscape: Moving Forward, Looking Back* (Cambridge University Press 2015).

equal pay, among many others. The ILO's tripartite structure incorporates both employer and employee concerns and is dedicated to the improvement of workplace conditions; therefore, these standards are a natural point of reference for TNCs, as borne out by the frequency of reference indicated in Section 2. There is a great deal of overlap between ILO instruments and the UDHR in terms of rights addressed. None of the ILO conventions, however, place a duty on corporate actors to observe the standards set out therein and, in line with traditional international law, the onus lies on states to enforce convention standards. While the duty on states is clear, the number of states ratifying the individual conventions varies wildly; thus the TNC at the top of the supply chain and the suppliers toward the bottom will not necessarily be party to the same, if any, of the ILO conventions. Furthermore, many of the most technical forms of guidance by the ILO are issued in non-binding form. For example, the ILO adopted the Tripartite Declaration of Principles Concerning Multinational Enterprises and Social Policy (ILO MNE Declaration), and it is incumbent on all ILO Member States to observe the principles set down therein. The 2017 iteration of the Declaration generally tracks the development of the business and human rights discourse at the international level. It is intended to address key issues in the context of global supply chains and the recent revision expressly incorporates the 2030 Sustainable Development Goals and the UNGPs. The document aims to encourage multinational enterprises to make positive contributions to economic and social progress through the realisation of decent work. Equally, the ILO Declaration on Fundamental Principles and Rights at Work and its concomitant follow-up procedure commits its Member States to respect and promote core rights that are intrinsic to responsible supply chain management, including freedom of association and the prohibition against forced and child labour, among many others.[31] Furthermore, the ILO has examined the issue of global supply chains and adopted express conclusions on work in global supply chains.[32] Due to the tripartite nature of the ILO and its substantive engagement with employers, it is not surprising that general references to its standards are frequently made by corporations in their supply chain management policies.

3.2.3 UN Global Compact

Our assessment of the supply chain policies confirms that the UN Global Compact is another key point of reference used by TNCs. It is the longest-running and largest voluntary corporate sustainability initiative providing a minimum level of social and environmental standards through its Ten Principles.[33] The Ten

31 ILO, 'Declaration on Fundamental Principles and Rights at Work' (18 June 1998), updated Annex 15 June 2010.

32 ILO, *Resolution Concerning Decent Work in Global Supply Chains*, 'Conclusions'.

33 *Ten Principles of the UN Global Compact*, 'Introduction' <www.unglobalcompact.org/what-is-gc/mission/principles> accessed 21 August 2018.

Principles[34] are drawn from the UDHR and the ILO Declaration on Fundamental Principles and Rights at Work, as well as environmental and anti-corruption agreements.[35] The Principles expressly track the four core labour rights set out in the ILO Declaration on Fundamental Principles and Rights at Work. The Compact aims to guide businesses at every stage of the value chain and its Guide to Corporate Sustainability further clarifies that a healthy business demands that businesses proactively manage their value chains to ensure the well-being of workers, the communities in which they operate and the planet.[36] The sheer reach of the Global Compact network justifies the high level of reference in supply chain management policies.

3.2.4 UN Guiding Principles on Business and Human Rights

No examination of contemporary reference points for CSR standards and supply chain management would be complete without introducing the UNGPs. While not the most often directly referenced standards in the supply chain management codes of conduct we examined, the frequent reference to ILO policies and the Global Compact indirectly incorporate the UNGPs. Both explicitly have aligned with the guidance set out in the UNGPs, providing a framework for how to action the UN Protect, Respect and Remedy Framework on Business and Human Rights. The 2011 endorsement of the UNGPs by the Human Rights Council was viewed as a "watershed" moment in the heretofore fractious relationship between human rights and the business community.[37] Government and business community support quickly coalesced to render the UNGPs the primary focus in business and human rights discourse and the foundation from which the future of the field would proceed.[38] The UNGPs were incorporated almost verbatim into the OECD *Guidelines for Multinational Enterprises* and are used as a point of reference for a growing number of international corporate social responsibility schemes.[39]

34 The ILO also expressly acknowledges the UN Global Compact as a partner in its work on global supply chains.
35 For example, Rio Declaration on the Environment and Development, UN Doc A/RES/66/288 (2012); UN Convention against Corruption (31 October 2003) 2349 UNTS 41.
36 UN Global Compact, 'Guide to Corporate Sustainability: Shaping a Sustainable Future' (December 2014) 7.
37 Human Rights Council, Resolution 17/4 'Human Rights and TNCs and other Business Enterprises' UN Doc A/HRC/RES/17/4 (16 June 2011); Economist Intelligence Unit, *The Road from Principles to Practice: Today's Challenges for Business in Respecting Human Rights* (2015).
38 See, generally, Rodríguez-Garavito, (n 29); Sanders (n 31).
39 OECD, *OECD Guidelines for Multinational Enterprises* (OECD Publishing 2011). For the UNGPs as a point of reference, see Global Reporting Initiative (GRI), 'G4 Guidelines and ISO 26000:2010 How to Use the GRI G4 Guidelines and ISO 26000 in Conjunction' (January 2014), <www.iso.org/files/live/sites/isoorg/files/archive/pdf/en/iso-gri-26000_2014-01-28.pdf> accessed 20 May 2018; European Commission, 'Commission Staff Working Document on Implementing the UN Guiding Principles for Business and Human Rights' SWD (14 July 2015) 144.

3.2.5 *Summary*

The repeated reference to international standards supports the consolidation of consensus regarding the minimum standards of practice for businesses and human rights, which is at the heart of responsible supply chain management. In our sample, TNCs refer to a number of different international standards in their supplier codes of conduct. For example, Vodafone and Anglo American list, inter alia, the UDHR and ILO conventions as references for their codes.[40] This combination of different standards suggests that companies base their codes on the most widely recognised international standards for issues of CSR. Whilst the combination *per se* does not have any contractual effect, it is probably used by the buyer companies to demonstrate both to the public (particularly consumers) and to their suppliers that CSR is important. Also, some of the standards have a slightly different focus and coverage (e.g. by definition, the ILO focuses on labour standards, whereas the Global Compact also addresses bribery) and therefore the combination ensures that the TNC seems to cover key CSR issues.

3.3 *Overcoming the international barriers*

In direct response to the growing international initiatives and the continuous stream of reports of businesses aggravating human rights, a number of states and an even greater number of civil society voices have called for an international treaty addressing business and human rights.[41] This proposal has been met with criticism and, as currently framed, it is not difficult to see why, as it does little more than add to an already substantial library of international treaties that are designed to protect human and labour rights.[42] A stronger approach would be to address incorporation of existing human rights obligations at the domestic level. Preventative domestic law can take two forms: national regulation or private contract. While there are examples of national regulations addressing issues of supply chain governance, they rest predominantly on self-reporting and transparency requirements, which are often ineffective or the law is riddled with loopholes that permit maintenance of the status quo.[43] Recent examples of national regulation

40 See Vodafone *Code of Ethical Purchasing, Version 2.0* and Anglo American, *Responsible Sourcing Standard for Suppliers* (November 2016) <www.vodafone.com/content/dam/sustainability/pdfs/vodafone_code_of_ethical_purchasing_with_guidance.pdf> accessed 20 May 2018.

41 Human Rights Council, 'Elaboration of an International Legally Binding Instrument on TNCs and Other Business Enterprises with Respect to Human Rights' UN Doc A/HRC/26/L.22/Rev.1 (26 June 2014); see Rodríguez-Garavito (n 29) 32 et seq; H Cantu Rivera, 'Negotiating a Treaty on Business and Human Rights: The Early Stages' (2017) 40(2) UNSW Law Journal 1200; J Ford & C M O'Brien, 'Empty Rituals or Workable Models? Towards a Business and Human Rights Treaty' (2017) 40(2) UNSW Law Journal 1223.

42 J G Ruggie, 'A UN Business and Human Rights Treaty?' (2014) An Issues Brief: Harvard University.

43 See for an assessment of the UK Modern Slavery Act: A Okoye, 'Corporate Enterprise Principles and UK Regulation of Modern Slavery in Supply Chains' (2017) 28(5) International Company and Commercial Law Review 196.

focused on improving supply chain governance include the US Dodd-Frank Wall Street Reform and Consumer Protection Act;[44] the 2017 French Due Diligence Law;[45] and the 2015 UK Modern Slavery Act.[46] These regulatory acts each represent a step in the right direction, yet they fall short of promising comprehensive and effective supply chain management. In order to give tangible effect to the standards produced at the international level, responsible businesses are increasingly relying upon contracts to demand higher levels of socially sustainable performance from their suppliers.

3.4 Contract law perspectives

From a contract law perspective, the use of and reference to international CSR standards raises issues such as the mode of incorporation, the drafting of the contractual terms related to CSR and enforcement. These will be addressed insofar as they are relevant to the underlying question of using international standards in private supply contracts.

3.4.1 Incorporation of the international CSR standards into supply chains

The review of the 30 companies' codes of conduct will show in this section a range of different ways in which companies incorporate international CSR standards into their supply chains.[47]

The first and seemingly most frequent method is using the international standards as a reference point for the supplier code of conduct that the TNC imposes on its suppliers. The supplier codes of conduct of the TNCs at the top of the chain stipulate CSR obligations for their suppliers on issues such as forced and child labour, based on the principles found in the international standards that they used as 'reference point'. The stringency of the language in the codes themselves varies from more binding forms that require the contractual partners to meet these standards to more aspirational forms such as 'strive to … '[48] or 'we have established the aspiration that the working conditions in our supply chain should meet standards based on international guidelines'.[49] An example of this approach can

44 Dodd-Frank Wall Street Reform and Consumer Protection Act, s 1504, 'Disclosure of Payments by Resource Extraction Issuers'.
45 Loi n° 2017–399 du 27 mars 2017 relative au devoir de vigilance des sociétés mères et des entreprises donneuses d'ordre (1).
46 UK Modern Slavery Act 2015, s 54(1).
47 See for a general assessment of CSR in supply chain contracts in English law A Rühmkorf, *Corporate Social Responsibility, Private Law and Global Supply Chains* (Edward Elgar 2015) Chapter 3.
48 See Anglo American, *Responsible Sourcing Standards for Suppliers*, 2. *Safety and Health*: 'Suppliers therefore must: 2.1 Strive to eliminate fatalities, work-related injuries and health impairment of the workforce … '.
49 See British Telecom, *Generic Standard 18 Sourcing with Human Dignity*, 1 *Background*.

be found in the supplier code of conduct of the company Anglo American, which states,

> External reference points: The following have been used as reference points and may be referred to by suppliers if additional detail is required: [then list of international standards follows].[50]

A further example of the reference to international standards in the supply chain documents is the following statement from Burberry:

> We require all our supply chain partners, whether they are providing products or services, to agree with our Responsible Business Principles. These include the Burberry Ethical Trading Code of Conduct, Migrant Worker and Homeworker Policy. The Ethical Trading Code of Conduct is underpinned by the United Nations Universal Declaration of Human Rights, the Fundamental Conventions of the International Labour Organization and the Ethical Trading Initiative Base Code.[51]

Unilever takes a similar line by saying that the principles in its Responsible Sourcing Policy (RSP) are 'not a Unilever "creation". They are anchored in internationally recognised standards'.[52]

The second mode of incorporation is that the buyer companies require their suppliers to conduct their operation in a way that respects specific international CSR standards. For example, British American Tobacco states,

> As such, we expect our suppliers to conduct their operations in a way that respects the fundamental human rights of others, as affirmed by the Universal Declaration of Human Rights.[53]

The wording used here is vague in that 'respect' does not mean "comply with", so it can be argued that it falls short of a binding legal requirement. However, given that the buyer expects the supplier to respect these documents, there is room for discussion about the actual legal effect of this wording. Still, it can be argued that the buyer could request its suppliers to "comply with" a standard. So, at least, the examples here can be considered to be a business requirement. A question that we cannot assess by our documentary analysis is whether or not the buyer companies

50 See Anglo American, *Supplier Sustainable Development Code*, 4 <www.angloamerican.com/~/media/Files/A/Anglo-American-PLC-V2/documents/supplier/Supplier_SD_Code_english.pdf> accessed 28 May 2018.

51 Burberry, 'Areas of Work: Labour and Human Rights' <www.burberryplc.com/en/responsibility/areas-of-work/labour-and-human-rights.html> accessed 23 May 2018.

52 Unilever, *Unilever Responsible Sourcing Policy: Working in Partnership with Our Suppliers*, 6.

53 British American Tobacco, *Supplier Code of Conduct*, 5.

react differently in practice to the breach of a business and a legal requirement respectively.

The third approach is similar to the second approach, but it uses more stringent language, as, in this scenario, the company expressly requires their suppliers to comply with international standards. For example, AstraZeneca (pharmaceuticals) declares,

> We expect our third parties to meet these strict standards, as set out in our Global Standard Expectations of Third Parties. Our Global Standard incorporates our Code of Conduct and key international standards, such as those published by the International Labour Organization (ILO).[54]

This overview demonstrates that international companies at the top of the supply chain make use of international CSR instruments vis-à-vis their suppliers in different ways. Whilst some of them use these documents as a source that underpins the content of their supplier code of conduct, others require respect of the principles of such standards while then again others expressly require compliance with them.

A related issue is the question of under what circumstances CSR policies can become contractual terms. It would go beyond the scope of this chapter to address the issue in detail and this issue will therefore only be touched upon here briefly.[55] Insofar as UK TNCs are concerned, the primary means of making CSR clauses contractual between buyers and suppliers is through the terms and conditions of purchase of the buyer.[56] Some companies include express CSR clauses directly in their terms and conditions, whereas others incorporate their supplier code of conduct into the terms and conditions by way of reference which then, in turn, often refers to the international law standards in the ways presented previously.[57]

An example of the first approach, i.e. to include express CSR clauses, is in the terms and conditions of purchase from GlaxoSmithKline. Clause 21, entitled 'Ethical Standards and Human Rights', contains a list of CSR obligations that are imposed on their suppliers. For example, the clause stipulates that the supplier warrants that 'it does not employ engage or otherwise use any child labour in any circumstances … ' and 'that it does not use forced labour in any form … '.[58]

An example of the latter approach can be found in the purchase order terms and conditions of Rio Tinto. Clause 10 stipulates that 'the supplier will … (b) comply with Rio Tinto's policy titled "The Way We Work"'.[59] In this case, the code of conduct is not a term of the contract, but a reference document, which will help to determine whether the contractual term that refers to it is a condition, warranty

54 AstraZeneca, *Global Standard Expectations of Third Parties.*
55 For further discussion on this, see Chapters 3 and 4 in this volume.
56 Rühmkorf (n 47) 87.
57 Ibid.
58 GlaxoSmithKline, *GlaxoSmithKline Terms and Conditions of Purchase*, clause 21.
59 Rio Tinto London Limited, *Purchase Order for the Supply of Goods, Terms and Conditions*, clause 10 ('Compliance with Law and Policies').

or innominate term.[60] It is necessary to assess the provisions of the supplier code of conduct in order to determine whether or not the supplier has breached this contractual term. If the CSR clauses are effectively incorporated into the contract, then the supplier code of conduct can become enforceable on the supplier, depending on the wording of the CSR provisions.

The following section will assess some examples of provisions in supplier codes of conduct in order to assess whether or not these constitute contractual terms that can be breached. Contract law has the power to give binding effect to otherwise soft and voluntary CSR instruments, such as codes of conduct or international law soft instruments, if it meets three criteria: first, such CSR clauses need to be effectively incorporated into the contract; second, the CSR provisions must be drafted in a binding way, so that alleged breaches by the supplier can be verified; and, third, the wording of the CSR provisions must be clear and unambiguous, as discussed in the next section. From a contract law point of view, these three issues are central; the status and purpose of the underlying standards in international law do not matter for their incorporation and enforcement in private contracts.

3.5 Are the CSR provisions binding and enforceable?

As noted, the issue of whether or not the CSR clauses are binding and enforceable depends on the way they are drafted in the contracts between buyers and suppliers. Due to the focus on publicly available documents in our analysis, we can only assess terms and conditions of purchase here and not individual contracts, as these are not published. This section will therefore critically assess some examples of such CSR provisions. We will consider three scenarios here. The first one is the direct inclusion of CSR clauses into the terms and conditions by GlaxoSmithKline. They contain some clear, binding and verifiable CSR clauses, such as that the supplier 'does not employ engage or otherwise use any child labour' and that 'it does not use forced labour in any form'.[61] The second scenario is that of the incorporation of the supplier code of conduct by reference, such as by Rio Tinto. However, although many companies seem to incorporate their supplier code of conduct into the contract by reference, it is important to consider that the wording of the supplier codes appear to differ significantly in terms of their stringency, so it is not possible to generalise. In the case of Rio Tinto, the section on 'labour and human rights' states the following:

> We support the United Nations' Universal Declaration of Human Rights. We work with suppliers who uphold fundamental human rights including: Ensuring all work is freely chosen; without the use of forced and compulsory labour.[62]

60 See Rühmkorf (n 47) 87.
61 GlaxoSmithKline, *GlaxoSmithKline Terms and Conditions of Purchase*, clause 21.
62 Rio Tinto, *The Way We Work*, clause 1.3.

Whilst Rio Tinto's statement indicates that it works with suppliers that do not use forced labour, it is a question of interpretation as to whether this provision requires suppliers to comply with this provision. This wording in Rio Tinto's code does not amount to the level of bindingness that we find in the first scenario in GlaxoSmithKline's terms and conditions, which require the suppliers *warrant* that they do not employ forced labour.[63] Similarly, there is a significant difference between 'We support the Universal Declaration of Human Rights' and a wording that would state "we comply with … ". Therefore, it can be concluded that it might be difficult to prove a breach of the contractual CSR terms by Rio Tinto's suppliers. This situation raises the question of whether or not these terms can be enforced in practice.

However, another company, Unilever, demonstrates that it is, in principle, possible to impose binding CSR obligations on suppliers through a supplier code of conduct that is incorporated into the contract by reference. Unilever's terms and conditions of purchase stipulate that

> Each supplier … acknowledges that it has reviewed Unilever's Responsible Sourcing Policy ("RSP") and agrees that all of their activities shall be conducted in accordance with the RSP.[64]

Still, the question of whether or not the CSR obligation is binding depends on the wording of the provision in Unilever's RSP. In case it is not firm and clear, it may be that there is a mismatch between the stringent incorporation of the policy into the contract and the wording of the actual policy itself. In the case of Unilever, the sourcing policy contains mandatory requirements and continuous improvement benchmarks. One of the mandatory requirements is the following provision:

> Work is conducted on a voluntary basis: Forced labour, whether in the form of indentured labour, bonded labour or other forms, is not acceptable. Mental and physical coercion, slavery and human trafficking are prohibited.[65]

This provision is binding on the supplier and a violation of this wording can be verified, as the supplier 'agrees that all of their activities shall be conducted in accordance with the RSP'. Therefore, Unilever is an example where the supplier code of conduct contains clear and binding obligations that it imposes on the supplier and that can be used to determine whether or not the supplier has breached a contractual term.

Finally, the third scenario concerns that of compliance with an international CSR standard. An example of this approach can be found in the code of conduct of British American Tobacco (BAT), which states,

63 Ibid.
64 Unilever, *General Terms & Conditions of Purchase of Goods of Unilever Supply Chain Company AG* ('Conditions'), clause 13.
65 Unilever, *Responsible Sourcing Policy: Working in Partnership with Our Suppliers.*

> … As such, we expect our suppliers to conduct their operations in a way that respects the fundamental human rights of others, as affirmed by the Universal Declaration of Human Rights.[66]

Their terms and conditions of purchase are not available online, but BAT states on its website that its supplier code of conduct defines 'the minimum standards we expect our suppliers to adhere to in order to supply goods or services to BAT and any BAT Group company'.[67] Therefore, it appears that suppliers have to adhere to the principles of the UDHR and that it is down to the wording of this document to determine whether or not a BAT supplier has violated the company's supplier code of conduct. UDHR Article 4 reads: 'No one shall be held in slavery or servitude; slavery and the slave trade shall be prohibited in all their forms'. This wording is clear and strict and a violation of it can thus be verified. It therefore can be argued that suppliers are obliged to comply with this article, given that BAT establishes an expectation to adhere to the principles of the UDHR. This is an important finding, as the Declaration thereby gains binding legal effect between the contractual parties of the supply agreement (i.e. the TNC as the buyer and its supplier) through contract law. BAT is therefore able to enforce this principle by applying the usual instruments of contract law, which are primarily damages in the case of English law.[68] Also, in those cases where the breach of a contractual term concerns a condition, the breach is considered to be repudiatory and the non-breaching party gains the right to terminate the contract.[69]

3.6 Enforcement of the CSR provisions down the chain and by third parties

The next issue is how these contractual CSR provisions can be enforced. Here, two scenarios must be distinguished. First, the enforcement down the chain onto suppliers and sub-suppliers; second, the enforcement by the employees of the suppliers, who are the intended beneficiaries of the contractual CSR terms in the contracts between buyers and suppliers. Enforcement is only possible if the terms and conditions of purchase that contain the CSR provisions are indeed part of the contract. In English law, the rules on unfair commercial contract terms cannot make invalid CSR policies included in the contracts between buyers and their suppliers, as these rules primarily focus on business-to-consumer relationships.[70] The validity of such clauses is, however, discussed in other legal systems, such as in German law.[71]

66 British American Tobacco (n 53) 5.
67 British American Tobacco, 'Policies, Principles and Standards' <www.bat.com/principles> accessed 23 May 2018
68 See N Andrews, *Contract Law* (2nd edn, Cambridge University Press 2015) Chapter 18.
69 See Rühmkorf (n 47) 108.
70 See the statutory framework The Unfair Contract Terms Act 1977, The Unfair Terms in Consumer Contracts Regulation 1999, The Sale of Goods Act 1979, The Supply of Goods and Services Act 1982 and The Consumer Credit Act 1974.
71 See B Spießhofer & F Graf von Westfalen, 'AGB-Recht, CSR-Klausel, Corporate Social Responsibility, Inhaltskontrolle' (2015) Betriebs-Berater 75.

In case the supplier is in breach of a contractual CSR term, the buyer can procure a remedy. However, here it must be noted that in English law (and in common law generally) the primary remedy against the party that is in breach of a contractual obligation is the right to demand damages.[72] If the seller has breached a condition then the buyer can procure the right to repudiate the contract, i.e. terminate it.[73] This situation differs from civil law jurisdiction, where the usual remedy is to force the defaulting party to perform the contract.[74] The remedy of specific performance is rarely awarded in English law.[75]

The enforcement down the chain onto sub-suppliers is an important issue for the actual reach of the CSR commitments, as global supply chains are often complex and long. Many TNCs at the top of the chain do not directly contract with all the suppliers in their chain. Rather, the supply chain management often establishes a complex supply chain, consisting of different tiers of suppliers and sub-suppliers.

However, contract law concerns, first and foremost, the parties of the contract. The privity of contract doctrine stipulates that it is a general rule that third parties cannot be subjected to a burden by a contract to which they are not a party.[76] Therefore, the sub-suppliers that are not party to contract between the TNC and their direct contractual partners are not bound by the supplier code of conduct. This means that they are beyond the direct reach of this contract. It is not possible for the corporation at the top of the chain to directly impose CSR obligations onto sub-suppliers. This situation significantly limits the practical effects and thus the power of contract law as an instrument of promoting CSR.[77]

The second scenario concerns the issue of enforcement by third parties, in particular, the employees of the suppliers, who could be seen as the intended beneficiaries of the contractual CSR clauses.[78] The practical effect of these CSR clauses across the chain would be stronger if these third parties were to acquire a right to enforce them. Traditionally, in English law, third parties were unable to enforce a contract that they are not party to, even if that contract has been expressly entered into for their benefit, due to the privity of contract doctrine.[79]

The Contracts (Rights of Third Parties) Act 1999 opens up the possibility for such third parties to derive a right of enforcement. The first avenue for such a right is that a term of the contract expressly provides that the third party may

72 JM Smits, *Contract Law: A Comparative Introduction* (Edward Elgar 2014) 194.
73 J Poole, *Textbook on Contract Law* (11th edn, Oxford University Press 2012) 57–59.
74 Smits (n 72) 194.
75 R Stone, *The Modern Law of Contract* (9th edn, Routledge 2011). para. 15.9.
76 Andrews (n 68) 175.
77 It is often argued by civil society that, due to their size and the numbers of their orders, TNCs have a strong bargaining power in practice, which they could use to impact on working conditions further down their supply chain, irrespective of the actual reach of their contracts with their direct suppliers. This issue is beyond the analysis of contract law here, however.
78 For detailed discussion, see Chapter 4 in this volume.
79 See *Dunlop Pneumatic Tyre Co. Ltd v Selfridge & Co Ltd* [1915] AX 847.

enforce a right in its own right.[80] However, none of the terms and conditions of purchase of the companies analysed here contained such a provision. Alternatively, a third party who is not party to a contract may enforce a contractual term if the term purports to confer a benefit on him.[81] The third party must be expressly identified in the contract by name, as a member of a class or as answering a particular description but need not be in existence when the contract is entered into.[82] In *Prudential Assurance Co Ltd v. Ayres*, these conditions were interpreted as meaning that 'on a true construction of the term in question its sense has the effect of conferring a benefit on the third party in question'.[83] It can be argued that, for example, the terms and condition of GlaxoSmithKline purport to confer a benefit on the supplier's employees as a third party. Examples of this are the clauses in their terms and conditions that state that the supplier warrants that 'it does not use forced labour in any form' and that it 'complies with the laws on working hours ... in the countries in which it operates'. As these clauses clearly refer to the working conditions that the supplier provides, its employees can be identified as the beneficiaries. However, in practice, this interpretation does not seem to have much of an impact, as this provision does not apply if on a proper construction of the contract it appears that the parties did not intend the term to be enforceable by the third party.[84] In fact, the assessment of the contractual documents from the 30 FTSE 100 companies shows that an exclusion clause in the terms and conditions seems to be common practice, such as this one from GlaxoSmithKline:

> Except for any rights granted to GSK Affiliates, which the parties hereby designate as intended third party beneficiaries to the Agreement, no person who is not a party to the Agreement shall have any rights under the Contracts (Rights of Third Parties) Act 1999 to enforce any term.[85]

This situation means that the third parties who are the beneficiaries of the CSR clauses in the supply contracts do not derive a right to enforce these, such as the right to form and to join a trade union, which is also found in the core ILO conventions. In practice, this exclusion of third party rights significantly limits the impact of contract law as a tool for the promotion of CSR in global supply chains.

80 Contracts (Rights of Third Parties) Act 1999, s1 (1) (a).
81 Contracts (Rights of Third Parties) Act 1999, s1 (1) (b).
82 Contracts (Rights of Third Parties) Act 1999, s3.
83 *Prudential Assurance Co Ltd v Ayres* [2007] EWHC 775 (Ch); [2007] 3 All ER 946.
84 Contracts (Rights of Third Parties) Act 1999, s2. See also N Andrews, 'Strangers to Justice No Longer: The Reversal of the Privity Rule under the Contracts (Rights of Third Parties) Act 1999 and its Implications for Commercial Contracts' (2000) The Cambridge Law Journal 540, 545.
85 GlaxoSmithKline, *GlaxoSmithKline Terms and Conditions of Purchase*, section 25 ('General').

4 Implications of the interaction of "the international" with "the national" in the context of CSR in global supply chains

In this section, we will discuss the implications of this interaction of international soft law with national private contract law under four headings: first, the hybridisation of law in this system of CSR promotion; second, the role that TNC home-states play for the use of contract law through legislation, as their legislative requirements can impact on the way in which TNCs choose to incorporate CSR issues into their supply chain contracts (i.e. in a more or less stringent way); third, the implications for the respective roles of private law and for public international law; fourth, the significance of enforcement mechanisms.

4.1 Hybridisation

The interaction of public international law and national contract law creates a hybrid regulatory system.[86] The reference to "hybrid regulatory system" means a system in which different forms of regulation interact, such as private law, public law, soft and hard law standards developed by international organisations and private regulation by and between companies. Heldeweg notes that the characteristic feature of such a system is 'a mix of origins'.[87] This hybridisation of CSR regulation is particularly based on the fact that contracts between private parties can give binding legal effect to CSR standards that are otherwise not binding on the parties. In this regulatory framework, we can observe that various regulatory models, such as direct regulation by government, regulation by contract and outsourcing of regulatory functions to third parties, coexist. This bears witness of a move from soft to hard law regulation of CSR without direct imposition by the state.

Within this system, the way CSR is incorporated into supply contracts and the way such contractual terms are monitored and enforced depends on the private parties. This shows that the hybrid system not only needs external steering through home-state legislation, but also effective enforcement mechanisms to hold TNCs accountable for the way they purport to promote CSR across their supply chains. Legislation by the home-states of TNCs steers how these companies make use of their contractual power to harden international CSR standards.[88] This system can thus create an accountability framework for the global supply chains. Whether or not contractual CSR clauses between buyers and suppliers are actually

86 See for a discussion of the term "hybrid" in relation to regulation: M Vrielink, C van Montfort, & M Bokhorst, 'Codes as Hybrid Regulation' in D Levi-Faur (ed), *Handbook on The Politics of Regulation* (Edward Elgar 2011), para. 35.5.2. See also A Kun, 'From Transnational Soft Law to National Hard Law? – Regulating Supply Chains' (2015) 8 Pecsi Munkajogi Kozlemenyek 53.

87 M A Heldeweg, 'Hybrid Regulation as a Legal Design Challenge' in A L B Colombi et al. (eds), *Law & Governance – Beyond the Public-Private Law Divide* (Eleven International Publishing 2013).

88 See G LeBaron & A Rühmkorf, 'Steering CSR through Home State Regulation: A Comparison of the Impact of the UK Bribery Act and Modern Slavery Act on Global Supply Chain Governance' (2017) 8(12) Global Policy 15.

enforced is an issue that is addressed in the following section. In any case, this hybrid system can contribute towards filling the regulatory gaps for CSR in global supply chains.[89]

4.2 The role of the home-states of TNCs

The second important implication of this interaction of international soft law and national contract law is that the home-states of TNCs assume a significant role in the hybrid regulatory system. They are important for the effectiveness of the hybrid system of promoting CSR, as their laws have the capacity to steer the way Western TNCs use their contractual power in supply chain contracts by "inducing" them to promote CSR in their private contracts.[90]

By establishing a statutory requirement to deal with CSR, home-state legislation can help to overcome the "fragmented approach" towards a level playing field where the TNCs have to promote CSR in a more uniform way. In recent years, home-states of TNCs have increasingly passed laws that impact CSR issues in global supply chains.[91] The majority of such laws are transparency laws, but we see a continuum of different types of laws that affect different issues (e.g. modern slavery, bribery) and have different levels of stringency (ranging from soft disclosure laws to stringent corporate criminal liability).[92]

In most cases, the home-states are 'regulating self-regulation'.[93] For example, the UK Modern Slavery Act leaves it to companies how they deal with modern slavery and trafficking. But there are examples of more stringent forms of regulation, such as the UK Bribery Act 2010 and the 2017 French *devoir de vigilance* law, where due diligence requirements are imposed on companies (although

89 See M P Vandenberg, 'The New Wal-Mart Effect: The Role of Private Contracting in Global Governance' (2007) 54 UCLA L Rev 913, 919.

90 See for a discussion of extraterritorial legislation A de Jonge, *Transnational Corporations and International Law: Accountability in the Global Business Environment* (Edward Elgar Publishing 2011) 91–126.

91 A recent study found that national governments have passed 19 pieces of national legislation in the last few years, which are aimed at combatting the business of forced labour in global supply chains. See N Phillips, G LeBaron, & S Wallin, 'Mapping and Measuring the Effectiveness of Labour-Related Disclosure Requirements for Global Supply Chains' working paper (2018) Geneva: ILO.

92 See A Rühmkorf, 'From Transparency to Due Diligence Laws? Variations in Stringency of CSR Regulation in Global Supply Chains in the "Home State" Of Multinational Enterprises' in J du Plessis, U Varottil, & J Veldman (eds), *Globalisation of Corporate Social Responsibility and its Impact on Corporate Governance* (Springer 2018) 177.

93 One perspective on this phenomenon is that of meta-regulation. Parker understands meta-regulation as the state regulating its own regulation, as well as any form of regulation that regulates any other form of regulation, for example legal regulation of self-regulation, non-legal methods of 'regulating' internal corporate self-regulation or management and the regulation of national law-making by transnational bodies; see C Parker, 'Meta-Regulation: Legal Accountability for Corporate Social Responsibility' in D McBarnet, A Voiculescu, & T Campbell (eds), *The New Corporate Accountability: Corporate Social Responsibility and the Law* (Cambridge University Press 2007) 210.

indirectly in the case of the UK Bribery Act, but still in a stringent form as a defence to a corporate offence). Thus far, there is little research on the question of how different forms of home-state legislation impact private governance relations between buyers and suppliers. A recent small-scale study, co-authored by one of the two authors of this chapter, compared the way 25 FTSE 100 companies deal with bribery and modern slavery in their corporate documents respectively, and indicates that stronger home-state laws on bribery seem to result in stricter corporate policies on bribery than on modern slavery.[94] This, in turn, raises the question of how those policies translate into business practices. More research is therefore needed to analyse the interaction of public and private governance and, in particular, to analyse what kind of public governance leads to more effective forms of private CSR promotion.

4.3 Implications for the respective roles of private law and for public international law

The increasing frequency with which businesses are incorporating or referencing global human rights standards or social sustainability principles in their supply chain contracts indicates progress towards truly sustainable business from both a social and an environmental perspective, although the question remains to what extent companies walk their talk, i.e. do the TNCs that incorporate CSR standards into the contracts with their suppliers also ensure that these principles are followed throughout their supply chain, or do they rather use these standards for PR reasons? The trend recognises the growing understanding of the role played by business in respecting the rights of individuals and preventing human and labour rights abuse in concert with the state's duty to do so.[95] However, for the same reason that the implementation of human rights treaties has been ineffective, international standards as a reference point alone will be ineffective unless backed up by strong methods of redress. Contract law provides at least some potential measure of consequence for a supplier failing to uphold the referenced standards.

It is, however, an imperfect response for a number of reasons. Firstly, private law, contract or otherwise, was not designed to assume a public, regulatory function and may be ill-equipped to do so, particularly when the alleged conduct is legal in one state and not in another. For example, the minimum child labour age or working hours standards differ greatly among states. Secondly, a contract claim will only yield a result for the corporate claimant. Individuals remain victims without redress and the loss of the supply contract could have far-reaching repercussions for individuals suddenly faced with no employment as opposed to employment in substandard conditions. Finally, contract dispute decisions are not designed to be determined based on the perceived breach of a social standard that is not perfectly defined. Where contracts generally demand precision, human

94 G LeBaron & A Rühmkorf (n 88).

95 See the 'protect, respect, remedy' framework in the UN Guiding Principles on Business and Human Rights.

rights standards are framed in imprecise terms by necessity. Thus, while contracts present one of the best options from the point of holding businesses to account for poor business practices, the value to the rights holder remains enigmatic.

Equally, this hybrid system has implications for the role of private law. In this hybrid system, private parties act as the regulators that use private law, including contract law, as the instrument of regulation. Thus, private law assumes a regulatory function.[96] The way in which private law promotes CSR raises the question of whether the traditional understanding of private law as primarily regulating the legal relationships between private individuals, without pursuing any goals for the benefit of wider society, is still tenable. By providing mechanisms in contract law for the incorporation and enforcement of CSR commitments by private actors, private law indirectly also promotes the general public interest. The incorporation of CSR policies that we have analysed create a system of contract governance.[97] In the promotion of CSR, private law does not purely facilitate the use of individual rights between private parties, but it also de facto pursues public policy goals. This is a phenomenon that Smits refers to as 'private law 2.0'.[98] The advantage of contract law here is its ability to overcome territorial boundaries as, in the supply chain contracts that are concluded between companies from different countries, its effects are not restricted to the territory of one country. It thus helps to close the governance gap of global supply chains. It is law that goes 'beyond the state'[99] that contributes to the creation of a 'private legal world order'.[100]

Thus, here we witness a changing role for private law, away from the pure facilitation of private relationships to a more international and more public role with diverse uses of private law by private actors.[101] It can be argued that this changing role of private law has been pushed further by the UNGPs as they have led to a process where national governments are starting to contemplate how they can implement the recommendations of the Principles through national legislation and publishing National Action Plans.[102] Some of the recent home-state laws on

96 See H Collins, *Regulating Contracts* (Oxford University Press 1999) 56–93. See also K Peterkova Mitkidis, 'Using Private Contracts for Climate Change Mitigation' (2014) 2(1) Groningen Journal of International Law 65–76.

97 See, generally, S Grundmann, F Möslein, & K Riesenhuber (eds), *Contract Governance: Dimensions in Law and Interdisciplinary Research* (Oxford University Press 2015).

98 J M Smits, *Private Law 2.0: On the Role of Private Actors in a Post-National Society* (Hague Institute for the Internationalisation of Law and Eleven International Publishing 2011).

99 N Jansen et al., 'Beyond the State: Rethinking Private Law' (2008) 56(3) American Journal of Comparative Law 527.

100 S B Spießhofer, *Unternehmerische Verantwortung: Zur Entstehung einer globalen Weltordnung* (Nomos 2017) 593–596.

101 See for a discussion of 'regulatory contract law' R Brownsword, R A J van Gestel, & H-W Micklitz, 'Introduction – Contract and Regulation: Changing Paradigms' in R Brownsword, R A J van Gestel, & H Micklitz (eds), *Contract and Regulation: A Handbook on New Methods of Law Making in Private Law* (Edward Elgar 2017).

102 See, for example, H M Government, 'Good Business: Implementing the UN Guiding Principles on Business and Human Rights' (updated May 2016) Cm 9255.

CSR in global supply chains, such as nonfinancial information disclosure laws, are, therefore, at least indirectly, a consequence of this process. This means that although the UNGPs contain only recommendations, they are a key element of the interaction between international standards and national law considered here. Therefore, this international standard has directly impacted the way private law is used to pursue the recommendations set out therein.

4.4 Enforcement is central for the effectiveness of this international–national regime

Ultimately, the effectiveness of this hybrid system depends, to a large extent, on the issue of whether or not CSR obligations are enforced or, at least, potentially can be enforced. Whilst we have argued that a binding wording allows to verify breaches of contractual CSR obligations and thus gives the transnational corporation at the top of the chain a remedy for breach of contract, the situation for third parties is unsatisfactory. We argued that they could gain a right to enforce the contract, which would make CSR clauses a much stronger tool in practice, but found that their rights are commonly excluded by contract. It is argued that this exclusion should no longer be possible. The present situation can ultimately result in a mockery of the contractual CSR clauses, as such clauses can be used by TNCs as a pure public relations instrument with no danger of their being enforced by, for example, the employees of the suppliers.[103] The Contracts (Rights of Third Parties) Act 1999 makes it expressly possible for a third party to enforce a contractual term if the term purports to confer a benefit on him. If the parties do not want a third party to gain a right to enforce a contract, then they should choose not to include such a term. Otherwise, TNCs gain reputational benefits through their CSR policies, whilst they do not risk any legal enforcement.[104]

5 Conclusions

This chapter demonstrates that through contract law, international law and national law interact in the promotion of CSR in global supply chains. Contract law is the tool that gives otherwise non-binding international CSR standards binding legal effect. Whether or not the TNCs as the buyers in global supply chains decide to enforce the contractual CSR clauses is their choice. Our analysis of 30 FTSE 100 companies reveals that the most widely used international standards are the UDHR and the ILO core conventions, followed by the UN Global Compact. There are also some, but fewer, references to the Ethical Trading Initiative Base Code, the UNGPs and the OECD Guidelines for Multinational Enterprises.

103 See for a detailed discussion of third-party rights A Beckers (n 9) 147–148. Further, see Chapters 4 and 5 in this volume.
104 See Chapter 1 in this volume.

We find that private law is used to fill the gaps left by natural parameters of public international law in the area of CSR. The adjudicatory mechanisms of international law continue to focus on states and, in the realm of human rights, are open to individuals in claims against states. As it is at present not possible to access justice against a transnational corporation directly at the international level, other legal approaches, including tort and contract law, are necessary for the development of an accountability framework. The question of whether or not such contractual CSR terms are, in fact, enforceable depends on two key issues: first, the incorporation of the CSR clauses into the contract; second, the way they have been drafted (i.e. are these clauses binding, precisely worded and not just aspirational?). This chapter suggests that the contractual reach of the CSR clauses and their enforcement is limited in practice, as the CSR clauses are only directly effective between TNCs and their direct suppliers. They cannot impose a contractual obligation onto third parties outside the contract due to the privity of contract doctrine. Sub-contracting therefore constitutes a significant challenge for the promotion of CSR through contract. Also, the right of enforcement is, in practice, limited to the parties of the contract – the transnational corporation and its direct suppliers. Third parties such as the employees of the supplier, who are supposed to benefit from the contractual CSR clauses, can gain a right of enforcement in English law in accordance with the Contracts (Rights of Third Parties) Act 1999, but our research demonstrates that this right is usually excluded in the supply contracts.

Despite these limitations, the use of international law in the supply chain, governed by national contract law, is a significant phenomenon. First, it leads to a hybrid system of promoting CSR, where different regulatory techniques and forms of regulation interact – national and international law, hard and soft law, public and private law, public regulation with private regulation. The various interactions within this hybrid system are ripe for further research. Second, home-state legislation is central for the effectiveness of this hybrid system of promoting CSR in global supply chains. Third, the interaction of public international law and contract law that we have discussed here is part of a broader trend that sees the roles of these areas changing. Finally, this chapter has demonstrated that contract law is one potential option for developing the common understanding of CSR and an alternative route to access justice for rights breaches when it is otherwise denied.

Bibliography

Abou-Nigm V R, McCall-SmithK, & FrenchD, *Linkages and Boundaries in Private and Public International Law* (Hart Publishing 2018) 147–173.

Andrews N, Chapter 18, in *Contract Law* (2nd edn, Cambridge University Press 2015).

Andrews N, 'Strangers to Justice No Longer: The Reversal of the Privity Rule under the Contracts (Rights of Third Parties) Act 1999 and its Implications for Commercial Contracts' (2000) 60(2) *The Cambridge Law Journal* 540, 545.

Aspremont J, *Formalism and the Sources of International Law: A Theory of The Ascertainment of Legal Rules* (Oxford University Press 2011).

Beckers A, *Enforcing Corporate Social Responsibility Codes: On Global Self-Regulation and National Private Law* (Hart Publishing 2015).
Boyle A & Chinkin C, *The Making of International Law* (Oxford University Press 2007) 212–213.
Brownsword R, van Gestel R A J, & Micklitz H, 'Introduction – Contract and Regulation: Changing Paradigms' in Brownsword R, van Gestel R A J, & Micklitz H (eds), *Contract and Regulation: A Handbook on New Methods of Law Making in Private Law* (Edward Elgar 2017).
Cafaggi F, 'Regulation Through Contracts: Supply-Chain Contracting and Sustainability Standards' (2016) 12(3) *European Review of Contract Law* 1.
Campbell K & Vick D, 'Disclosure Law and the Market for Corporate Social Responsibility' in McBarnet D *et al.* (eds), *The New Corporate Accountability* (Cambridge University Press 2007) 242.
Cantu Rivera H, 'Negotiating a Treaty on Business and Human Rights: The Early Stages' (2017) 40(2) *UNSW Law Journal* 1200.
Cerone J, 'Regional Human Rights Law Beyond Regional Frontiers: The Inter-American Commission on Human Rights and US Activities in Iraq' (2005) 9(32) *ASIL Insights* 32.
Chander A, 'Unshackling Foreign Corporations: Kiobel's Unexpected Legacy' (2013) 107 (4) *American Journal of International Law* 829.
Chopra S & Meindl P, *Supply Chain Management: Strategy, Planning, and Operation* (5th edn, Pearson Education 2013).
Collins H, *Regulating Contracts* (Oxford University Press 1999) 56–93.
De Jonge A, *Transnational Corporations and International Law: Accountability in the Global Business Environment* (Edward Elgar Publishing 2011) 91–126.
Du Plessis J et al., *Globalisation of Corporate Social Responsibility and its Impact on Corporate Governance* (Springer Publishing 2018).
Ford J & O'Brien M C. 'Empty Rituals or Workable Models? Towards a Business and Human Rights Treaty' (2017) 40(2) *UNSW Law Journal* 1223.
Gereffi G, Humphrey J, & Sturgeon T, 'The Governance of Global Value Chains' (2005) 12(1) *Review of International Political Economy* 78.
Gereffi G & Lee J, 'Economic and Social Upgrading in Global Value Chains and Industrial Clusters: Why Governance Matters' (2016) 133(1) *Journal of Business Ethics* 25.
Grant SM & Zilka D, 'The Rise of Foreign Investors in Federal Securities Class Actions' (2004) *Securities Litigation & Enforcement Institute PLI Corp. Law & Practice, Course Handbook* Ser. No. B-1442 91, 96.
Griggs D, 'Sustainable Development Goals for People and Planet: Planetary Stability Must Be Integrated with United Nations Targets to Fight Poverty and Secure Human Well-Being' (2013) 495(7441) *Nature* 305.
Grundmann S, Möslein F, & Riesenhuber K (eds), *Contract Governance: Dimensions in Law and Interdisciplinary Research* (Oxford University Press 2015).
Heldeweg A M, 'Hybrid Regulation as a Legal Design Challenge' in Colombi, A L Bet al. (eds), *Law & Governance – Beyond the Public-Private Law Divide* (Eleven International Publishing 2013).
Higgins R, *Problems & Process: International Law and How to Use It* (Clarendon Press 1995) 12.
Jansen N et al., 'Beyond the state: Rethinking Private Law' (2008) 56(3) *American Journal of Comparative Law* 527.
Kun A, 'From Transnational Soft Law to National Hard Law? – Regulating Supply Chains' (2015) 8*Pecsi Munkajogi Kozlemenyek* 53.

LeBaron G & Rühmkorf A, 'Steering CSR through Home state Regulation: A Comparison of the Impact of the UK Bribery Act and Modern Slavery Act on Global Supply Chain Governance' (2017) 8(12) *Global Policy* 15.

Martin J & Bravo K, *The Business and Human Rights Landscape: Moving Forward, Looking Back* (Cambridge University Press 2015).

McBarnet D & Kurkchiyan M, 'Corporate Social Responsibility through Contractual Control? Global Supply Chains and "Other Regulation"' in McBarnet D, Voiculescu A, & Campbell T (eds), *The New Corporate Accountability: Corporate Social Responsibility and the Law* (Cambridge University Press 2007) 59.

McCall-Smith K & Rühmkorf A, 'Reconciling Human Rights and Supply Chain Management through Corporate Social Responsibility' in Abou-Nigm V R, McCall-Smith K, & French D (eds), *Linkages and Boundaries in Private and Public International Law* (Hart Publishing 2018) 147–173.

McKendrick E, *Contract Law* (8th edn, Palgrave Macmillan 2009) 10.

Millington A, 'Responsibility in the Supply Chain' in Crane A et al. (eds), *The Oxford Handbook of Corporate Social Responsibility* (Oxford University Press 2008) 365.

Monczka M R*et al.*, *Purchasing & Supply Chain Management* (South-Western2010).

Murphy S D, 'Does International Law Obligate states to Open Their National Courts to Persons for the Invocation of Treaty Norms That Protect or Benefit Persons?' in Sloss D (ed), *The Role of Domestic Courts in Treaty Enforcement* (Cambridge University Press 2009).

Okoye A, 'Corporate Enterprise Principles and UK Regulation of Modern Slavery in Supply Chains' (2017) 28(5) *International Company and Commercial Law Review* 196.

Parker C, 'Meta-Regulation: Legal Accountability for Corporate Social Responsibility' in McBarnet D, Voiculescu A, & Campbell T (eds), *The New Corporate Accountability: Corporate Social Responsibility and the Law* (Cambridge University Press 2007) 210.

Peterkova Mitkidis K, 'Using Private Contracts for Climate Change Mitigation' (2014) 2(1) *Groningen Journal of International Law* 65–76.

Peterkova Mitkidis K, *Sustainability Clauses in International Business Contracts* (Eleven International Publishing 2015).

Phillips N, LeBaron G, & Wallin S, 'Mapping and Measuring the Effectiveness of Labour-Related Disclosure Requirements for Global Supply Chains' working paper (ILO2018).

PooleJ, *Textbook on Contract Law* (11th edn, Oxford University Press 2012) 57–59.

Rodríguez-Garavito C, 'Business and Human Rights: Beyond the End of the Beginning' in Rodríguez-Garavito C (ed), *Business and Human Rights: Beyond the End of the Beginning* (Cambridge University Press 2017) 14.

Ruggie J G, 'A UN Business and Human Rights Treaty?' (2014) *An Issues Brief: Harvard University.*

Rühmkorf A, Chapter 3, in *Corporate Social Responsibility, Private Law and Global Supply Chains* (Edward Elgar Publishing 2015).

Rühmkorf A, 'From Transparency to Due Diligence Laws? Variations in Stringency of CSR Regulation in Global Supply Chains in the "Home state" Of Multinational Enterprises' in du Plessis J J, Varottil U, & Veldman J (eds), *Globalisation of Corporate Social Responsibility and its Impact on Corporate Governance* (Springer 2018) 147–173.

Sanders A, 'The Impact of the "Ruggie Framework" and the United Nations Guiding Principles on Business and Human Rights on Transnational Human Rights Litigation' in Martin, J & Bravo, K E (eds), *The Business and Human Rights Landscape: Moving Forward, Looking Back* (Cambridge University Press 2015).

Smits J M, *Private Law 2.0: On the Role of Private Actors in a Post-National Society* (Hague Institute for the Internationalisation of Law and Eleven International Publishing 2011).

Smits J M, *Contract Law: A Comparative Introduction* (Edward Elgar Publishing 2014) 194.

Spießhofer B *Unternehmerische Verantwortung: Zur Entstehung einer globalen Weltordnung* (Nomos 2017) 593–596.

Spießhofer B & Graf von Westfalen F, 'AGB-Recht, CSR-Klausel, Corporate Social Responsibility, Inhaltskontrolle' (2015) *Betriebs-Berater* 75.

Steinitz M, 'The Case for an International Court of Civil Justice' (2014) 37 *Stanford Law Review Online* 75, 78.

Stone R, *The Modern Law of Contract* (9th edn, Routledge 2011).

Strand R, Freeman R E, & Hockerts K, 'Corporate Social Responsibility and Sustainability in Scandinavia: An Overview' (2015) 127(1) *Journal of Business Ethics* 1, 2.

Thorsen S S, 'Are Current Approaches to Responsible Supply Chain Management Working?' (12 August 2010) *Institute for Human Rights and Business*, 12 August 2010. <www.ihrb.org/focus-areas/commodities/commentary-current-approaches-responsi ble-supply-chain-management-working> accessed 25 May 2018.

Thorsen S S & Jeppensen S, 'Changing Course – A Study into Responsible Supply Chain Management' (2011) *Global CSR and Copenhagen Business School for the Danish Ministry* 9.

Van Opijnen M & Oldenziel J, *Responsible Supply Chain Management: Potential Success Factors and Challenges for Addressing Prevailing Human Rights and other CSR Issues in Supply Chains of EU-based Companies* (CREM and SOMO for the European Commission 2011).

Vandenbergh M, 'The New Wal-Mart Effect: The Role of Private Contracting in Global Governance' (2007) 54(4) *UCLA Law Review* 913.

Vrielink O M, van Montfor C, & Bokhorst M, 'Codes as Hybrid Regulation' in Levi-Faur D (ed), *Handbook on The Politics of Regulation* (Edward Elgar 2011).

Vytopil A L, *Contractual Control in the Supply Chain: On Corporate Social Responsibility, Codes of Conduct, Contracts and (Avoiding) Liability* (Eleven International Publishing 2015).

Webley L, 'Qualitative Approaches to Empirical Legal Research' in Cane P & Kritzer H (eds), *The Oxford Handbook of Empirical Legal Research* (Oxford University Press 2010) 938.

Zerk J, 'Corporate Liability for Gross Human Rights Abuses: Towards a Fairer and More Effective System of Domestic Law Remedies. A Report Prepared for the Office of the UN High Commissioner for Human Rights' (2012) *Office of the High Commissioner for Human Rights* 44, 94.

Zumbansen P, 'Defining the Space of Transnational Law: Legal Theory, Global Governance, and Legal Pluralism' (2012) 21(2) *Transnational Law & Contemporary Problems* 305, 305.

3 Contractual enforcement of CSR clauses and the protection of weak parties in the supply chain

Vibe Ulfbeck, Ole Hansen and Alexandra Andhov

1 Introduction

The previous chapter described how CSR obligations found in international law instruments, both soft law and hard law, are implemented into companies' codes of conduct. This chapter takes the next step and asks under what circumstances CSR obligations that are found in the supply chain leader's code of conduct or elsewhere may become enforceable by means of contract. CSR literature often focuses on the desirability of legal enforcement and support of legal enforcement rather than on its viability. In other words, numerous arguments from ethical and social perspectives are proposed. It is the aim of this chapter to present not only what, in the light of respect for human rights, ought to be achieved, but what legal constructs may be used in order to achieve enforceability of CSR clauses.[1]

The focus of this chapter is on enforcing CSR clauses in the relationship between a supply chain leader and a supplier. Overall, the chapter focuses on two different aspects, i.e. both the need to enforce CSR provisions in the relationship between the chain leader and the supplier and the possible need to *avoid* enforcement of CSR clauses in order to protect the supplier as the weaker party to the contract. The discussion will unfold as follows. Section 2 describes some examples of CSR clauses and implementation models. Section 3 then focuses on two issues: a) the ways in which CSR clauses can become part of the contract between the chain leader and the supplier, b) the interpretation of such clauses, including the problem of "vagueness" of such clauses. In contrast, Section 4 asks to what extent the supplier may need to be protected against enforcement of CSR clauses

1 A number of studies with regard to different national legal systems have already been carried out within recent years. Major works, on which the following presentation will rely, include with regard to international contract law K P Mitkidis, *Sustainability Clauses in International Business Contracts* (Eleven International Publishing 2015), with regard to Dutch law, UK law and Californian law: A L Vytopil, *Contractual Control in the Supply Chain. On Corporate Social Responsibility, Codes of Conduct, Contracts and (Avoiding) Liability* (2015), and with regard to German law and UK law in particular, A Beckers, *Enforcing Corporate Social Responsibility Codes: On Global Self-Regulation and National Law* (Hart Publishing 2015); A Rühmkorf, 'Corporate Social Responsibility' in *Private Law and Global Supply Chains* (Edward Elgar 2015).

through doctrines of unconscionability. Finally, Section 5 analyses the extent to which the relational character of the contract may impact on these questions.

2 Some examples of CSR clauses and models for implementation

Empirical studies reveal that the inclusion of CSR clauses in contracts in the supply chain has become quite common.[2] CSR clauses may have different forms and be formulated in many different ways. Often, CSR obligations are found in a code of conduct. In the following some examples of various formulations are presented.

A clause used by Bombardier in its code of ethics and business conduct ('Bombardier code') is formulated in the following way:

> Bombardier conducts its operations in a sustainable way and in compliance with the environmental laws and regulations. Bombardier expects that environmental protection is a priority for the supplier in all significant aspects of its activities. As a minimum the supplier must comply with all applicable environmental laws, regulations and standards ... [3]

This is an example of a clause that simply requires the observance of national legislation.[4] This type of clause does not seem to impose any obligations on the seller that did not already exist. Probably the only effect of the clause – if implemented into the contract – is that non-observance of environmental legislation is also turned into a contractual matter, so that potentially the contract and contractual remedies can also be used for enforcing the legal requirements. This may be valuable if the activities of the seller take place in a jurisdiction where governmental enforcement of environmental protection legislation is weak, as is common in developing countries.[5]

The Bombardier code continues,

2 See M P Vandenbergh 'Private Environmental Governance' (2013) 99(1) Cornell Law Review 129, 157 with reference to two studies.

3 See <www.bombardier.com/content/dam/Websites/bombardiercom/supporting-documents/BInc/Bombardier-Supplier-Code-of-Conduct-en.pdf> accessed 10 August 2018.

4 A similar clause is found in the *Code of Vendor Conduct* used by Gap Inc. According to Section 5, all factories must 'comply with all applicable environmental laws and regulations' see <http://www.gapinc.com/content/dam/gapincsite/documents/CodeofVendorConduct_FINAL.pdf > accessed 28 August 2018; also Accenture in its code of business ethics as its second principle stipulates that 'we comply with all laws, whether local, national or regional. Accenture people, and those acting on our behalf, are responsible for understanding the applicable rules and must work with legal to ensure compliance', see <www.accenture.com/t20171023T034348Z__w__/dk-en/_acnmedia/PDF-63/Accenture-CoBE-Brochure-English.pdf#zoom=50> accessed 31 August 2018.

5 On problems with regard to changing legislation during the duration of the contract, see below in Section 3.4.

> The supplier shall strive to reduce the impacts of its activities and products on the environment and work towards a “total life cycle” view in product design, while maintaining its competitiveness.[6]

By requiring the buyer not only to adhere to national law but also to ‘strive to achieve a “total life cycle view”’ this clause goes further than the first one.[7]

Another example of an environmental protection provision is the following, also found in a code of conduct:

> Worley Parsons favours Suppliers or Contractors who conduct their business operations in a way that protects the environment and have.... b) a written environmental policy, c) a written environmental management plan to identify risks from their activities and minimize their impacts on the environment.[8]

This provision does not in fact impose any obligations on the supplier, but merely states the buyer’s preference in selection of suppliers.

As explained in Chapter 2, codes of conduct may also make reference to the UN Global Compact or other soft law international principles.[9] By making such reference to non-binding international law, these codes go further than the one in the first example, as the expected regulatory compliance comprises both hard law and soft law principles. Also the supplier’s own environmental policy may go further than the requirements found in applicable hard law.

Clauses like the ones described here can gain contractual force in several different ways. Roughly four different models can be distinguished. Under these models, CSR obligations can be dealt with in a number of different ways and combinations between the models also exist.

A: The express terms model

Under the express terms model, CSR obligations of a supplier may be written directly into the main contract. Alternatively, they may be found as express terms in the terms and conditions of the contract, i.e. the standard terms used by the company.[10]

6 See <www.bombardier.com/content/dam/Websites/bombardiercom/supporting-documents/BInc/Bombardier-Supplier-Code-of-Conduct-en.pdf> accessed 15 August 2018.

7 On the interpretation of clauses like this, see Section 3.3.

8 See <http://www.worleyparsons.com/AboutUs/Opportunities/Documents/Supply%20Chain%20Code%20of%20Conduct.pdf > accessed 10 August, 2018. Similar statements have been expressed by, i.e., Rio Tinto < https://www.riotinto.com/procurement/doing-business-with-us-17809.aspx> accessed 4 September 2018.

9 <http://saabgroup.com/about-company/saab-supplier-portal/Supplier-code-of-conduct/> accessed 17 August 2018.

10 If there is a reference to these terms and conditions in the main contract, the setup may be seen as a combination of the reference model and express terms model.

B: The reference model

Under the reference model, a reference to CSR obligations may be found in the main contract or in the terms and conditions of the contract. The reference may be to the company's code of conduct or CSR obligations formulated elsewhere, for instance in international soft law instruments. The main contract may also contain a reference to the standard terms and conditions, which, again, contain a reference to CSR obligations (*a double reference system*).

C: The stand alone model

Under the stand alone model, the agreement, containing the CSR obligations of suppliers – for instance a code of conduct – is signed aside the "main" supply contract. CSR obligations may be more or less specifically described and the document may be turned into a separate agreement in different ways. Parties to the main supply contract may stipulate additional contractual terms or their respective rights and obligations, including those of CSR, in a separate agreement that they sign. Alternatively, the supplier may be found to have accepted the CSR commitments in the document by confirming this electronically when accessing the buyer's webpage.

D: The implied terms model

Under the implied terms model, CSR obligations are considered part of the contract although not explicitly mentioned in the contract on the basis that such terms are commonly regarded as part of the type of contract in question.[11]

3 Enforcement and classical contract law

3.1. The characteristics of classical contract law

Classical contract law takes as a starting point that two parties have voluntarily assumed well-defined obligations vis-à-vis each other.[12] The contract is regarded as a bi-polar relationship and since the contract only concerns the parties, the parties are free to decide on the content of the contract according to the principle of freedom of contract. This view of the contract affects all parts of contract law, including rules on formation, interpretation and validity of contracts. However, the inclusion of CSR clauses in commercial contracts changes the contract. Thus, CSR clauses do not just concern the parties but societal interests that are external

11 See also C Poncibò, 'The Contractualisation of Environmental Sustainability' (2016) 12(4) European Review of Contract Law 335, 342–344, where Poncibò discusses the possibility of interpreting sustainability goals as implied terms.

12 For the use of the term "classical contract law", see for instance P S Atiyah, *The Rise and Fall of Freedom of Contract* (Oxford University Press 1979) 405.

to the parties. This is one of the reasons why enforcement of CSR clauses by means of classical contract law may often give rise to difficulties. In the following sections, some of the basic challenges are described.

3.2 Is the clause part of the contract at all?

First of all, it needs to be assessed whether the relevant provision is in fact part of the contract. As described in the introduction, one of the ways in which CSR obligations can gain contractual force is by direct implementation into the contract (the express terms model). There are several examples of this in practice.[13] In general, express provisions may be preferred if non-compliance with the specific CSR obligation by a supplier imposes severe economic risks on the buyer. For this reason, for instance, anti-bribery clauses are often included as express terms in a contract.[14]

If the anti-corruption or other CSR provision appears as one of the provisions of the main contract itself it does not give rise to doubt that it is to be considered as a part of the parties' agreement alongside with other (commercial or industrial) terms.[15]

However, empirical research suggests that most often CSR clauses are found outside the commercial terms of the contract, mainly in the company's code of conduct.[16] One of the reasons for this may be that CSR clauses can be long and detailed.[17] If the CSR obligations are found in a code of conduct the relevant provisions can be considered binding in two ways. First, a code of conduct may become binding by way of reference (*the reference model*), meaning that a reference to the code of conduct in the main contract or in the terms and conditions has the effect of incorporating the code of conduct into the contract and thus giving it contractual force.[18] Different national jurisdictions have different

13 Mitkidis (n 1) 155. For more examples, visit <www.lawinsider.com/clause/sustainability> accessed 4 September 2018, which provides a number of CSR clauses that can be used for direct incorporation into different types of contracts.

14 Mitkidis (n 1) 156. The International Chamber of Commerce (ICC) drafted in 2012 a model anti-corruption clause to be included in contracts under which parties intend to comply with the ICC Rules on Combating Corruption (ICC Rules, *ICC Rules on Combating Corruption* 2011) <https://iccwbo.org/publication/icc-rules-on-combating-corruption>. The ICC Rules represent a voluntary tool that business parties may decide to refer to in order to limit their possible exposure to national anti-corruption laws. However, the fact that this clause is rather long and detailed may also lead to its being incorporated by reference.

15 A different question is whether the CSR clauses, due to their content, may be challenged by other fundamental principles of contract law. This question is dealt with in Sections 3.3 –3.4.

16 Mitkidis (n 1) 157.

17 An example is the model corruption clause mentioned in n 14.

18 See G H Treitel, *The Law of the Contract* (10th edn, Sweet & Maxwell 1999) 198 on the incorporation of exemption clauses contained in standard form contracts. For the position in Nordic Law, see U Bernitz, *Standardavtalsrätt* (7th edn, Juristförlaget 2010) 58–63.

thresholds for regarding a provision as incorporated by reference.[19] The content of the CSR provision and the extent to which the reference is highlighted in the text may be relevant to deciding whether a code of conduct must be regarded as incorporated into the contract or not.[20]

Second, the CSR provisions within a code of conduct will be binding if the code of conduct itself is signed or in another way agreed upon by the parties and in this way turned into a separate contract (*the stand alone model*).[21] In contrast, it must be assumed that a code of conduct that is solely found on, e.g., the buyer's webpage, stating certain requirements that all suppliers must live up to (at any time) will most often not be regarded as tacitly accepted by a supplier that enters into a contract with the buyer.[22] A recent empirical study with regard to labour clauses shows that such 'weak' implementation is not uncommon.[23] Accordingly, references to general commercial policies, "values" or "goals" displayed in advertising materials or elsewhere by the buyer will generally not constitute a legally binding contractual commitment on the part of the supplier. In legal literature, it has also been considered whether a code of conduct found on, e.g., the chain leader's webpage is in reality a public declaration that must be considered as an offer that gains contractual force once it is accepted by the beneficiaries of the code of conduct, such as, for instance, employees of the supplier.[24] In English law the doctrine of consideration stands in the way of this construction,[25] which also does not seem viable in German law.[26]

Finally, CSR obligations may be regarded as part of a contract even if neither of the previously described models apply, but it is possible to argue that such commitments are commonly regarded as part of the type of contract in question and consequently should be regarded as implied terms (the implied terms model).[27] A similar argument can be made if conforming to CSR requirements has become an established practice between the parties in a long-term relation.[28] It can also be considered whether certain CSR commitments can be regarded as industry practice.[29] Making this argument

19 See A L Vytopil (n 1) 76, 91, 107, on Dutch law, UK Law and Californian law.
20 Vytopil (n 1) 109.
21 In an empirical study, this model proved to be less frequently used; see Vytopil (n 1) 128.
22 Vytopil (n 1) 139.
23 Ibid.
24 Beckers (n 1) 82.
25 Beckers (n 1) 93.
26 Beckers (n 1) 97.
27 A related line of thinking is presented by M C Menting, 'Industry Codes of Conduct, the Foundations of Contract Law and Regulation: A Bottom-Up Perspective' in R Brownsword, R A J van Gestel, & H-W Micklitz (eds), *Contract and Regulation. A Handbook on New Methods of Law Making in Private Law* (Edward Elgar Publishing 2017) 39, 67, with regard to industry codes, making the point that such codes can be 'enforced in a more indirect fashion when used as a specification for and interpretation of open-ended legal standards in contract law … '
28 Mitkidis (n 1) 163.
29 Mitkidis (n 1) 164.

would require proof that an industry practice has actually been established. Such proof will often be difficult to provide.[30]

3.3 Interpretation: Vagueness of language, intention not to have legal effect and contradictions

It is recognized as a general principle of contract law that for a contract to be enforceable, the content of the clause must live up to a certain minimum of precision.[31] This means that unspecified and generic promises might be not be considered as contractual terms. This principle is also applicable to isolated parts of an agreement, i.e. to specific provisions or clauses, that may be denied legal effect due to vagueness or imprecision, even if the parties by the time of the completion of the contract in fact were aware of their inability to describe their respective obligations with precision. E. Allan Farnsworth expresses the position in this way:

> A third cause of indefiniteness is the parties' inability at the time of the agreement to foresee all of the problems that may arise. Instead of a simple, discrete transaction to be consummated in the near future, there may be a complex of transactions to be spread over a period of time. . . . The extent to which the requirement of definiteness can be accommodated to such situations . . . will affect in an important way the utility of contract law in contemporary economic life.[32]

This is of particular importance with regard to CSR clauses that may often be vague or imprecise in their wording. To take one of the examples mentioned in Section 2, it would not be clear what it would take to satisfy the requirement in the Bombardier code to strive for a 'total life cycle view' in product design.

The meaning of a 'total life cycle view' is uncertain and open to interpretation in the light of specific understandings within the industry and activities of both the chain leader and the supplier. For instance, it is not clear whether the supplier is to observe the 'total life cycle view' from a cost perspective or from a management perspective.[33] One could even argue that only the chain leader is able to properly

30 Mitkidis (n 1) 164, on different ways of proving an industry practice.
31 See, for instance, on this general rule Treitel (n 18), 46, and Halson (n 18) 190–193, both referring to the House of Lords decision in *G Scammel & Nephew Ltd v. Ouston* (1941), and Vytopil (n 1) 68 for Dutch law with reference to article 6:227 DCC, 81 with regard to English law, 97–98 with regard to Californian law. See for Nordic Law O Hansen & V Ulfbeck, *Lærebog i aftaleret* (Jurist-og Økonomforbundets Forlag 2014) 83 and 121 and O Lando et al., *Restatement of Nordic Contract Law* (Djoef Publishing 2016) 185–186, explaining the principle that when a contract is interpreted, preference will be given to an interpretation that renders a term effective (enforceable) rather than ineffective. The rule can be traced back to the Roman law principle s*implex commendation non obligat* (an unspecific recommendation does not bind).
32 See E A Farnsworth, *Contracts* (Little Brown & Co Law & Business 1990) 210.
33 M Pullman & M Sauter, *Sustainability Delivered: Designing Socially and Environmentally Responsible Supply Chains* (Business Expert Press 2014) 109–132.

carry out the life cycle analysis.[34] Therefore, the obligation to 'work towards a "total life cycle view"' on the part of the supplier would require close and unspecified collaboration with the chain leader.

Formulations like these expose the supplier to rather undefined financial and legal risks. At the same time, since it is highly uncertain what obligation the supplier has actually undertaken it will also be difficult for a court to evaluate under which conditions there is a breach of the contract with regard to such clauses. Consequently, it may not be possible to enforce this type of clause by means of ordinary contractual remedies, such as claims for damages and rescission of the contract.[35]

Another barrier to enforcement of CSR provisions as contractual terms of a contract may be found in express terms of the contract to the effect that the CSR obligations are "not intended to have legal effect". Some legal systems have developed specific doctrines of law clarifying that the parties have the right to determine whether certain provisions in a contract are to be considered legally binding or not. Such doctrines are found in Dutch, English and US law.[36] This type of disclaimer is sometimes used with regard to industry codes.[37] As a starting

34 It is often the product designer of the entire product that, knowing the components, can carry out a coherent life cycle analysis in order to assess the costs over the full life span period of a specified of good, service, structure or system. It is usual that the total life cycle assessment includes (full) manufacturing costs, installation costs, operating costs, maintenance and upgrade costs and remaining value at the end of ownership or its useful life; see Pullman and Sauter (n 33) 53–78 and J Browne, I Hunt, & J Zhang, 'The Extended Enterprise' in A Molina, J M Sánchez, & A Kusiak (eds), *Handbook of Life Cycle Engineering: Concepts, Models and Technologies* (Kluwer Academic Publishers 1998) 4–5.

35 Hence, with regard to drafting, one could argue that, given the broad scope of CSR – human rights, labour rights, environmental protection and anti-corruption – the parties, if it is their true intention to apply and enforce these clauses, should draft these clauses in specific contractual language. The corruption clause mentioned in n 14 could be mentioned as an example of a clause that is drafted in rather specific language. An exerpt of the clause follows: "...(3) If a Party, as a result of the exercise of a contractually-provided audit right, if any, of the other Party's accounting books and financial records, or otherwise, brings evidence that the latter Party has been engaging in material or several repeated breaches of Paragraphs 2.1 and 2.2 above, it will notify the latter Party accordingly and require such Party to take the necessary remedial action in a reasonable time and to inform it about such action. If the latter Party fails to take the necessary remedial action or if such remedial action is not possible, it may invoke a defence by proving that by the time the evidence of breach(es) had arisen, it had put into place adequate anti-corruption preventive measures, as described in Article 10 of the ICC Rules on Combating Corruption 2011, adapted to its particular circumstances and capable of detecting corruption and of promoting a culture of integrity in its organization. If no remedial action is taken or, as the case may be, the defence is not effectively invoked, the first Party may, at its discretion, either suspend or terminate the Contract, it being understood that all amounts contractually due at the time of suspension or termination of the Contract will remain payable, as far as permitted by applicable law."

36 Vytopil (n 1) 67, 80, 98.

37 Menting (n 27) 63, stating that 'Some industry codes include in this respect a disclaimer that explicitly states that the code rules are not legally binding or uses similar words to that effect'.

point one might think this type of clause would also be relevant with regard to CSR obligations.[38] However, empirical studies do not mention the existence of such clauses with regard to CSR obligations.[39] One of the reasons for this may be that the buyer (chain leader), who in reality sets the terms of the contract, may not have an interest in making CSR obligations non-binding to the supplier. However, in parallel to the previous discussion on the incorporation of CSR obligations into the contract as implied terms of the contract one might also raise the question whether a "no intent to be legally bound" clause could be considered impliedly part of the contract between the parties with regard to CSR obligations.[40] If it is assumed that CSR obligations largely do not form part of the contract but are most often only stipulated in, e.g., codes of conduct, this could support this argument.[41] A long-standing practice between the parties not to rely on legal tools in the enforcement of CSR obligations in the contract could further support the view that the CSR obligations are only to be regarded as non-binding soft law commitments between the parties, even if they are incorporated into the contract.

Finally, a basic problem that courts may face in interpreting a supply chain contract is whether the interpretation of the CSR requirements in the contract may affect the interpretation of the commercial terms of the contracts and vice versa.[42] Thus, if a contract contains not only commercial terms but also CSR terms (which may be categorized as 'regulatory terms'[43]) these two types of terms may often in reality be in conflict with one another. For instance, the commercial part of the contract may require a high speed of delivery and low prices while the regulatory part of the contract at the same time demands that the supplier lives up to far reaching CSR obligations. Both things may not be possible at the same time.[44] This gives rise to the question of which terms should be given precedence over the other ones. In contemporary commercial court practice it must be assumed that there will be a tendency to place the

38 Vytopil (n 1) 67.
39 Vytopil (n 1) 67, 80, 98.
40 See Menting (n 27) 77, with reference to Dutch case law where it has been found that an industry code incorporated into a franchise agreement could not be considered to include legally binding obligations but 'amount [ed] to a standard of decency at the most'.
41 Vytopil (n 1) 98: 'If the promises concern a subject matter that is generally dealt with in a legally binding manner, unless the MNC and the supplier state that they do *not* wish to be legally bound, they will be legally bound'.
42 See F Cafaggi, 'The Regulatory Functions of Transnational Commercial Contracts: New Architectures'(2013) 36(6) Fordham International Law Journal 1557, 1610, arguing that the regulatory part of the contract will affect the entire contract.
43 Cafaggi (n 42) 1558.
44 According to an empirical study buyers sometimes force suppliers to break the code with demanding production schedules; see J Phillips & S K Lim 'Their Brother's Keeper: Global Buyers and The Legal Duty to Protect Supplier's Employees' (2009) 61(2) Rutgers Law Review 209, 349.

most weight on the commercial parts of a contract, thus preventing the enforcement of CSR obligations as a "defence" against the chain leader.

4 Invalidity: CSR clauses and unconscionability doctrines in classical contract law

Legal systems contain various rules on invalidity of contracts.[45] With regard to CSR obligations, in particular, rules on unconscionability may be relevant.

Thus, CSR clauses are often one-sided, where the economically more powerful party – the chain leader – obliges an economically weaker party – the supplier – to carry out activities that are burdensome. Given the inequality of bargaining power, a supplier may have no choice but to accept the buyer's terms, including CSR obligations.[46] Moreover, a supplier may risk sanctions consisting in exclusion from the supply chain if the supplier does not live up to contract requirements. This raises the question of the possible need to protect the supplier as the weaker party in the supply chain.[47]

Particularly problematic are situations where implemented systems of rules directly or indirectly are under the unilateral control of one of the parties.[48] CSR clauses may be formulated in this way, giving the chain leader the power to unilaterally change or decide what is the acceptable level of compliance.[49] This places an – in principle – unlimited and undefined risk on the supplier.

45 For Nordic law, see Lando et al. (n 31) Chapter 4 on such grounds of invalidity as coercion, fraud, undue influence and exploitation, etc. See also the Draft Common Frame of Reference (DCFR), Chapter 7.

46 Cafaggi (n 42) 1567, noting that 'The main contractor the seller is forced to assume contractually binding obligations towards the buyer not only for himself but also for the parties located upstream'. See also Menting (n 28) 87, mentioning the problem of imbalanced industry codes.

47 D Leczykiewicz, 'Private Regulation, Compliance and Reviewability of Contracts' in R Brownsword, R A J van Gestel, & H-W Micklitz (eds), *Contract and Regulation. A Handbook on New Methods of Law Making in Private Law* (Edward Elgar Publishing 2017) 323, 344, puts it this way: ' . . . Incentives for compliance may stem from fear about one's reputation or economic pressure from existing contractual partners, potential future partners or a trade organization to which the non-complying party belongs. The role of state law is to determine when such pressures are legitimate . . . '

48 This situation is well-known from long term contracts entered into between public authorities and private suppliers of goods or services where the public entity may have the power to unilaterally bring about a change of the legal requirements underlying the contract.

49 Cafaggi (n 42) 1570, stating that 'Often the content of the contracts between main contractors and suppliers depends upon the contract between the retailer and contractor, and unilateral modifications to the latter contract are automatically transferred to those upstream'. On delegation of unilateral power to one contracting party to decide the legal position of the other party in public contracts, see O Hansen, 'Public Law by Contract – The Reluctant Creation of Private Markets for Public Welfare Service' (2017) 25(3) European Review of Private Law 644. On the enforceability of contract modifications, see Halson (n 18) 323 ff.

In such situations, the supplier might look for a possible defence in other branches of the law. In the European Union, one solution to balance the bargaining powers has been sought in consumer protection law, which has provided additional tools for consumers against the terms favouring corporations that abuse their economic superiority and knowledge. Thus, at the EU level, the unfair contract terms directive applies to the relationships between companies and consumers.[50] However, even though one may claim similarity between consumers and small- and medium-sized companies (often the suppliers), the Court of Justice of the European Union (CJEU) interprets the concept of "consumer" restrictively.[51] The CJEU has consistently held that EU definitions of "consumer" must not be given any wider interpretation.[52] Consequently, the directive will hardly be relevant with regard to the relationship between the chain leader and the supplier.

With regard to a specific type of supply chain, namely the food supply chains, the European Commission has recently published a draft Directive on Unfair Trading Practices in Business-to-Business Relationships in the Food Supply Chain.[53] This Directive concerns the position of small- and medium-sized companies when negotiating and dealing with larger corporations with significant bargaining power that can impose pressure on other weaker operators in the food supply chains.[54] Thus, in general, the proposal reflects an increased awareness of the problem of unequal bargaining power in the relationship between the chain leader and the supplier.

If adopted, this Directive will prohibit certain specifically listed unfair trading practices, which are particularly harmful for small- and medium-sized operators in the food supply chain.[55] As an example serves the the prohibition against practices, according to which 'a buyer unilaterally and retroactively changes the terms of the

50 Council Directive 93/13/EEC of 5 April 1993 on unfair terms in consumer contracts, OJ EC L.95/29. The directive on unfair terms introduced the EU's notion of 'good faith' to prevent imbalances in the rights and obligations between sellers and consumers.

51 E.g. Case C-361/89 *Patrice Di Pinto* [1991] L 372–31.

52 E.g. C-541/99 *Cape Snc v. Idealservice Srl* [2001] ECR O-09049.

53 'Proposal for a Directive of the European Parliament and of the Council on Unfair Trading Practices in Business-To-Business Relationships in the Food Supply Chain' COM/2018/0173Final – 2018/082 (COD), available online at: <https://eur-lex.europa.eu/legal-content/EN/TXT/?uri=CELEX%3A52018PC0173>. This Directive is based on the previous Green Paper on 'Unfair Trading Practices in the Business-to-Business Food and Non-Food Supply Chain in Europe' COM/2013/037 final. The European Commission substantiated the rationale to limit the scope of the directive to the food supply chain with its research and finding that the food supply chain is particularly vulnerable to unfair trading practices due to large differences in bargaining power. Ibid., Preamble 7.

54 The European Commission, Competition in the food supply chain, 'Staff Working Document' (28 October 2009) 28 refers to 'stronger buyers', who are often perceived as gatekeeper to consumer markets. See also EY, Cambridge Econometrics Ltd, Arcadia International (2014), 'The Economic Impact of Modern Retail on Choice and Innovation in the EU Food Sector' study for the European Commission 45.

55 Ibid., Preamble 5.

supply agreement concerning the frequency, timing or volume of the supply or delivery, the quality standards or the prices of the food products'.[56] Such unfair trading practices are to be sanctioned by a special public authority empowered to impose fines on the operator conducting unfair trading practices.[57] Thus, only public law sanctions are prescribed in the proposal. Furthermore, the prohibitions only concern the commercial terms of the contract.[58] Thus, even if it is assumed that the public law regulation will have a spill over effect on private law sanctions and influence the extent to which courts will be willing to find that terms of a contract between the chain leader and the supplier should be regarded as unfair and consequently invalid under existing doctrines, the prohibitions in the directive will not be directly applicable to CSR clauses.[59]

The legal position on the issue of unconscionability with regard to business-to-business contracts varies considerably in the different legal systems[60] and different legal systems may also apply different techniques for protecting the weaker party to a contract.[61] However, although not entirely impossible, in general it is difficult to succeed in getting a business-to-business contract deemed invalid due to unconscionability.[62]

56 The proposal, art.3(1)c.

57 The proposal article 4. It is foreseen that the relevant authority will often be the national competition authority; see the comment to article 4 in the Explanatory Memorandum to the Proposal for a Directive of the European Parliament and of the Council on Unfair Trading Practices in Business-to-Business Relationships in the Food Supply Chain, COM/2018/0173Final – 2018/082 (COD), available online at: <https://eur-lex.europa.eu/legal-content/EN/TXT/?uri=CELEX%3A52018PC0173>.

58 The proposal art. 3.

59 On the connection between the commercial part of the contract and the CSR part, see Section 3.3.

60 Relevant general provisions include the German BGB §242 ('Treu un Glauben') and in the Common Nordic Contracts Act § 36 (on unreasonable agreements and agreements contradicting good faith). Under English law, the Unfair Contract Terms Act 1977 is applicable to business-to-business relationships, see R Lawson (ed), *Exclusion Clauses and Unfair Contract Terms* (11th edn, Sweet & Maxwell 2017). However, the name of the Act is a bit misleading given that it is applicable only in regard to the terms excluding or restricting liability in tort, not to other contractual terms, see *Chitty on Contracts, Volume I, General Principles* (31st edn, Sweet & Maxwell 2012) 1051–1053. The act does not seek to control unfair contract terms in general. In the US, the court is able to strike 'any clause of the contract' if the clause is unconscionable; see Section 2–302(1) of the UCC (2015), Farnsworth (n 32) §4.28.

61 Thus, courts have held that the terms of a contract did not become part of the contract at all (as described under Section 3.2). Sometimes courts have applied rules of strict construction, finding the terms unclear or ambiguous (as described under Section 3.3) and then interpreting them *contra proferentem* ("against the offerer") – and hence against the more powerful party; see E A Farnsworth, 'Comparative Contract Law' in M Reimann & R Zimmermann (eds), *The Oxford Handbook of Comparative Law* (Oxford University Press 2012) 912.

62 For instance, in Scandinavian law, art. 36 on unconscionability in the Danish Contract Act has been applied as a basis for setting aside contractual terms in purely commercial settings; see U 2001.284 V, U 2004.2400 H, U 2004.1968 V, U 2012 5235 H.

5 Adjusting the doctrines

5.1 Applying relational law and network contract theory

As described in the previous section, enforcement of CSR obligations under classical contract law faces a series of challenges. Based on traditional principles of formation of contract, it may not always be possible to view CSR commitments as forming part of the contract. To the extent that they do form part of the contract, interpreting the commitments may also pose difficulties and hinder enforcement. In contrast, in Europe, rules on unconscionability seem only to a limited extent to be available for the protection of the supplier against unfair contract terms in the contract with the chain leader. However, these observations need some supplementing, since the legal position between the contracting parties may be influenced by factors that lie outside the formal requirements of the contract, such as the party's long-term interests or the overall contractual pattern established to enable supply. At least two independent – yet interrelated – lines of contract law theory have addressed this issue and can be said to provide arguments for adjustments of the previously mentioned principles of fundamental contract law.

5.2 Relational contract theory: Lowering the bars for contracting

Relational contract theory may be seen as providing arguments for an inclusion of CSR commitments into the sphere of the binding obligations of the parties.

Put simply, contractual obligations and remedies against breach derive from the existence of a binding contract and the ability and willingness of a court system to give legal effect to the contractual content of the agreement. Classical contract law sought to tie any legal obligation of a party to a contract to the (objective) wording of the contract terms[63] or – in civil law systems – to the (subjective) intentions of the parties.[64] It regarded the contract as a matter concerned solely with the interests of the contractual parties. This model of understanding developed in societies where day-to-day exchange of generic goods and services without further involvement (sometimes called "discrete contracts"[65]) was the primary type of market transaction. Thus, as laid out, a classical contract law approach to CSR clauses will often be restrictive and exclude CSR commitments from the core part of the agreement rather than interpreting them as being a part of the binding contract.

The characteristics of modern trade and market activity, however, differ substantially from the classical picture of the market. Supply chains are typically established on the basis of long-term agreements setting the legal framework for current exchanges between the parties. Long-term commitments are often chosen either because the performance of the supplier or the conditions for exchange are

63 See Farnsworth (n 32) 503.
64 See Atiyah (n 11) 405.
65 See, e.g., Farnsworth (n 32) 210, M A Eisenberg, 'Why There is no Law of Relational Contracts' (2000) 94(3) Northwestern University Law Review 813.

of a complex or uncertain nature, causing transaction costs to increase.[66] In addition, establishing long-term relations within the supply chain often serves the purpose of building and protecting the reputational value of the product.

For a long time it has been acknowledged that uncertainty and complexity of obligations establish an interdependence between the parties.[67] The risk of non-performance of a party and a disruption of the transaction as a whole creates a need for adjustments or variations of the contract terms to secure the common goals and long-term interest of the parties, i.e. their contractual relation.[68] On the basis of these observations relational contract theory decades ago pointed to the fact that governing contractual norms often exists outside the contract documents and impacts on the behaviour of the parties and their actual legal position.[69] Although a separate "relational contract law" was never developed as a specific set of rules applying to a specific type of contract, relational law thinking has arguably to some extent influenced general contract law.[70] In fact, today different legal systems (though with considerable variations) more willingly accept contract interpretation as being under the influence of external normative factors.[71] The relational character of the transaction may to some degree push the main terms of the contract into the background, e.g. by lowering the bars set by existing doctrines of contract formation and widening the frames set for contract interpretation.[72]

In light of the relational element of supply chain contracts, it could be assumed that courts would *more willingly accept* the contractual character of CSR clauses when those are incorporated into the contract by reference (*the reference model*) or agreed upon in a separate document (*the stand alone model*); see in general Section 3.2.

Likewise, it could be expected that courts would be *less reluctant* to give legal effect to CSR clauses by way of interpretation[73] or to consider CSR terms to be implied (*the implied terms model*); see in general Section 3.3.

66 See, e.g., S Grundmann, F Caffagi, & G Vettori, 'The Contractual Basis for Long-Term Organization – The Overall Architecture' in S Grundmann, F Caffagi, & G Vettori (eds), *The Organizational Contract* (Routledge 2013) 10–11.
67 See O E Williamson, 'Transaction-Cost Economics: The Governance of Contractual Relations' (1979) 22(2) Journal of Law & Economics 233–262.
68 See I R Macneil, 'Contracts: Adjustment of Long-Term Economic Relations under Classical, Neoclassical, and Relational Contract Law' (1978) 72 North Western University Law Review 854–905.
69 See S Macaulay, 'Non-Contractual Relations in Business: A Preliminary Study' (1963) 28(1) American Sociological Review 55–67; I R Macneil (n 66), 854ff, 895ff.
70 Leczykiewicz (n 47) 238–239. See also E Tjong Tjin Tai, 'Networks and Informal Contract Law' in R Brownsword, R A J van Gestel, & H-W Micklitz (eds), *Contract and Regulation. A Handbook on New Methods of Law Making in Private Law* (Edward Elgar Publishing 2017) 235, 238–239, describing the Dutch legal system as reflecting a more contextual approach on the basis of relational law theory.
71 For an overview, see R E Scott, 'The Promise and the Peril of Relational Contract Theory' in J Braucher, J Kidwell, & W C Whitford (eds), *Revisiting the Contracts Scholarship of Stewart Macaulay* (Hart Publishing 2013) 105–139.
72 Ibid., 266.
73 See, e.g., Beckers (n 1) 284–290.

One relevant argument against such expected effect of the supply chain's relational character is, however, that CSR commitments in fact may *not* be reflecting the parties' actual common goals or expectations, but rather merely a need for the chain (leader) to express a social concern as a part of an advertising concept or to avoid negative public attention or to comply with applicable law, such as reporting and due diligence law.[74] Nevertheless, some legal scholars have recently drawn upon the heritage of the relational contract theorists to show how, for instance, sustainability clauses are or might be implemented into supply chains.[75] Modern relational contract theory points to digitalization of markets and transaction structures as the solution to the problem for collaboration of the geographical distance between the parties in global business networks.[76] In fact, the insertion of CSR clauses in a contract may have the effect of reinforcing the relational character of the contract.[77] A CSR clause may often reflect the fact that there is considerable reputational value connected to the product and/or to supply chain members themselves (typically the chain leader).

5.3 Network theory: Raising the level of protection of weak network participants?

As mentioned in Section 3.4, general principles of contract law provide only limited protection against CSR clauses placing, e.g., undefined economical risks upon the supplier and/or placing it within the unilateral power of the chain leader to determine the content of the supplier's performance. The structure of modern supply chains may, however, express an inequality of bargaining power, which often exists between downstream and upstream supply chain links. Relational contract law theory was not designed to handle such situations. It evolved from sociological studies of the behaviour of businessmen and on the basis of economic theory. Generally, it was not concerned with the protection of contracting parties considered to be weak or in the need of social protection, such as consumers, for example.[78]

74 See Chapters 4 and 7 in this volume.
75 See F Cafaggi, 'Regulation through Contracts: Supply-Chain Contracting and Sustainability Standards' (2016) 12(3) European Review of Contract Law 1–40, and, e. g., Beckers (n 1) 284–290. Relational contract law theory has also been used to show how social welfare policies are protected through housing development contracts; see N Davidson, 'Relational Contracts in the Privatization of Social Welfare: The Case of Housing' (2006) 24 Yale Law & Policy Review 263.
76 See T Dietz, 'Relational Contracts 2.0 – Efficiency and Power' in A C Cutler & T Dietz (eds), *The Politics of Private Transnational Governance by Contract* (Routledge 2017) 116–123, and T Dietz, 'Contract Law, Relational Contracts, and Reputational Networks in International Trade: An Empirical Investigation into Cross-Border Contracts in the Software Industry' (2011) 37(1) Law & Social Inquiry 53.
77 Mitkidis (n 1) 94–95.
78 Leib (n 72) 267–268. More recent parts of legal scholarship have aimed to draw upon relational contract theories in relation to contract laws possible social dimensions; see, e.g., T Wilhelmsson, *Critical Studies in Private Law* (Kluwer Academic Studies 1992).

However, transnational supply chain contracts are not only examples of relational contracts, but also of a contractual network. Even before the evolution of the internet and the general globalization of markets, some legal scholars have pointed to the fact that the network structure of business transactions impacted on fundamental principles of private law. For instance, it has been suggested, that due to the common interdependence in contractual networks, an increased duty of loyalty may be assumed to exist between network participants.[79] As an example, network leaders may under the circumstances be assumed to be under an implied duty to treat other network participants fairly and under due consideration of the common network interests.[80]

Recent scholarship – combining network theory with relational contract law thinking – points at digitalization as a prominent fertilizer for relational contracting in global supply chains.[81] The digital exchange of information shapes new and efficient means for supply chain management.[82] These new means for monitoring and exchange of information must be assumed to include a potential control with CSR compliance.[83] As an example, a real-time camera monitoring of the production site may give the chain leader information that would otherwise be unachievable in the relation between independent contractors, not only with respect to compliance with the commercial terms, but also with respect to abuses covered by CSR standards, such as, e.g., the use of child labour. However, digitalization of global supply chains may also increase the gap in bargaining power between chain leaders and suppliers, e.g. because suppliers may find themselves forced to accept full transparency of their business sphere towards the chain leader. Due to the immense economic value of the product's reputation, sanctions in the case of non-compliance with both commercial and CSR terms (such as rescission of the contract and exclusion from the chain /network), may be unbearable.

This imbalance created between contracting parties by new business models and the risk of unconscionable results even in these purely commercial settings may support the view that there is a need to rethink existing principles on unconscionability or even more generally, the foundations of modern general contract law.[84] Thus, modern transnational supply chains are based upon substantial reputational values and close interaction and knowledge sharing among the chain participants. The contracting parties and the transactions will often be subject to

79 See, e.g., H Collins, 'Introduction to Networks as Connected Contracts' in G Teubner & H Collins (eds), *Networks as Connected Contracts* (Hart Publishing 2011) 14–15.

80 See, e.g., M Bianca, 'Good Faith Related Duties of Disclosure and a View on Franchising' in S Grundmann, F Caffagi, & G Vettori (eds), *The Organizational Contract* (Routledge 2013) 181–196.

81 See Dietz (n 76) 113–129.

82 Dietz 2017 (n 76) 113.

83 See T Dietz, *Global Order Beyond Law* (Hart Publishing 2016) 84–88, and in Chapter 7.

84 Along the same line of thought, A Beckers, 'Corporate Codes of Conduct and Contract Law: A Doctrinal and Normative Approach' in R Brownsword, R A J van Gestel, & H-W Micklitz (eds), *Contract and Regulation. A Handbook on New Methods of Law Making in Private Law* (Edward Elgar Publishing 2017) 89, 130 ff.

considerable internal transparency. Consequently, the commercial background is significantly different from the now relatively well-known business-to-consumer setting, and will imply a much more complex fairness evaluation. Moreover – and illustrative of the complexity – as touched upon in Chapter 7, the aim to protect suppliers considered to be commercially weak or inferior vis-à-vis the chain leader may further collide with the interests of third parties in holding the chain members responsible for compliance with CSR policies.

6 Conclusion

CSR provisions are increasingly incorporated into contracts in the supply chain. However, to the extent that suppliers do not live up to these obligations, contractual enforcement may become relevant. The analysis shows that such enforcement may face severe difficulties. Firstly, CSR clauses are often found in codes of conduct and it is not always clear that these codes are part of the contract at all. Secondly, if the clauses are written in a vague and imprecise language, they may be difficult to enforce. However, to the extent that the clauses are in fact to be considered part of the contract between the parties, the use of CSR clauses in contracts may also pose problems of a different kind. For example, the clauses may give the buyer a unilateral right to change requirements in the contract, rendering the contract severely unbalanced. Moreover, rules on unconscionability can only be expected to protect the supplier as the weak party to a limited extent. Basically this means that, although contracts seem to be used as a tool for achieving CSR goals, the traditional (classical) contract law enforcement mechanisms may prove less useful both with regard to conveying contractual force to the clause and with regard to offering protection of the weak party in the contractual relationship. In general, contract law may face a challenge in adapting to a new role as facilitator of the use of CSR clauses. Inspiration may be sought in relational contract law theory. In its origin, relational contract theory sprung from sociological observations and economic theory aiming to understand the dynamics of long-term and complex transactions. Thus, relational law theory may provide a basis for arguing that the bars with regard to contract formation should be lowered and that vague CSR clauses could be given some meaning through flexible interpretation. However, relational contract theory evolved long before the digital revolution of transnational trade and was only little aware of a possible need for protection of weak contracting parties. It is insufficient for dealing with the imbalance created between contracting parties by new business models. The risk of unconscionable results even in these purely commercial settings may indicate that there is a need to revitalize the idea of the social and protective elements as forming part of general contract law.

Bibliography

Beckers A, *Enforcing Corporate Social Responsibility Codes: On Global Self-Regulation and National Law* (Hart Publishing 2015).

Bernitz U, *Standardavtalsrätt* (7th edn, Juristförlaget 2010).

Bianca M, 'Good Faith Related Duties of Disclosure and a View on Franchising' in Grundmann S, Caffagi F, & Vettori G (eds), *The Organizational Contract* (Routledge 2013), 181–196.

Browne J, Hunt I, & Zhang J, 'The Extended Enterprise' in Molina A, Sánchez J M, & Kusiak A (eds), *Handbook of Life Cycle Engineering: Concepts, Models and Technologies* (Kluwer Academic Publishers1998) 4–5.

Cafaggi F, 'The Regulatory Functions of Transnational Commercial Contracts: New Architectures'(2013) 36(6) *Fordham International Law Journal.*

Cafaggi F, 'Regulation through Contracts: Supply-chain Contracting and Sustainability Standards' (2016) 12(3) *European Review of Contract Law* 1–40.

Chitty J et al., *Chitty on Contracts, Volume I, General Principles* (31st edn, Sweet & Maxwell 2012).

Collins H, 'Introduction to Networks as Connected Contracts' in TeubnerG & CollinsH (eds), *Networks as Connected Contracts* (Hart Publishing 2011) 14–15.

Davidson N, 'Relational Contracts in the Privatization of Social Welfare: The Case of Housing' (2006) 24 *Yale Law & Policy Review* 263.

Dietz T, 'Contract Law, Relational Contracts, and Reputational Networks in International Trade: An Empirical Investigation into Cross-Border Contracts in the Software Industry' (2011) 37(1) *Law & Social Inquiry* 53.

Dietz T, 'Relational Contracts 2.0 – Efficiency and Power' in Cutler A C & Dietz T (eds), *The Politics of Private Transnational Governance by Contract* (Routledge 2017) 116–123

Farnsworth E A, *Contracts* (Little Brown & Co Law & Business 1990) 210.

Farnsworth E A, 'Comparative Contract Law' in Reimann M & Zimmermann R (eds), *The Oxford Handbook of Comparative Law* (Oxford University Press 2012) 912.

Grundmann S, Caffagi F, & Vettori G, 'The Contractual Basis for Long-Term Organization – The Overall Architecture' in Grundmann S, Caffagi F, & Vettori G (eds), *The Organizational Contract* (Routledge 2013) 10–11.

Halson R, *Contract Law* (2nd edn, Pearson 2013).

Hansen O & Ulfbeck V, *Lærebog i aftaleret* (Jurist-og Økonomforbundets Forlag 2014) 83 and 121.

Lando O *et al.*, *Restatement of Nordic Contract Law* (Djoef Publishing 2016) 185–186.

Lawson R (ed), *Exclusion Clauses and Unfair Contract Terms* (11th edn, Sweet & Maxwell 2017).

Leczykiewicz D, 'Private Regulation, Compliance and Reviewability of Contracts' in Brownsword R, van Gestel R A J, & Micklitz H-W (eds), *Contract and Regulation: A Handbook on New Methods of Law Making in Private Law* (Edward Elgar Publishing 2017) 323.

Leib E J, 'Relational Contract Theory and Consumer Form Contract' in Braucher J, Kidwell J, & Whitford W C (eds), *Revisiting the Contracts Scholarship of Stewart Macaulay* (Hart Publishing 2013).

Macaulay S, 'Non-Contractual Relations in Business: A Preliminary Study' (1963) 28(1) *American Sociological Review* 55–67.

Macneil I R, 'Contracts: Adjustment of Long-Term Economic Relations under Classical, Neoclassical, and Relational Contract Law' (1978) 72 *North Western University Law Review* 854–905.

Mitkidis K P, *Sustainability Clauses in International Business Contracts* (Eleven International Publishing 2015).

Phillips J & Lim S-K, 'Their Brother's Keeper: Global Buyers and The Legal Duty to Protect Supplier's Employees' (2009) 61(2) *Rutgers Law Review* 209, 349.

Poncibò C, 'The Contractualisation of Environmental Sustainability' (2016) 12(4) *European Review of Contract Law* 335, 342–344.

Pullman M & Sauter M, *Sustainability Delivered: Designing Socially and Environmentally Responsible Supply Chains* (Business Expert Press 2014) 109–132.

Scott R E, 'The Promise and the Peril of Relational Contract Theory' in BraucherJ, KidwellJ, & WhitfordW C (eds), *Revisiting the Contracts Scholarship of Stewart Macaulay* (Hart Publishing 2013).

Tai E T T, 'Networks and Informal Contract Law' in Brownsword R, van Gestel R A J, & Micklitz H-W (eds), *Contract and Regulation. A Handbook on New Methods of Law Making in Private Law* (Edward Elgar Publishing 2017) 235.

Treitel G H, *The Law of the Contract* (10th edn, Sweet & Maxwell 1999).

Vandenbergh M P, 'Private Environmental Governance' (2013) 99(1) *Cornell Law Review* 129, 157.

Vytopil A L, *Contractual Control in the Supply Chain. On Corporate Social Responsibility, Codes of Conduct, Contracts and (Avoiding) Liability* (Eleven Internationla Publishing 2015).

4 Enforcement of sustainability contractual clauses in supply chains by third parties

Kateřina Mitkidis

1 Introduction

The incorporation of sustainability-related provisions into supply chain agreements became a widespread practice among companies seated in developed countries.[1] On the face, these provisions primarily aim to protect the environment, secure upholding of human and labour rights in suppliers' operation and/or prevent corruption (hereinafter "sustainability contractual clauses" or "SCCs"). In other words, the beneficiaries of these provisions are parties external to the supply chain agreement, those being primarily suppliers' employees, local communities and global population as a whole.

However, for companies with international supply chains, sustainability contractual clauses serve other important functions. First, companies seated in developed countries are under public scrutiny in respect to their sustainable and ethical conduct.[2] News reporting unsustainable or unethical behaviour in a company's supply chain draws attention and threatens the company's brand, and thus sales.[3]

1 See in respect to environmental provisions M P Vandenberg, 'The New Wal-Mart Effect: The Role of Private Contracting in Global Governance' (2007) 54(4) UCLA Law Review 913; D McBarnet & M Kurkchiyan, 'Corporate Social Responsibility Through Contractual Control? Global Supply Chains and "Other-Regulation"' in D McBarnet, A Voiculescu, & T Campbell (eds), *The New Corporate Accountability: Corporate Social Responsibility and the Law* (Cambridge University Press 2007) 59; Pace University School of Law and International Association for Commercial Contracts and Management, 'The Triple Bottom Line: The Use of Sustainability and Stabilization Clauses in International Contracts' (2010) at 26; K P Mitkidis, *Sustainability Clauses in International Business Contracts* (Eleven International Publishing 2015) 153–155; see in respect to human rights provisions K Mitkidis, S Perkovic, & P Mitkidis, 'Tendencies in Contractual Governance to Promote Human and Labour Rights in Transnational Supply Chains', working paper, on file with the authors.

2 See for example Human Rights Watch, <www.hrw.org/topic/business> accessed 20 July 2018.

3 On the relationship between CSR and financial performance, see Q Wang, J Dou, & S Jia, 'A Meta-Analytic Review of Corporate Social Responsibility and Corporate Financial Performance: The Moderating Effect of Contextual Factors' (2016) 55(8) Business & Society 1083. On the relationship between media attention and companies' environmental performance, see J Haddock-Fraser & I Fraser, 'Assessing

Second, companies are facing a threat of increasing legalisation of the relevant areas. If we take child labour within international supply chains as an example, it used to be regulated primarily by international law that is not directly applicable on private subjects.[4] Recently, an increasing number of legal obligations has been imposed on businesses at the EU and national levels in this area. With effect from 2017, the EU has obliged large companies to report on their human rights policies, including respective implementation tools (such as due diligence) and key performance indicators.[5] Reporting obligations are also prescribed by the California Transparency in Supply Chains Act of 2010 and the UK Modern Slavery Act 2015 (namely its Transparency in Supply Chain Provisions). The Dutch parliament has, in 2017, adopted the Child Labour Due Diligence Law (currently within the senate).[6] France followed the same year, adopting a due diligence law aiming to prevent serious human rights abuses, including child labour, in supply chains.[7] By implementing human rights provisions into their supply chain contracts, companies may secure (partial) compliance with these laws; in other words, contracts attempt to implement and operationalise the new legal obligations. They also aim to create a safe harbour.[8] Moreover, by including these issues into supply chain contracts, companies signal to the regulators that no more hard law is necessary, as the problems are already taken care of by the companies themselves.

However, while there is much motivation to include sustainability clauses into supply chain contracts, there is much less motivation to enforce them. Sustainability clauses are often disconnected from the subject matter of a specific contract.[9] As such, if a sustainability clause is breached, the specific contract can still be performed without major disturbance.[10] In other words, the

Corporate Environmental Reporting Motivations: Differences Between “Close-to-Market” and “Business-to-Business” Companies’ (2008) 15(3) Corporate Social Responsibility and Environmental Management 140.

4 ILO Convention No. 138 Minimum Age Convention 1973, adopted in Geneva 1973, entered into force 1976; International Labour Organization (ILO) Convention No. 182 Worst Forms of Child Labour Convention 1999, adopted in Geneva 1999, entered into force 2000.

5 Directive 2014/95/EU amending Directive 2013/34/EU as regards disclosure of non-financial and diversity information by certain large undertakings and groups [2014] OJ L 330/1. The Directive had partly built on existing national legislation, especially those in the UK (2006) and Denmark (2008).

6 Wet Zorgplicht Kinderarbeid. Information on the legislative process available at <www.eerstekamer.nl/wetsvoorstel/34506_initiatiefvoorstel_van_laar> accessed 11 June 2018. For more information, see Chapter 6 in this volume.

7 Loi no. 2017–399 du 27 Mars 2017 relative au devoir de vigilance des sociétés mères et des entreprises donneuses d’ordre.

8 On the concept of safe harbour, see more in Chapter 6 in this volume.

9 M Andrecka & K Mitkidis, ‘Sustainability Requirements in EU Public and Private Procurement: A Right or an Obligation?’ (2017) 1 Nordic Journal of Commercial Law 57–89, 65–69.

10 An exception to this is the situation where a sustainability contractual clause is connected to a certification scheme. See F Cafaggi, ‘The Regulatory Functions of Transnational Commercial Contracts: New Architectures’ (2013) 36(6) Fordham International Law Journal 1557.

breach does not directly interfere with parties' transactional interests. Thus, a major issue in respect to sustainability contractual clauses remains the interaction of their aim on the face towards third parties on the one hand and the companies' motivations to enforce their commercial contracts for the benefit of third parties on the other. Although there is ample legal and business literature and theory on aligning these interests (for example the stakeholder theory or competitive advantage theory in CSR),[11] those have proven to be difficult to operationalise in practice.[12]

The gap between diverse interests is broadened by the beneficiaries of the sustainability contractual clauses not having an obvious legal standing to enforce the provisions. As third parties do not sign the supply chain agreement that benefits them, they lack privity and, thus, also available contractual remedies. The enforcement of supply chain contracts remains in the hands of the contractual parties, which often do not prefer to strictly enforce sustainability contractual clauses, especially not through courts.[13] This is not only due to the fear of public exposure of any unsustainable or unethical conduct in international supply chains that could harm the involved company or its brand, but is also due to the facts that (i) the regulatory purpose[14] of sustainability contractual clauses may often be achieved more slowly over time through relational enforcement tools (although harming individuals and communities 'on the way'); (ii) remedies available to companies enforcing sustainability contractual clauses on their suppliers are unsuitable to remedy the harms that can occur;[15] and (iii) often, sustaining the business relationship is simply more important for the contractual parties than the possible benefits of the business relationship to external subjects.[16]

As a result, third parties that should benefit from sustainability contractual clauses have been exploring legal strategies to enforce these provisions directly. One of the more successful strategies so far has been using false advertising

11 R Edward Freeman, *Strategic Management: A Stakeholder Approach* (Pitman 1984); M E Porter & M R Kramer, 'Strategy & Society: The Link Between Competitive Advantage and Corporate Social Responsibility' (2006) 84(12) Harvard Business Review 78.

12 See, e.g., Wang, Dou and Jia (n 3).

13 McBarnet and Kurkchiyan (n 1) 79; F Cafaggi, 'The Architecture of Transnational Private Regulation' (2011) EUI Working Paper, LAW 2011/12, European University Institute, 9; L-W Lin, 'Legal Transplants through Private Contracting: Codes of Vendor Conduct in Global Supply Chains as an Example' (2009) 57(3) American Journal of Comparative Law 711, 725; Mitkidis (n 1) 7; P Verbruggen, 'Private Regulatory Standards in Commercial Contracts: Questions of Compliance' in H-W Micklitz, R A J Van Gestel, & R Brownsword (eds), *Contract and Regulation: A Handbook on New Methods of Law Making in Private Law* (Edward Elgar Publishing 2017) 301.

14 Cafaggi (n 10).

15 Mitkidis (n 1) 216–230.

16 A L Vytopil, *Contractual Control in the Supply Chain. On Corporate Social Responsibility, Codes of Conduct, Contracts and (Avoiding) Liability* (Eleven International Publishing 2015) 126; N Affolder, 'Looking for Law in Unusual Places: Cross-Border Diffusion of Environmental Norms' (2018) Transnational Environmental Law 22.

claims.[17] Use of contract law-based claims has been sporadic and has had a lower success rate.[18] There are basically two contract law concepts that come to mind. First, the legal concept of unilateral contract has been invoked as a possible route for enforcing unilaterally adopted CSR policies and codes of conduct.[19] However, strictly speaking, using the unilateral contract claim does not constitute enforcement of a contract by a third party. Rather, a party asserting the existence of a unilateral contract claims that a contract, in fact, exists in a situation where offer and acceptance have not been formally exchanged, but rather implicitly understood from the statements and behaviours of the parties. The second contract law concept is the third-party beneficiaries claim . The concept of third-party beneficiaries refers to a situation when a party has the right to sue on contract despite not being an original party to the contract. This legal concept is in focus here, while the unilateral contract is discussed only marginally for the sake of completeness. Moreover, the discussion in this chapter centres on the possibility of enforcing sustainability contractual clauses by third parties against chain leaders. While it might be theoretically easier to succeed with a third-party claim against the respective supplier, practically, such claims have much less value. This is because victims of human/labour rights abuses and other unethical/unsustainable conduct in international supply chains are most often citizens of countries providing only limited protection to those concerns. Thus, while using the third-party beneficiaries claim, they also move the dispute to supply chain leaders' jurisdictions, which generally have more favourable policies in the areas of human/labour rights abuses and other unethical/unsustainable conduct, as well as (possibly) stronger judicial systems.

The chapter proceeds as follows: it discusses the issue in general and a third-party beneficiary claim in detail, both from a substantive and procedural law perspective (Section 2). After that, the chapter provides normative arguments for crediting the legal standing of third parties in enforcement of the sustainability contractual clauses that they are supposed to benefit from (Section 3). The author, however, acknowledges that there are also valid and strong arguments against the recognition of third parties' standing in respect to sustainability contractual clauses in supply chain contracts. Those arguments are also reviewed and discussed (Section 4) before providing conclusions (Section 5).

2 Third-party beneficiaries

Contract law establishes a framework for compelling the performance of legally given promises between contractual parties, thus effectuating the Roman rule of *pacta sunt servanda*.[20] There are two main reasons for this: efficiency and

17 European Center for Constitutional and Human Rights (ECCHR), 'Complaint re Fair Working Conditions in Bangladesh: Lidl Forced to Back Down', available at <www.ecchr.eu/en/case/complaint-re-fair-working-conditions-in-bangladesh-lidl-forced-to-back-down> accessed 17 July 2018; *Kasky v. Nike, Inc.*, 45 P.3d 243 (Cal. 2002); *Bellissiomo v. Tony's Factory*, Rb. Amsterdam, 6 February 2007, IER 2007, 53; the possible use of false advertisement claims is dealt with in Chapter 6 in this volume.
18 Relevant case law is reviewed in later parts of this chapter.
19 Most famously in the *Walmart case* (see n 40), discussed further in Section 2.1.1.
20 'Promises should be kept'.

fairness.[21] Traditionally, private parties have been free to maximise their wealth through entering into bargains of their choice with the backup of the state's enforcement if the given promise is breached. States have their particular reasons to enforce private promises, smooth functioning of their economy standing at the forefront.[22] Already the Romans understood that a well-organised, efficient trade can only happen if contracts are kept.[23] While efficiency seems to be an overarching goal of contract law, fairness does not lag behind. As Wehberg wrote, '[f] ew rules for the ordering of Society have such a deep moral and religious influence as the principle of the sanctity of contract …'[24]

In commercial contracts, parties pursue their own private interests. The core of a contract is that a party perceives the performance by its contractual partner to be worth paying the agreed price or fulfilling its own contractual obligations; the party thus perceives the contract as contributing to its wealth creation. 'The "two-parties bargaining" dimension of contract is so prominent' that involving a third party into a contract is considered an anomaly'.[25] It is considered to disrupt the balance of the contractual relationship between the two parties,[26] to be irreconcilable with the two main aims of contract law. Yet, it will later be argued that these positions do not hold true in respect to sustainability contractual clauses and their possible enforcement by third parties.

2.1 *Substantive law*

The recognition of third parties' right to enforce a contract has puzzled contract law theory and practice.[27] Yet, it has become a generally accepted principle across national jurisdictions, including European ones.[28] Even the international law of contracts accepts the possibility that contractual parties may stipulate a right in favour of a third party.[29]

21 M Eisenberg, 'The Bargain Principle and its Limits' (1982) 95(4) Harvard Law Review 741.
22 Ibid., 744.
23 H Wehberg, 'Pacta Sunt Servanda' (1959) 53(4) The American Journal of International Law 775, 775.
24 Ibid.
25 A N Hatzis, 'Rights and Obligations of Third Parties' in B Bouckaert & G De Geest (eds), *Encyclopedia of Law & Economics, Vol. III: The Regulation of Contracts* (1st edn, Edward Elgar Publishing 2000) 200.
26 J Gathii, 'Incorporating the Third Party Beneficiary Principle in Natural Resource Contracts' (2014) 43(1) Georgia Journal of International Comparative Law 93, 133.
27 Hatzis (n 25) 201.
28 For the European and national levels, see O Lando, H Beale, & Commission on European Contract Law (eds), *Principles of European Contract Law: Parts I and II – Combined and Revised* (Kluwer Law International 2000) 322; J Hallebeek, 'Contracts for a Third-Party Beneficiary: A Brief Sketch From the *Corpus Iuris* to Present-Day Civil Law' (2007) 13(2) Fundamina 11, 53; H Verhagen, 'Contemporary Law' in J J Hallebeek & H Dondorp (eds), *Contracts for a Third-Party Beneficiary: A Historical and Comparative Account* (Brill Nijhoff 2008) 138 and 143.
29 For the international level, see UNIDROIT Principles of International Commercial Contracts (2016 edition), Articles 5.2.1–5.2.6. The major international law instrument regulating commercial contracting – the United Nations Convention on

Looking at the various regulations of third-party beneficiaries to contracts, we can deduce three main requirements that must be present for a third party to be able to enforce the promise given to her: the contractual parties must *intend* to grant a *specific right* to an *identified or identifiable third party.* These requirements and their relevance to the subject of sustainability contractual clauses will now be discussed in detail. Some jurisdictions impose additional conditions for the creation of a third party's right. For example, under the UK Contracts (Rights of Third Parties) Act 1999, reliance by a third party is a trigger for contractual liability to that party.[30] Under the Dutch Civil Code, an acceptance by the third-party beneficiary is necessary.[31] While these additional requirements are certainly relevant to sustainability contractual clauses in these specific contexts, the discussion here focuses on the aspects of third-party beneficiaries that are common to most jurisdictions.

Before delving into the analysis of the three main requirements for third-party beneficiaries' standing, it is important to note that it might be difficult to talk about application of these requirements to SCCs in general, as SCCs differ significantly in respect to form, length and content, depending on the specific company's business profile, strategy and the industry it belongs to.[32] In particular, the clauses' content will affect their enforceability by third parties, meaning that not only the issue at stake, but also the actual wording and the strength of the commitment are relevant. Some of the differences are pinpointed in the following text.[33] Moreover, and more importantly, enforceability will naturally depend on the applicable law and its peculiarities as outlined previously.

2.1.1 Intention

The first requirement for the application of the third-party beneficiaries concept is the *intention* of contractual parties to bestow a right on a third party. It is widely recognised that ' . . . the mere fact that a contract may benefit a third party in some way or another is generally insufficient to assume that parties have intended that the third party acquires a claim.'[34] This is rather logical, as basically any contract benefits not only the contractual parties, but also certain external subjects. For example, a license agreement for the use of a trademark does not only give

Contracts for the International Sale of Goods (CISG), adopted in Vienna 1980, entered into force 1988, 1489 UNTS 3 – does not provide for third-party beneficiaries' rights. However, it has been argued that this does not mean that third parties' rights are not admissible under the CISG, but rather that this topic should be treated as falling outside the Convention's scope.

30 S A Smith, *Contract Theory* (Oxford University Press 2004) 91.

31 Dutch Civil Code, art. 6.253.

32 Mitkidis, supra, n 1, Chapter 7.

33 For a more detailed discussion on enforceability, see Chapter 3 in this volume.

34 Verhagen (n 28) 145. Similarly, S Vogenauer & J Kleinheisterkamp, *Commentary on the Unidroit Principles of International Commercial Contracts (PICC)* (Oxford University Press 2009) Article 5.2.1, para 10; Hatzis (n 25) 209 (noting that '. . . a contract's unintentional beneficial effect for a third party should not be the source of enforceable rights for third parties who benefit from it').

rights translating to economic gains for the contractual parties, but also benefits consumers of the product on which the trademark is placed, as they are for example able to quickly distinguish the product from other products in a shop. Consumers would in this situation be classified as incidental beneficiaries.

The intention to bestow a right on a third party may be expressed in the contract. While this is often the case in the area of financial law, for example in credit agreements, it is rarely (if ever) present in supply chain agreements in respect to CSR issues. An intention can, however, be incorporated into the contract impliedly and deduced by contract interpretation. What can be used for contract interpretation depends on the governing law of the contract. Some jurisdictions require very clear evidence of the intention.[35] Other jurisdictions are more liberal. This is also the case with the international law of contracts, where a third party's right can be deduced from the contractual text, usages and practices, the principle of good faith and other documents and principles.[36]

However, one must be aware of other contractual clauses that may basically nullify any possible reading of an implied intention of contractual parties in the contract. This is primarily a no-third-party clause.[37] For example, GlaxoSmithKline's standard terms and conditions of purchase of goods and services (2017) for Egypt includes in its title 21 'Ethical Standards and Human Rights'; among others, the supplier's warranty that it does not use child and/or forced labour. However, title 26, 'General', includes provision 26.8, which reads,

> Except for any rights granted to GSK Affiliates, which the parties hereby designate as intended third party beneficiaries to the Agreement, no person who is not a party to the Agreement shall have any rights under the Contracts (Rights of Third Parties) Act 1999 to enforce any term.[38]

With such a provision present in the contract, third parties lose their ability to enforce any sustainability clause. While this is specifically legislated for in the UK context,[39] the same conclusion is most likely to be reached by contract interpretation also in other jurisdictions.

Based on this, it is evident that the contractual parties' intention to bestow a right on a third party is possibly the crucial aspect in the application of the third-party beneficiaries concept in the CSR area. This requirement (together with

35 This is the case in common law countries in general, as determining contractual content is limited by the parol evidence rule. See also Verbruggen (n 13) 312–316.

36 Vogenauer and Kleinheisterkamp (n 34) Article 5.2.1, para. 15.

37 A Beckers, *Enforcing Corporate Social Responsibility Codes: On Global Self-Regulation and National Private Law* (Hart Publishing 2015) 144.

38 GlaxoSmithkKine *Terms And Conditions Of Purchase (Goods & Services) Egypt* (February 2017), <https://supplier.gsk.com/irj/go/km/docs/pccshrcontent/procurement_terms/gsk-terms-conditions-of-purchase-goods-services-egypt.pdf> accessed 20 June 2018.

39 Contracts (Rights of Third Parties) Act 1999, section 1(4).

third-party beneficiaries standings in general) was tested in the *Walmart case.*[40] The plaintiffs (Walmart's suppliers' employees) in this class-action lawsuit brought by the International Labor Rights Fund against Walmart, Inc. claimed that they were third-party beneficiaries of the contract between Walmart and its suppliers. The contract incorporated Walmart's code of conduct, titled 'Standards for Suppliers' by reference. Relying on the Standards, the plaintiffs asserted that Walmart had breached its obligation to duly inspect compliance of the suppliers in respect to human and labour rights. The court held that the suppliers' intention to enter into a contract including the Standards was primarily to benefit themselves;[41] thus, it essentially stated that suppliers' employees were incidental and not intentional beneficiaries.[42] The decision has, however, been criticised by some authors, stating that it is the objective aim of companies' codes of conduct to benefit third parties, namely suppliers' employees.[43] Phillips and Lim argue that '[c]ircumstances surrounding the origination, development, and publication of buyers' codes indicate an intention to benefit workers'.[44]

2.1.2 *Right*

The second requirement for the application of the third-party beneficiaries concept common to most jurisdictions is that the parties intend to bestow *a specific right* onto a third party and this right is to be found in the contract. A lack of a specific right was the second reason for the dismissal in the *Walmart case*. The court held that the plaintiffs failed to prove a clear promise made by Walmart to audit its suppliers' performance. In the court's opinion, Walmart had merely a right, but not an obligation, to audit its suppliers and thus to protect suppliers' employees.[45] However, a parallel could be made here to the *Wolfgang case*,[46] where the court extended the right of the defendant to cancel a race in the case of bad weather (unsafe racing) conditions into an obligation to do so. Drivers were thus found to be third-party beneficiaries to a contract between a speedway owner and a motorsports sanctioning body. Therefore, at least in some jurisdictions we have seen that courts were more flexible in finding the rights of third-party beneficiaries. This creative interpretation of contract law and contracts amounts to court activism – creating law where there is none. In the civil law context, Verhagen states that:

40 *Doe v. Wal-Mart Stores, Inc.*, 572 F.3d 677 (9th Cir. 2009), referred to as the *Walmart case.*

41 J J Brudney, 'Envisioning Enforcement of Freedom of Association Standards in Corporate Codes: A Journey for Sinbad or Sisyphus?' (2012) 33(4) Comparative Labor Law & Policy Journal 555, 578.

42 J Phillips & S-J Lim, 'Their Brothers' Keeper: Global Buyers and the Legal Duty to Protect Suppliers' Employees' (2009) 61(2) Rutgers Law Review 333, 369.

43 Brudney (n 41) 580; Beckers (n 37) 126–129.

44 Phillips and Lim (n 42) 369.

45 Decision in the *Walmart case*, 684.

46 *Wolfgang v. Mid-America Motorsports, Inc.*, 111 F.3d 1515, 1524 (10th Cir. 1997).

> [i]n order to fill certain gaps in the civil code, courts have sometimes more or less 'invented' the existence of a clause in favour of a third party, although there was neither an expressed nor an implied intention of the parties to create rights in his favour.[47]

It is not unimaginable that courts would take such an active position in the CSR area, where victims of suppliers' unsustainable or unethical behaviour do not have access to justice. Courts' activism is, however, not the optimal solution, as it upsets the balance of division of the state's powers and may lead to unexpected results. Yet, even one decision of one court in one jurisdiction in these lines may cause a global wave of positive activism and raise the enforcement of international obligations by states, as we have seen in the area of climate law in the Dutch *Urgenda case*.[48]

Moreover, in respect to the bestowed right, a discussion has been raised over whether third parties may derive a claim both from a promissory obligation to benefit third parties and from an obligation not to harm others. Smith purports that only the former is possible;[49] however, some courts have decided otherwise. A prominent example here is the decision of a French court of cassation, in which the court found that a patient who received contaminated blood administered by a public hospital was a third-party beneficiary to a contract between the national transfusion service and the public hospital.[50] This was a surprising decision, as there was no expressed provision in the contract granting such a claim to patients. One would thus expect a tort claim instead. However, this decision was probably rendered as it seemed more fair to the patient.[51] While, according to French law, in a tort claim, the patient would have to prove negligence of the transfusion service, in a contract law claim, the burden of proof is reversed and the transfusion service had to prove that there was no negligence on their side. Again, this decision could potentially be translated into the CSR area, where, so far, third-party beneficiary claims have only been considered in respect to individual and positively formulated (human and labour) rights.

Taking inspiration from such creative application of law by courts, a third-party right could be found even in cases where third parties are not granted any specific right, but instead the promisor agrees not to harm others. This is typical for the environmental area. If a duty of care is recognised as a source of third-party beneficiaries' claims, the actual promise can be found in various documents and/or actions. In the *Walmart case*, claimants argued that the duty of care could be deduced firstly from the company's code of conduct and secondly from the substantial control that Walmart exercised over its suppliers. Both of those arguments

47 Verhagen (n 28) 146.
48 Information and case documents are available at <www.urgenda.nl/en/> accessed 4 December 2018.
49 S A Smith, 'Contracts for the Benefit of Third Parties: In Defence of the Third-Party Rule' (1997) 17(4) Oxford Journal of Legal Studies 643, 646.
50 Cass. civ. 2e, 17 December 1954, D. 1955.269Z.
51 Verhagen (n 28) 146.

were dismissed by the court. In respect to the first one the court stated that the company reserved merely a right to audit the suppliers' performance rather than promising to do so. In respect to the latter, the court stated that audits aimed at securing suppliers' compliance with the contract rather than directing their daily activities. Maryanov thus concludes that '[i]n sweatshop litigation, plaintiffs have yet to establish that a duty to workers arises from the relationship between a corporation and its suppliers.'[52,53] Another possible avenue to establishing that a company has embraced a duty of care is to read the contract in connection with the company's public statements, such as CSR reports.

Looking back to the *Walmart case*, we observe that not only the question of positive/negative obligation, but also the question of the actual wording of the contractual clause matters. The plaintiffs in the case relied on the following wording in the 'Standards for Suppliers', under a section titled 'Right of Inspection': 'Wal-Mart will undertake affirmative measures, such as on-site inspection of production facilities, to implement and monitor said standards.' While in general, headlines and titles in contractual documents do not determine their legal status, the text of the section was interpreted by the court within the context of the whole document. The Standards further elaborated on the possibility of Walmart's cancelling orders if a supplier fails to cooperate during an on-site inspection. There were no possible remedies provided for the supplier or its employees if an on-site audit is not performed or is deemed insufficient. The interpretation exercise conducted by the court reveals the Achilles' heel of most CSR documents, standards and codes directed to suppliers – the vague language that prevents their enforcement by the intended beneficiaries.[54]

2.1.3 Identification

Finally, the presence of a clear intention of the contractual parties to benefit others and recognition of a specific right may not be enough to trigger the application of third-party beneficiary claims if the third party or parties are not identified. This does not mean that a third party must be individually stated, but that the relevant third parties must be identifiable at least as members of a specific group or class.[55] This might not cause problems when concerning suppliers' employees (*Walmart case*),[56] patients (*"blood transfusion" case*) or racers (*Wolfgang case*), but is more

52 D C Maryanov, 'Sweatshop Liability: Corporate Codes of Conduct and the Governance of Labor Standards in the International Supply Chain' (2010) 14(1) Lewis & Clark Law Review 397, 430.

53 For further discussion on this topic, see Chapter 5 in this volume, specifically the section on 'assumption of responsibility'.

54 See also K P Mitkidis, 'Life-Cycle Based Climate Regulation Through Supply Chain Contracts' working paper, presented at the SMART conference 'Life-Cycle Based Management and Reporting for Sustainable Business', 29–30 November 2016, University of Oslo Faculty of Law Legal Studies Research Paper Series No. 2017–21 9–10.

55 Vogenauer and Kleinheisterkamp (n 34) Article 5.2.2, para 3–5.

56 The question of whether the supplier's employees can be considered as a group of third-party beneficiaries did not raise problems.

complex to achieve in respect to a contractual duty of care where the number of potential beneficiaries is indefinite.[57] An example here could be a situation when a company promises to lower carbon dioxide emissions to a certain level within its supply chain.[58] However, such use of the third-party beneficiary claim could also hinder any positive efforts of companies in this area.[59]

The question of who is identifiable as a third-party beneficiary to a contract is, thus, of special relevance when a third-party right is derived from a general obligation "not to harm others", as discussed previously. One argument against the recognition of such a practically indefinite group of third parties is the blurring of boundaries between contract and tort in disputes concerning breaches of the duty of care,[60] potentially leading to erosion of both. This blurring became very obvious in the French *"blood transfusion" case*.[61] As shown in this case, it depends not only on the applicable law, but also on the attitude of the deciding judge(s) how these cases will be treated. In this connection, Smith speaks about 'contract-as-tort' theory and warns that privity of contract may become an anachronism.[62] Another argument against recognition of such broad groups of third-party beneficiaries when those are not specifically identified or identifiable is the economic consequences. Geis states that by not identifying third-party beneficiaries clearly, the negotiation costs are externalised on the judiciary.[63] While this is certainly true, not recognising the rights would harm third parties rather than sanction costs' externalisation. Finally, third-party beneficiaries do not need to exist at the time of conclusion of the contract that benefits them. It is generally accepted to stipulate in favour of future beneficiaries.[64]

2.2 Procedural aspects

Third parties may face not only substantive but also procedural law hurdles when enforcing sustainability contractual clauses.

The first issue may arise regarding the venue. Here, plaintiffs need to consult private international law rules. Of special interest is the doctrine of *forum non conveniens*, applicability of choice of venue clauses on third parties and the possibility to sue a mother company for the actions of its subsidiaries.

57 Vogenauer and Kleinheisterkamp (n 34) Article 5.2.1, para 24; the German courts acknowledge the existence of so-called 'contracts with protective effects for third parties', which could be appropriate for use in the CSR area.
58 For now, it proves difficult to establish a direct liability of companies for climate change consequences. A major case is being heard in Germany, *Saúl v. RWE*; more information available at <https://germanwatch.org/en/huaraz> accessed 21 June 2018.
59 For further discussion on climate change and liability, see the special issue of Journal of European Tort Law: Climate Change and Environmental Liability (2017) 8(2).
60 Vogenauer and Kleinheisterkamp (n 34) Article 5.2.1, para 24.
61 Cass. civ. 2e, 17 December 1954, D. 1955.269.
62 Smith (n 49) 647.
63 G S Geis, 'Broadcast Contracting' (2012) 106(3) Northwestern University Law Review 1153, 1194–1195 and 1198.
64 For a comparative perspective, see Verhagen (n 28) 152–153.

The *forum non conveniens* doctrine gives a court the possibility to dismiss a case when a more appropriate venue exists to hear the case. The doctrine, being prevalent in common law jurisdictions, has been applied to a much lesser extent in civil law jurisdictions and is basically refused within the EU.[65] In jurisdictions accepting the *forum non conveniens* doctrine, it can play a decisive role for success in efforts to enforce sustainability contractual clauses by plaintiffs from developing countries, who cannot rely on their home courts to protect their rights. As Maryanov states, '[f]or a foreign sweatshop worker from a country with low labor standards, dismissal from a U.S. court is likely fatal to the case.'[66]

Moreover, the choice of venue clause in a contract may come into question. Is this clause also binding for third parties who have effectively not agreed to it? This question has been discussed namely in relation to arbitration clauses.[67] A third party, such as a supplier's employee, does not often have the knowledge of the existence of an arbitration clause, which may even have the form of a separate arbitration agreement. Bagot and Henderson claim that, considering the consensual character of arbitration agreement, third parties should be given notice of the arbitration agreement before the contract is entered into.[68] However, this proves practically impossible if the third parties are not known at the time of the contract conclusion or are identified only as members of a specific group or class. For these reasons, it might be considered unreasonable to uphold an arbitration agreement in face of third parties enforcing sustainability contractual clauses.

Finally, successful enforcement of sustainability standards in commercial contracts might be prevented by corporate structures.[69] If it is a corporation's local subsidiary that has a direct contract with a supplier rather than the corporation itself, access to courts in the mother company's jurisdiction will most probably be hindered.[70] This could, however, in effect account to a refusal of justice.

The second major procedural hurdle relates to the governing law of a contract. The choice of law made by the contractual parties is essential to determining

65 Case C-281/02 *Owusu v Jackson and Others* [2005] ECR I-1383. For a deeper analysis of the doctrine in the European Union, see Sarah Wall, 'The End of Forum non Conveniens: Has the European Court of Justice Gone Beyond its Boundaries' (2012) 2 King's Inns Student Law Review 49.

66 Maryanov (n 52) 415.

67 See, e.g., M H Bagot Jr. & D A Henderson, 'Not Party, Not Bound – Not Necessarily: Binding Third Parties to Maritime Arbitration' (2002) 26(2) Tulane Maritime Law Journal 413; J J Sentner Jr., 'Who Is Bound by Arbitration Agreements? Enforcement by and against Non-Signatories' (2005) 6(1) Business Law International 55; J M Hosking, 'The Third Party Non-Signatory's Ability to Compel International Commercial Arbitration: Doing Justice without Destroying Consent' (2004) 4(3) Pepperdine Dispute Resolution Law Journal 469.

68 Bagot and Henderson (n 67) 460.

69 While fascinating, this issue is not dealt with in detail here, as it goes beyond the scope of this chapter.

70 A parallel example, although not related to contract but tort, can be drawn from the case between Shell Plc. and Nigerian villagers, *Okpabi and others v. Royal Dutch Shell Plc and another* (2018) EWCA Civ 191, 14 February 2018. The plaintiffs now aim to take the case to the UK Supreme Court.

whether the contract grants a right to a third party. As we have seen in the previous discussion, there are some differences in respect to the admissibility of third-party beneficiary claims in various jurisdictions.

2.3 Unilateral promises as a sub-category of third-party beneficiary claims[71]

The third-party beneficiary doctrine goes hand-in-hand with theories of the binding effects of unilateral promises. It could even be seen as their specific modification.[72] The distinguishing factor is that, while a unilateral promise can create a separate contract between a promisor and a promisee, third-party beneficiaries rely on a contract to which they are not the signatory parties.

The unilateral contract doctrine has been, same as the third-party beneficiary doctrine, tested in the *Walmart case*. The plaintiffs in this case used various arguments to hold the corporation liable for inadequate working conditions in its suppliers' factories. Thus, in addition to claiming that they are third-party beneficiaries to the contract between Walmart and its supplier, they also claimed that the 'Standards for Suppliers' incorporated in the contract amounted to a separate contract concluded directly between Walmart and themselves. They relied on the US 'employee handbook doctrine',[73] under which unilateral statements may have a contractual character although the subjects making them did not intend to extend a contractual offer to the addressees. The court dismissed this claim for the same reasons as the third-party beneficiary claim: the plaintiffs failed to establish a clear promise from Walmart to conduct on-site audits.[74] The case, however, represents an important point in the history of sustainability standards' enforcement, as the judge did not refute that a supplier's code of conduct may in fact constitute a direct contract of a corporation with its supplier's employees if it is clear enough and disseminated in such a manner that employees knew of its contents and reasonably relied on it.

The unilateral contract doctrine has not been tried in relation to sustainability standards within the European context yet. The possibility of success may, however, be expected to be even lower than in the US, as European jurisdictions generally require expressed intention of the proclaiming party to be bound by the unilateral statement.[75] The text of most supplier codes of conduct, though, remain vague in respect to the obligations on the side of the corporations.

71 For more detailed analysis of the unilateral contract doctrine and its relevance in the CSR area, see Mitkidis (n 1) 194–196.
72 Vogenauer and Kleinheisterkamp (n 34) Article 5.2.1, para 8.
73 See, e.g., R H Winters, 'Employee Handbooks and Employment-At-Will Contracts' (1985) Duke Law Journal 196.
74 For a detailed analysis, see K E Kenny, 'Code or Contract: Whether Wal-Mart's Code of Conduct Creates a Contractual Obligation between Wal-Mart and the Employees of its Foreign Suppliers' (2007) 27(2) Northwestern Journal of International Law & Business 453.
75 See, e.g., Commission on European Contract Law, Principles of European Contract Law (PECL), Article 2:107: '(a) promise which is intended to be legally binding without acceptance is binding'.

3 Normative arguments for third parties' legal standing in sustainability-related contractual claims

This section moves the discussion to a more normative space, presenting the author's arguments for why third-party standing in respect to sustainability contractual clauses should be recognised.

3.1 Effectuating contractual parties' intention

The first argument follows the reasoning of Gathii, who in relation to natural resources contracts, purports that ' . . . allowing third parties to sue is necessary to effectuate the intentions of the parties to the contract'.[76] In other words, recognising a third-party beneficiary claim is not meant to circumvent the contractual party's will, but to realise it.[77] The function of a third-party beneficiary claim is thus not substantive (to find whether a contract creates a right for a third party), but remedial (to give effect to the original intentions of the contractual parties).[78] Naturally, this presumes that the parties intended to give a third party (third parties) a specific right, as discussed previously. In the area of CSR, it is hard to imagine that companies' activities do not aim to benefit third parties. Safeguarding human and labour rights is always related to certain individuals. The purpose of benefiting others has been found by some courts from circumstances surrounding a specific claim. In *Chen v. Street Beat Sportswear*, the US Supreme Court found that the aim to benefit third parties was 'strikingly obvious' although not expressly stated in the contract.[79] If we consider a common situation – when a company adopts a policy (such as a code of conduct) for their suppliers to pay minimum wage to the employees and for reports on the existence and enforcement procedure of this policy, including its incorporation into supply chain contracts in its publicly available sustainability report and on its website – the purpose seems rather obvious: the company wants to benefit the suppliers' employees.

The perception that companies' CSR activities aim at benefiting third parties is further strengthened if the company is a member of an industry-wide initiative. For example, the pharmaceutical industry organises itself into the Pharmaceutical Supply Chain Initiative (PSCI), with the '… vision of better, social, environmental and economic outcomes in the communities where we buy.'[80] The PSCI has issued 'Pharmaceutical Industry Principles for Responsible Supply Chain Management' for the members to implement throughout their supply chains. Regardless of the motivation for participation in the PSCI, members benefit not only through sharing information and knowledge, but also through reputation building as

76 Gathii (n 26) 114.
77 Ibid., 97.
78 Eisenberg (n 21) 1386.
79 *Chen v. Street Beat Sportswear, Inc., U.S.*, 226 F. Supp. 2d 355, 363 (E.D.N.Y. 2002); Phillips and Lim (n 42) 369–370.
80 Pharmaceutical Supply Chain Initiative, <https://pscinitiative.org/> accessed 22 June 2018.

sustainable companies.[81] If a court refused to recognize third-party beneficiaries' rights to plaintiffs, who could show that the PSCI members have actually not implemented the principles throughout the supply chain, the court would leave a fraud unidentified. Here, contract law comes close to tort law again, as public proclamations about using contracts in a specific way are used for brand building. As such they may be susceptible to false advertisement claims.[82]

However, a court cannot decide for a third party if the specific contract contains a no-third-party clause. That would go straight against the parties' expressed intention. The existence of a no-third-party clause remains most often hidden from public site, in comparison to the sustainability contractual clauses regularly discussed in corporate public statements. The question is whether companies should be blamed for such an imbalance of provided information or whether the legal requirement of non-financial reporting on supply chain governance tools basically forces companies to do so. As the situation is now, companies may reap the benefits of publicly committing themselves, without any effective control over their actual behaviour and with the possibility of retracting the commitment confidentially through a simple contractual clause.[83] Regulators could thus consider whether the application of a no-third-party clause could be disabled in respect to sustainability contractual clauses.[84] This would allow for third parties and the public to rely on companies' commitments when enforcing their rights and would avoid companies' inadequate public statements about the use of supply chain agreements.

3.2 Aligned with public policy

Recognising third-party beneficiaries' rights in the case of sustainability contractual clauses would be in line with public policy. In 2015, the United Nations (UN) set forth 17 goals to achieve a sustainable future.[85] No goal is more important than another one; they are 'integrated and indivisible'.[86] Multiple goals are relevant to situations in international supply chains.[87] For example, under 'Goal 8: Decent Work and Economic Growth', the signatories establish a target to '[t]ake immediate and effective measures to eradicate forced labour, end modern slavery and human trafficking …' The *2030 Agenda for Sustainable Development* is globally accepted and supported as a guidance to public policy. Many signatories, including the EU and the US, have adopted policy documents clarifying their understanding of the goals and their commitments to pursue those. For example,

81 Geis (n 63) 1179.
82 *LIDL* (n 17).
83 Geis (n 63) 1182.
84 See, similarly, Chapter 2 in this volume.
85 United Nations, General Assembly, *Transforming Our World: The 2030 Agenda for Sustainable Development*, A/RES/70/1 (2015) adopted in New York.
86 *2030 Agenda for Sustainable Development*, primarily para 6 and 18.
87 UN Global Compact, 'Sustainable Supply Chains: Through the Lens of the 17 SDGs' webinar, <www.unglobalcompact.org/library/4211> accessed 22 June 2018.

the EU declared support for the *2030 Agenda for Sustainable Development* and stated that together with its Member States, it will 'implement the 2030 Agenda across all internal and external policies in a comprehensive and strategic approach.' To that end, and among others, '[t]he EU and its Member States will continue to support responsible business practices and responsible management of supply chains, respecting tenure rights and integrating human and labour rights, financial probity and environmental standards and accessibility'.[88]

In order for the policy not to be (yet another) empty promise to workers in countries with weaker human and labour rights protection and citizens influenced by the outsourcing practices of large companies, the EU and other countries need to find ways to impact the activities of their companies extraterritorially. Reporting and due diligence obligations are possible tools to enhance sustainable behaviour in international supply chains. However, there is a lack of effective monitoring and sanctioning. Recognising third-party rights would complement already available tools by incentivising companies to exert bigger efforts to control suppliers' conduct and discourage those companies who simply take advantage of lower social and environmental standards in developing countries. It would be a background rule against which contracts are negotiated and business relationships in supply chains are built.[89] Moreover, countries requesting that companies report on their sustainable supply chain management practices and/or conduct risk-based due diligence should in the view of the author recognise third-party beneficiary claims to avoid the current schizophrenic situation when they require their companies to contract basically on behalf of workers and citizens in other countries, but do not recognise those workers' and citizens' right to enforce the contract afterwards.

An argument could be put forward that contract law policy underpinnings are 'more concerned with enforcing privately made bargains than with coercing behaviour'.[90] The word 'more' is important here. Over its history, other concerns were implemented into contract law, primarily under the principle of fairness. A prominent example here is the protection of the weaker party. When stepping outside of the world of commercial contracts, we see plenty of instances of protection of the weaker party, especially in consumer and labour contracts. However, protection of the weaker party can also be found in the commercial world, for example, in the case of unconscionable contractual terms when a stronger business partner imposes her terms on the weaker one.[91] Therefore, an introduction of a new policy of recognition of third-parties' rights in respect to sustainability contractual clauses could be accepted based on the principle of fairness. Yet again, the same argument comes to mind; if a company publicly proclaims that it uses its contracts for pursuing sustainability goals – in fact, includes such clauses in the

88 Joint Statement by the Council and the Representatives of the Governments of the Member States Meeting Within the Council, the European Parliament and the European Commission, The New European Consensus on Development, 'Our World, Our Dignity, Our Future' (7 June 2017) para 54.

89 Gathii (n 26) 138.

90 Ibid., 42.

91 J M Perillo, *Calamari and Perillo on Contracts* (6th edn, West 2009) para 3.6.

contracts and reaps the reputational benefits from this – it is fair to allow protected subjects to enforce the contracts. Moreover, this is also respecting the values of justice and morality. As developed countries are proclaiming to support global sustainability, their citizens are also those consuming most of the goods produced in international supply chains, while criticising the human rights situation, labour conditions and insufficient environmental protection in developing countries. Allowing for third parties to enforce sustainability contractual clauses would contribute to aligning the contradicting claims and attitudes of our society.

3.3 Access to justice

The background of this chapter is the impeded access to justice for workers and citizens of (primarily) developing countries for breaches of their rights from supply chain contracts between a buyer from a developed country and a supplier from a developing country. The problem has been widely discussed within and regulated in the soft UN framework for business and human rights – the 'protect, respect and remedy' framework – and the follow-up implementation of the guiding principles (UNGP).[92] The discussion of access to remedy for victims of unsustainable conduct in international supply chains brings us back to the analysis of procedural aspects of third-party beneficiary claims. The already-examined question of *forum non conveniens* is especially relevant here.[93] The UNGP prescribe that

> [i]n order to meet their responsibility to respect human rights, business enterprises should have in place policies and processes appropriate to their size and circumstances, including: … (c) Processes to enable the remediation of any adverse human rights impacts they cause or to which they contribute.[94]

And it has so far been the corporate remediation actions that we mainly rely on. Companies developed best practice for the monitoring and enforcement of sustainability requirements in supply chains. The best practice comprises suppliers' self-assessment, internal and/or external on-site audits, action plans and, eventually, contract termination.[95] However, the best practice is largely focused on risk management in respect to companies' possible complicity in unethical practices rather than on remediation of damage caused to third parties. Moreover, even

92 UN Human Rights Council, 'Report of the Special Representative of the Secretary-General on the issue of Human Rights and Transnational Corporations and Other Business Enterprises'; J Ruggie, 'Protect, Respect and Remedy: A Framework for Business and Human Rights' (2008) UN Doc. A/HRC/8/5, para 84: 'Effective grievance mechanisms play an important role in the State duty to protect, in both its legal and policy dimensions, as well as in the corporate responsibility to respect'. J Ruggie, 'Guiding Principles on Business and Human Rights: Implementing the United Nations "Protect, Respect and Remedy" Framework' (2011) UN Doc. A/HRC/17/31.
93 See infra Section 2.2.
94 UNGP, para 15.
95 Mitkidis (n 1) 231.

when a company has the best intentions, it may become involved in unintentional rights abuse.[96] That is the reason why states remain primarily responsible for securing access to remedy.[97] Given that developing countries may lack the necessary resources and capabilities to secure effective access to remedy, developed countries should step up when companies based in their jurisdictions become complicit in any abuse of human rights or other unsustainable behaviour. Recognising third-party beneficiary rights is one possible tool to live up to this expectation. Moreover, facilitating such claims, rather than refusing them based on procedural obstacles, is recommended.[98] In this respect, the European Union Agency for Fundamental Rights suggests simplifying the evidentiary obligations of human rights violation victims by a rebuttable presumption of 'a certain level of evidence' and shifting the burden of proof 'from a victim to a company to prove that a company did not have control over a business entity involved in the human rights abuse.'[99]

4 Arguments against allowing third parties to sue on sustainable contractual clauses

The previous section presented three normative arguments for recognising third-party beneficiary rights, namely that third-party beneficiary rights are effectuating contractual parties' intent, that they are in line with public policy, and that they would secure better access to remedy for victims of unsustainable behaviour in international supply chains. Nevertheless, though those arguments may be persuasive, arguments to the opposite effect should be considered.

Possibly the strongest argument against accepting third-party beneficiary rights to sustainability contractual clauses is the risk of opening the floodgates to cases.[100] As clauses often benefit an indefinite number of people, there is a fear that companies would be exposed to an endless line of litigation.[101] Moreover, a concern has been expressed that many such litigations would be started by factually unaffected parties and disaffected members of the community,[102] thus turning contract law-based cases into a strategic litigation tool rather than remedying damages done.[103] The concern may be exaggerated, though, as parties from developing countries most probably do not have the resources to see such cases through and strategic litigation has already been taking place through, for

96 UNGP, Commentary to para 22.
97 UNGP, para 25.
98 'Improving Access to Remedy in the Area of Business and Human Rights at the EU Level', Opinion of the European Union Agency for Fundamental Rights, FRA Opinion – 1/2017 [B&HR].
99 Ibid., 7.
100 *DAS v. George Weston Limited* (see Chapter 5).
101 Gathii (n 26) 135.
102 Geis (n 63) 1178.
103 BSR Conversations with Newsmakers, Call Summary – December 19, 2005, 'Legal Perspectives and Interpretation of the *ILRF v. Wal-Mart* Lawsuit', featuring Andrew Boling, Philip H Rudolph, and Dana Veeder.

example, false advertising cases.[104] The recognition of third-party rights may thus serve a more symbolic and psychological function.

Hand-in-hand with the first line of reasoning goes the argument that allowing third parties to sue on contract for breach of sustainability contractual clauses could be disproportionately detrimental and costly to buyers in comparison with the benefits they were supposed to receive.[105] As sustainability contractual clauses are not directly connected to the subject matter of a contract, buyers might feel discouraged from risking their business for protecting (legally) unrelated subjects. We could thus be afraid that companies may abandon the practice of inserting SCCs into their contracts. A counter-argument here can be that it is not probable that companies will relax in their sustainable supply chain management efforts, as the area is increasingly legalised.

Another criticism of allowing third-party claims on sustainability contractual clauses is that by doing so, we basically rely on companies to regulate the fields of human rights, labour conditions and environmental protection (among other CSR topics) in their supply chains. Thus, we accept and expect that companies substitute states in their regulatory role.[106] This is, however, in conflict with both existing law and soft regulation. As was stressed in the UNGP, states are primarily responsible for these areas of public interests; this is also reflected in the three pillars of the UN's approach to business and human rights: states must "protect" rights while companies must "respect" them. Yet, even by not recognising third-party rights, we will not avoid companies' "legislating" through contracts. Finally, this is not a new phenomenon. Already in 1943 Kessler wrote, 'Freedom of contract enables enterprises to legislate by contract and, what is even more important, to legislate in a substantially authoritarian manner without using the appearance of authoritarian forms'.[107] Therefore, it seems that recognising third-party rights in respect to sustainability contractual clauses will not change this practice for better or for worse.

Finally, as already discussed, the use of contracts for managing public interests may be deemed to distort the underlying premise of contract law. Geis answers this concern by saying that contracts for the benefit of third parties may in fact lead to wealth maximisation of all involved subjects: 'A promisor may seek to tie her hands to signal an incremental commitment broadly and thereby gain new customers, better employees, fewer competitors, or some other strategic benefit. Similarly, the promisee to a broadcast contract may realize private gains'.[108] While this argument holds true, using an already existing legal institution (contract) to explain a new one (extraterritorial access to justice) may lead to 'a denaturalization of both'.[109] An important question to ask is thus whether contract law is equipped

104 *Kasky v. Nike, Inc* (n 17).
105 Eisenberg (n 21) 1407.
106 Geis (n 63) 1169 and 1173.
107 F Kessler, 'Contracts of Adhesion – Some Thoughts about Freedom of Contract' (1943) 43(5) Columbia Law Review 629, 640.
108 Geis (n 63) 1188.
109 Verhagen (n 28) 158.

to secure sustainable supply chain management or whether we may destroy it on the way.

5 Discussion and conclusion

This chapter discussed the legal requirements for the application of the contract law third-party beneficiary doctrine in respect to sustainability contractual clauses. While investigating the main requirements prescribed by the majority of legal systems – (i) the *intention* of contractual parties to (ii) grant a *specific right* to (iii) an *identified or identifiable third party* – it has been shown that, although difficult, the success of a third-party claim is not unimaginable (and while mostly unsuccessful in courts, it has not been refuted by them either). However, possible success will much depend, first, on the right of the third party. Positive and individual rights might be better adept at the realisation of such a claim. In contrast, negatively defined (a company's commitment not to harm others) and collective rights will be hard to defend through a third-party beneficiary claim due to the challenge of proper identification of the intended beneficiaries. Second, success will also much depend on the wording of the specific contractual clause. So far, the wording of sustainability contractual clauses and suppliers' codes of conduct, often incorporated into contract by reference, remains largely vague, making it difficult for third-party beneficiaries to prove the intention of the contractual parties and the content of the right they claim. Still, with increasing pressure – both societal and legislative – on companies to adopt sustainable management practice throughout their supply chain, one can expect that the language of contracts and codes will be sharpened.

Sections 3 and 4 then put forward arguments for the recognition of third-party beneficiaries' rights and its criticisms. Both groups of arguments are strong. While contract law's foundations may be shaken by a permissive third-party beneficiary rule, which may hypothetically lead to plentiful (strategic) litigation, recognising third-party beneficiary rights in respect to sustainability clauses may tilt corporate efforts toward addressing sustainability issues in international supply chains more seriously.

One may, however, ask if applying third-party beneficiary doctrine to these new realities will not dismantle the hardly achieved agreement over third-party beneficiary claims. Moreover, it would seem that contract law is used as a tool in need rather than for its particular suitability to these problems. As was shown in the French *"blood transfusion" case*, the third-party beneficiary right was used as a construct where tort law would not normally be used, but where the results of tort law seemed unfair. Similarly, the third-party beneficiary rule can possibly be applied to a situation where tort law might not be impossible, but difficult to apply. On the one hand, this "substitution" is questionable in regard to its effectiveness and appropriateness, as it may lead to the corrosion of established legal principles and rules. On the other hand, it may be a natural development of law in times when society is searching for transnational law capturing cross-border private law-based realities, an expression of freeing us from the conceptual public/private understanding of law we are locked in.[110]

A separate issue to consider is the interplay between contract law, CSR reporting and risk-based due diligence laws, and tort law. CSR reporting and risk-based due diligence laws aim to enhance, among others, sustainability behaviour in international supply chains. Since international law is not applicable to private parties while the reach of national law is geographically limited, states adopt these meta-regulations to drive changes extraterritorially. While there are certainly some positive results of these meta-regulations, the fact that they rely on contract as the ultimate means of enforcement can be seen as a major weakness. The law requires large companies to conduct risk-based due diligence and/or to report on it; in effect, it requires them to include sustainability contractual clauses into their supply chain contracts. However, it does not require them to enforce the contractual commitment. Companies thus include sustainability contractual clauses into their contracts and report on doing so, but can also include a no-third-party rights clause into the same contracts. The existence of the latter, of course, does not appear in CSR reports. We may thus ask, is this enough? Or even, is this possibly a ground for a false advertisement claim? Yet, this is not meant to blame companies (as they may have many valid and legal reasons for doing this), but rather to question the design of current regulation. Are we asking companies through both hard and soft law to adhere to some practices that they can be sanctioned (legally and otherwise, e.g. reputationally) for? In other words, are we driving the companies by incompatibility between policy and legal requirements to tort? CSR reporting and risk-based due diligence laws aim to protect third parties, but possibly not to 'arm' them against companies. We thus need to keep searching for more appropriate legal solutions to drive sustainable supply chain management.

Overall, it is the opinion of the author that, on the one hand, the potential of third parties' enforcing sustainability contractual clauses has not been exhausted yet, namely in the area of human and labour rights. A recognition of third parties' standing to enforce sustainability contractual clauses in these areas might provide incentives for contractual parties to work with the issues more carefully and more sincerely, and also provide incentives for states to enforce international human and labour rights laws more diligently in order to protect their own companies.[111] On the other hand, the author concludes that while enforcement by third parties could be potentially feasible in claims relating to individual positive rights, namely human and labour rights, it may have a very low level of possible success in claims relating to collective and/or negatively formulated rights, e.g. in the area of environmental protection.

110 G Teubner, 'After Privatization? The Many Autonomies of Private Law' (1998) 51(1) Current Legal Problems 393, 395–396.

111 For similar arguments in respect to natural resources contracts concluded between states and foreign investors, see Gathii (n 26) 98–99.

Bibliography

Andrecka M & Mitkidis K, 'Sustainability Requirements in EU Public and Private Procurement: A Right or an Obligation?' (2017) 1 *Nordic Journal of Commercial Law* 57–89.

Affolder N, 'Looking for Law in Unusual Places: Cross-Border Diffusion of Environmental Norms' (2018) *Transnational Environmental Law* 1.

Bagot M H Jr. & Henderson D A, 'Not Party, Not Bound – Not Necessarily: Binding Third Parties to Maritime Arbitration' (2002) 26(2) *Tulane Maritime Law Journal* 413–461.

Beckers A, *Enforcing Corporate Social Responsibility Codes: On Global Self-Regulation and National Private Law* (Hart Publishing 2015).

Brudney J, 'Envisioning Enforcement of Freedom of Association Standards in Corporate Codes: A Journey for Sinbad or Sisyphus?' (2012) 33(4) *Comparative Labor Law & Policy Journal* 555–603.

Cafaggi F, 'The Architecture of Transnational Private Regulation' (2011) EUI Working Paper, LAW 2011/12.

Cafaggi F, 'The Regulatory Functions of Transnational Commercial Contracts: New Architectures' (2013) 36(6) *Fordham International Law Journal* 1557–1618.

Eisenberg M, 'The Bargain Principle and its Limits' (1982) 95(4) *Harvard Law Review* 741–801

Freeman R, *Strategic Management: A Stakeholder Approach* (Pitman1984).

Gathii J, 'Incorporating the Third-Party Beneficiary Principle in Natural Resource Contracts' (2014) 43(1) *Georgia Journal of International and Comparative Law* 93–139.

Geis G S, 'Broadcast Contracting' (2012) 106(3) *Northwestern University Law Review* 1153–1200.

Haddock-Fraser J & Fraser I, 'Assessing Corporate Environmental Reporting Motivations: Differences Between "Close-to-Market" and "Business-to-Business" Companies' (2008) 15(3) *Corporate Social Responsibility and Environmental Management* 140–155.

Hallebeek J, 'Contracts for a Third-Party Beneficiary: A Brief Sketch from the Corpus Iuris to Present-Day Civil Law' (2007) 13(2) *Fundamina* 11–54.

Hatzis A N, 'Rights and Obligations of Third Parties' in Bouckaert B & De Geest G (eds), *Encyclopedia of Law & Economics, Vol. III: The Regulation of Contracts* (Edward Elgar Publishing 2000).

Hosking J M, 'The Third Party Non-Signatory's Ability to Compel International Commercial Arbitration: Doing Justice without Destroying Consent' (2004) 4(3) *Pepperdine Dispute Resolution Law Journal* 469–587.

Kenny K E, 'Code or Contract: Whether Wal-Mart's Code of Conduct Creates a Contractual Obligation between Wal-Mart and the Employees of its Foreign Suppliers' (2007) 27(2) *Northwestern Journal of International Law & Business* 453–473.

Kessler F, 'Contracts of Adhesion – Some Thoughts about Freedom of Contract' (1943) 43(5) *Columbia Law Review* 629–642.

Lando O, Beale H, & Commission of European Contract Law, *Principles of European Contract Law: Parts I and II – Combined and Revised* (Kluwer Law International 2000).

Lin L-W, 'Legal Transplants through Private Contracting: Codes of Vendor Conduct in Global Supply Chains as an Example' (2009) 57(3) *American Journal of Comparative Law* 711–744.

Maryanov D C, 'Sweatshop Liability: Corporate Codes of Conduct and the Governance of Labor Standards in the International Supply Chain' (2010) 14(1) *Lewis & Clark Law Review* 397–450.

McBarnet D & Kurkchiyan M, 'Corporate Social Responsibility Through Contractual Control?' in McBarnet D, Voiculescu A, & Campbell T, *The New Corporate Accountability, Corporate Social Responsibility and the Law* (Cambridge University Press 2007).

McBarnet D, Voiculescu A, & Campbell T, *The New Corporate Accountability, Corporate Social Responsibility and the Law* (Cambridge University Press 2007).

Micklitz H, Van Gestel R A J, & Brownsword R, *Contract and Regulation: A Handbook on New Methods of Law Making in Private Law* (Edward Elgar Publishing 2017).

Pace University School of Law and International Association for Commercial Contracts and Management, 'The Triple Bottom Line: The Use of Sustainability and Stabilization Clauses in International Contracts' (2010).

Perillo J M, *Calamari and Perillo on Contracts* (6th edn, West 2009).

Peterková Mitkidis K, *Sustainability Clauses in International Business Contracts* (Eleven International Publishing2015).

Peterková Mitkidis K, 'Life-Cycle Based Climate Regulation Through Supply Chain Contracts' working paper, Life-Cycle Based Management and Reporting for Sustainable Business SMART Conference, 29–30 November 2016, University of Oslo Faculty of Law Legal Studies Research Paper Series No. 2017–21.

Phillips J & Suk-Jun L, 'Their Brothers' Keeper: Global Buyers and the Legal Duty to Protect Suppliers' Employees' (2009) 61(2) *Rutgers Law Review* 333–379.

Porter M E & Kramer M R, 'Strategy & Society: The Link Between Competitive Advantage and Corporate Social Responsibility' (2006) 84(12) *Harvard Business Review* 78–85.

Sentner J J Jr., 'Who Is Bound by Arbitration Agreements? Enforcement by and against Non-Signatories' (2005) 6(1) *Business Law International* 55–75.

Smith S, 'Contracts for the Benefit of Third Parties: In Defence of the Third-Party Rule' (1997) 17(4) *Oxford Journal of Legal Studies* 643–663.

Smith S A, *Contract Theory* (Oxford University Press2004).

Teubner G, 'After Privatization? The Many Autonomies of Private Law' (1998) 51(1) *Current Legal Problems* 393–424

Vandenbergh M, 'The New Wal-Mart Effect: The Role of Private Contracting in Global Governance' (2007) 54(4) *UCLA Law Review* 913–970.

Verbruggen P, 'Private Regulatory Standards in Commercial Contracts: Questions of Compliance' in Micklitz H, Van Gestel R A J, & Brownsword R, *Contract and Regulation: A Handbook on New Methods of Law Making in Private Law* (Edward Elgar Publishing 2017).

Verhagen H, 'Contemporary Law' in Hallebeek J J & Dondorp H (eds), *Contracts for a Third-Party Beneficiary: A Historical and Comparative Account* (Brill Nijhoff 2008).

Vogenauer S & Kleinheisterkamp J, *Commentary on the UNIDROIT Principles of International Commercial Contracts* (Oxford University Press 2009).

Vytopil A L, *Contractual Control in the Supply Chain: On Corporate Social Responsibility, Codes of Conduct, Contracts and (Avoiding) Liability* (Eleven International Publishing 2015).

Wall S, 'The End of Forum non Conveniens: Has the European Court of Justice Gone Beyond its Boundaries' (2012) 2*King's Inns Student Law Review* 49–69.

Wang Q, Dou J, & Jia S, 'A Meta-Analytic Review of Corporate Social Responsibility and Corporate Financial Performance: The Moderating Effect of Contextual Factors' (2016) 55(8) *Business & Society* 1083–1121.

Wehberg H, 'Pacta Sunt Servanda' (1959) 53(4) *American Journal of International Law* 775–786.

Winters R, 'Employee Handbooks and Employment-at-Will Contracts' (1985) *Duke Law Journal* 196–220.

Part II

TORT LAW

5 Direct and vicarious liability in supply chains

Vibe Ulfbeck and Andreas Ehlers

1 Introduction

The preceding chapters have been concerned with contract law aspects related to responsible supply chain management. However, tort law may also be relevant in this regard. Thus, the extent to which a chain leader may be held liable for the acts of the supplier may affect the incentives to establish responsible supply chain management.[1]

The extent to which enterprises should be liable for failing to establish a safe and healthy working environment is at the centre of much contemporary discussion in both law and politics. The same applies to the question of imposing liability on enterprises for causing damage to the environment. Politically, there seems to be a desire that private enterprises assume a still greater responsibility for protecting both their employees against work-related injuries and other third parties from incurring harm ensuing from pollution or some other environmental hazard. The political focus on protecting the employees and the environment from harm is hardly surprising given the obvious socio-economic benefits from reducing the occurrence of such harm.

Traditionally, an employee who has sustained an injury at work or a third party that has sustained environmental harm has merely been allowed to sue the enterprise that is directly responsible for such injury or harm. This is not surprising since it is a basic tenet of law that companies (as well as physical persons) can be held liable only for their own actions and omissions.

However, in recent years, the reach of tort law has been expanded in the sense that tort law has also been used as a tool in "foreign direct liability cases", in particular cases concerning the possible liability of a parent company for the acts and omissions of a subsidiary based abroad.[2]

1 On the interaction between contract and tort in this regard, see Chapter 7 in this volume.

2 For a recent account on foreign direct liability see L Enneking, *Foreign Direct Liability and Beyond: Exploring the Role of Tort Law in Promoting International Corporate Social Responsibility and Accountability* (Eleven International Publishing 2005). The following account in section 2.1. is based on V Ulfbeck, 'Supply Chain Liability for Workers' Injuries – Lessons to be learned from Products Liability?' (2018) 9(3) Journal of European Tort Law 12–15.

This chapter goes one step further and examines the extent to which tort law can be invoked to establish supply chain liability, i.e. liability of the chain leader for the acts and omissions of a supplier. More specifically, it examines to what extent an employee of a supplier or a third party, having incurred environmental harm due the actions or omissions of the supplier, may sue the enterprise pursuant to the tort law rules on fault-based liability (direct liability) and vicarious liability (indirect liability). Furthermore, it is explored to what extent work injury claims and claims for environmental damage give rise to different challenges in law.

2 Direct liability

2.1 Work injuries

At the moment, in 2018, one supply chain liability case is pending in Europe (Germany).[3] It concerns the possible liability of the chain leader, the German discount retailer KIK, for work injuries suffered by Pakistani workers due to a factory fire in Karachi in 2012. In European legal theory, it has been argued that such a claim could be based on the reasoning in the important decision *Chandler v. Cape*,[4] in which the employees of a subsidiary successfully sued the parent company for damages caused by exposure to asbestos at the workplace.[5] Although concerned with parent liability[6] for the acts of a subsidiary and not supply chain liability, it has been argued that the criteria set out in the *Chandler* decision ("the *Chandler* criteria") can also be relevant in a supply chain context.[7] In *Chandler*, the parent company was held liable on the basis that it had "assumed responsibility". It was crucial to the court's decision that Cape had omitted to advise the subsidiary as to what measures should be taken to reduce or avoid the potential negative effects of asbestos. The Court (Arden) explained in more detail:

> In summary, this case demonstrates that in appropriate circumstances the law may impose on a parent company responsibility for the health and safety of its employees. Those circumstances include a situation where, as in the present case, (1) the business of the parent and the subsidiary are in a relevant respect the same; (2) the parent has, or ought to have, superior knowledge on some

3 The KIK case in Germany; see <https://business-humanrights.org/en/kik> accessed 30 November 2018. For insights into this case and how it is being argued, see C Terwindt, S Leader, A Yilmaz-Vastardis, & J Wright, 'Supply Chain Liability: Pushing the Boundaries of the Common Law?' (2018) 8(3) Journal of European Tort Law 261.

4 [2012] EWCA Civ 525.

5 P Rott & V Ulfbeck, 'Supply Chain Liability of Multinational Corporations?' (2015) 3 European Review of Private Law 415, 432; see also Terwindt, Leader, Yilmaz-Vastardis, & Wright (n 3).

6 For a general account of parent liability for subsidiaries or the so-called foreign direct liability cases, see Enneking (n 2) Chapter 3; L Anker-Sørensen, 'Parental Liability for Externalities of Subsidiaries: Domestic and Extraterritorial Approaches' <http://SSRN.com/abstract=2506508> accessed 9 July 2018, section 7.

7 Rott and Ulfbeck (n 5), 432.

> relevant aspect of health and safety in the particular industry; (3) the subsidiary's system of work is unsafe as the parent company knew, or ought to have known; and (4) the parent company knew or ought to have known that the subsidiary or its employees would rely on its using that superior knowledge for the employees' protection. For the purpose of (4) it is not necessary to show that the parent is in the practice of intervening in the health and safety policies of the subsidiary. The court will look at the relationship between the companies more widely. The court may find that the element (4) is established where the evidence shows that the parent has a practice of intervening in the trading operations of the subsidiary, for example production and funding issues.[8]

As it appears, the court focuses in particular on the concepts of 'superior knowledge' and 'reliance' as relevant criteria for assessing whether the parent company can be said to have assumed liability.[9] It is worth noticing that the element of reliance, according to the court, can be established by looking at the case 'more widely' and that 'intervening' in, for example, trading and funding issues may be sufficient. Consequently, it seems that some degree of actual control of the subsidiary by the parent company can be relevant in establishing reliance. Whereas the criterion of "reliance" has been brought to attention in Canadian case law (see later in the chapter), it remains to be seen whether it will also be adopted in European case law on supply chain liability.

In Canada a recent case, *Das v. George Weston Limited*, [10] sheds light on the possible applicability of tort law principles in a supply chain context. The *Das case* concerned the Rana Plaza disaster in Bangladesh. Injured workers and dependents sued the Canadian chain leader, Loblaws, claiming damages on the basis of tort liability. The case was decided on the basis of the law of limitations, but certain liability issues were also addressed. In fact, the court examined the question under both Bangladeshi law (as including English law) and Canadian law.[11] With regard to Bangladeshi/English law, the court found that the basic

8 [2012] EWCA Civ 525, para 80.

9 Interestingly, the reasoning of the court seems detached from company law principles and based on a "pure" tort law. This makes the reasoning transferable to the supply chain situation. See further Rott and Ulfbeck (n 5) 432, on the "pure" tort law thinking in the case. Despite the fact that the decision is based on tort law thinking, it has been criticized for evading company law principles, i.e. for being a disguised circumvention of the principle of the separate entities. See, for instance, T Bullimore 'Sins of the Father, Sins of the Son' (2012) Professional Negligence 2012, 2014: ' … but the effect of the decision is to cast the veil aside, through the application of tortious principles'. As to "potential control", see also A Sanger 'Crossing the Corporate Veil: The Duty of Care Owed by a Parent Company to the Employees of its Subsidiary' (2012) 71(3) The Cambridge Law Journal 480.

10 [2017] ONSC 4129.

11 The court did not explain why it examined both legal systems. According to choice of law rules related to tort law, the applicable law is normally the place where the injury took place, i.e. in this case, Bangladeshi law, which is based on the common law. When the court chose to examine Canadian law, which is also a common law system, it may have been to show that Bangladeshi law is not necessarily different from Canadian law (although this might have been expected).

question was whether Loblaws owed a duty of care towards the plaintiffs. In examining this question, the court made a reference to the neighbour principle[12] and examined various liability tests, including the 'assumption of responsibility'.[13] The court reached the conclusion that neither of the tests was satisfied. With regard to the assumption of responsibility theory, the court found that the *Chandler* line of reasoning did not lead to liability in the concrete case. Thus, the court remarked,

> With no disrespect intended, the New Wave employees, many of them illiterate in Bangla and in English would not know about, depend upon, or be influenced by CSR standards . . . or the contractual arrangements . . . They would have come to work regardless of Loblaws CSR standards.[14]

Although the court reached the conclusion that liability could not be imposed, it is worth noticing that the court seemed to accept that the *Chandler* criteria could also be relevant in the supply chain setting. With regard to policy considerations, the court specifically noted the concern for an indeterminate liability and that such liability would 'inundate the court with claims'.[15] With regard to Canadian law, a similar line of reasoning was applied. Under Canadian law, the analysis of a case that does not belong to an already established category[16] involves a duty of care analysis focusing on 1) foreseeability, 2) proximity and 3) policy reasons.[17] The court reached the conclusion that neither the requirement of foreseeability nor the requirement of proximity was satisfied. With regard to policy considerations, the court noted that such considerations also argued against allowing a claim, mentioning specifically, the prospect of 'indeterminate liability' and 'massive extension of liability of purchasers'.[18]

Also, in the case *Doe v. Wal-mart*, [19] the feasibility of invoking tort law to establish liability for unsafe conditions at the workplace was addressed. The plaintiffs relied on the doctrine of the Good Samaritan, according to which someone who undertakes a duty to assist another assumes a duty to take reasonable care in doing so.[20] In particular, tort liability may be established in case of reliance of a

12 *Das* (n 10), para 395.
13 The court also examined the "Caparo test" and the "incremental liability test", *Das* (n 10), para 412.
14 *Das* (n 10), para 438. In reality, this line of reasoning would lead to a situation where illiterate employees enjoy a lower level of protection than other employees.
15 Ibid., para 452.
16 Ibid., para 520.
17 Ibid., para 523, 526, 536.
18 Ibid., para 536.
19 *Doe v. Wal-mart* 572 f.3d 677 (9th Cir. 2009).
20 See Restatement (third) of Tort, art. 42 and 43. Section 43, which concerns third party claims, reads as follows: 'An actor who undertakes to render services to another and who knows or should know that the services will reduce the risk of physical harm to which a third person is exposed has a duty of reasonable care to the third person in conducting the undertaking if: (a) the failure to exercise reasonable care increases the

third person upon the undertaking.[21] The plaintiffs argued that Walmart's code of conduct reflected the required undertaking of a duty and that reliance could be established, since the code had been made public in various languages in all Walmart's supplier factories. However, amongst other things, such as lack of day-to-day control, the court was worried about the floodgate implications of finding for the plaintiffs and said that, by the reasoning put forward by the plaintiffs, all businesses would 'be responsible for the employment conditions for their own workers and all the workers employed by their suppliers'.[22]

To sum up, in all of the supply chain liability cases concerning workers' injuries, the criterion of "reliance" on the part of the employees has been seen as relevant in determining whether or not to impose liability on the chain leader. Moreover, in this regard, the *Chandler* criteria have also been found relevant in a supply chain setting. Furthermore, it seems that, according to the *Chandler* decision, one way of establishing reliance is by showing some degree of actual control/intervention on the part of the parent company/chain leader. Finally, a general concern underlying all of the decisions concerning supply chain liability for workers' injuries is the fear of "opening the floodgates" for claims.[23]

2.2 Environmental damage

In the following, it will be examined to what extent supply chain liability can also be incurred for environmental damage. As of July 2018, no such cases have been brought before the courts.[24] However, two recent cases, appearing before the courts in Europe, concern parent company liability for acts and omissions of a subsidiary with regard to environmental liability. Interestingly, both cases adopt the *Chandler* criteria.

In *Lungowe & Others v. Vedanta Resources Plc & Konkola Copper Mines*[25] (*Vedanta*) the claimants, 1,826 citizens of Zambia, sued Vedanta, a multinational mining company domiciled in the UK, and its subsidiary, the Konkola Copper

risk of harm beyond that which existed without the undertaking, (b) the actor has undertaken to perform a duty owed by the other to the third person, or (c) the person to whom the services are rendered, the third party, or another relies on the actor's exercising reasonable care in the undertaking'. In J Phillips and S-K Lim 'Their Brothers' Keeper, Global Buyers and the Legal Duty to Protect Suppliers' Employees' (2009) 63(1645) Rutgers Law Review 333, 350 ff, the potential for liability in supply chains based on this doctrine is explored.

21 See H Revak, 'Corporate Codes of Conduct or Ideal Publicity?' (2012) 63(6) Hastings Law Journal 1645, 1662, emphasizing this.

22 This reasoning has been criticized; see Revak (n 21) and Phillips and Lim (n 20) 353ff. In the *Wal-mart case*, the theory of "joint employment" was also rejected as a basis for a tort law claim against Walmart on the grounds that there was no "day-to-day" authority on the part of Walmart over employment decisions in the supply chain.

23 Probably, the fear of "opening the floodgates" is of particular concern in the supply chain context, as opposed to the parent–subsidiary context.

24 Yet, the fear of such liability has led to the adoption of environmental management throughout organizations.

25 [2017] EWCA Civ 1528.

Mines, domiciled in Zambia. The claimants alleged that toxic liquid waste from a mine owned by Konkola had polluted their land and waterways, causing loss of income and numerous personal injuries. The defendants challenged that the English courts had jurisdiction to try the case, but in the Technology and Construction Court (Queen's Bench Division) the challenge was denied by (the then) Mr. Justice Coulson, finding that the case could be heard. On the appeal of this decision, which was dismissed by the court of appeal, also finding that the case could be heard, Simon made comments as to the substance of the case that are of interest to the assessment of the feasibility of third parties injured by a subsidiary to claim damages from their parent company:

> (1) The starting point is the three-part test of foreseeability, proximity and reasonableness. (2) A duty may be owed by a parent company to the employee of a subsidiary, or a party directly affected by the operations of that subsidiary, in certain circumstances. (3) Those circumstances may arise where the parent company (a) has taken direct responsibility for devising a material health and safety policy the adequacy of which is the subject of the claim, or (b) controls the operations which give rise to the claim. (4) *Chandler v. Cape Plc* and *Thomson v. The Renwick Group Plc* describe some of the circumstances in which the three-part test may, or may not, be satisfied so as to impose on a parent company responsibility for the health and safety of a subsidiary's employee. (5) The first of the four indicia in *Chandler v. Cape Plc*, requires not simply that the business of the parent and the subsidiary are in the relevant respect the same, but that the parent is well placed, because of its knowledge and expertise to protect the employees of the subsidiary. If both parent and subsidiary have similar knowledge and expertise and they jointly take decisions about mine safety, which the subsidiary implements, both companies may (depending on the circumstances) owe a duty of care to those affected by those decisions. (6) Such a duty may be owed in analogous situations, not only to employees of the subsidiary but to those affected by the operations of the subsidiary.[26]

Simon went on to say that at such an early state of the case it was, on the evidence presented, not possible to say whether Vedanta (the parent) and Konkola (the subsidiary) owed a duty of care to the Zambian claimants. However, the findings of Simon show that in English law there is a basis for parties having suffered environmental damage and personal injuries to sue the parent company of the tortfeasor. For present purposes it is important to note that Simon explicitly found that not only employees of the subsidiary but also third parties having been affected by its operations might sue.

In a similar case, *HRH Emere Godwin Bebe Okpabi and others v. (1) Royal Dutch Shell Plc and (2) Shell Petroleum Development Company of Nigeria and between Lucky Lalame and others v. (1) Royal Dutch Shell Plc and (2) Shell*

26 *Vedanta* (n 25), para 83.

Petroleum Development Company of Nigeria (*Okpabi*),[27] citizens of Nigeria sued the parent company of the Shell Group, claiming that the parent company should be held liable for pollution caused in Nigeria by its subsidiary. The court of appeal found that the criteria set out in *Vedanta*, including the *Chandler* criteria, were applicable.[28] However, in this case Simon found that the Nigerian citizens had not demonstrated that the parent company owed them a duty of care, either on the basis of an assumed responsibility or on the basis that it controlled or shared control of the operations. Notably, Simon stressed that

> [i]t is . . . important to distinguish between a parent company which controls, or shares control of, the material operations on the one hand, and a parent company which issues mandatory policies and standards which are intended to apply throughout a group of companies in order to ensure conformity with particular standards. The issuing of mandatory policies plainly cannot mean that a parent has taken control of the operations of a subsidiary (and, necessarily, every subsidiary) such as to give rise to a duty of care in favour of any person or class of persons affected by the policies.[29]

Obviously, these cases do not deal with the possible liability of a buyer for environmental harm and personal injury caused by a supplier, but they show that English courts are willing to adapt the duty concept to novel situations. And just as it has been argued in *Das*, described previously, that the *Chandler* criteria may be relevant in a supply chain context with regard to work injuries, it could on the basis of *Vedanta* and *Okpabi*, also described previously, be argued that the *Chandler* criteria should be applicable in a supply chain context with regard to environmental harm. Thus, although all of the supply chain liability cases have concerned injuries to employees of the supplier, it must be expected that the line of reasoning presented in these cases will also play a significant role in cases concerning environmental liability towards third parties. Obviously, however – and as illustrated by the remarks of Simon in *Okpabi* – it may be more difficult to show that the *Chandler* requirements are fulfilled in an environmental liability case. First, it is questionable how the criteria of reliance are to be applied to a wide range of third parties who have suffered environmental harm. In practice it will not be possible to show reliance by each individual but possibly reliance on the part of the supplier, which, according to the *Chandler* criteria, should also be sufficient. Second, the "floodgate" concern, which has been raised in all cases regarding workers' injuries, may be even more profound with regard to environmental liability. Thus, in these cases, the range of people who can potentially be affected is greater, fuelling the concern of establishing an indeterminate liability.[30]

27 [2018] EWCA Civ 191.
28 See explicitly, Ibid., *Okpabi* (n 27), para 192.
29 Ibid., para 89.
30 For parallel problems and distinctions with regard to the concept of third-party beneficiary law, see Chapter 2 in this volume.

3 Vicarious liability in supply chains

3.1 The nub of the concept of vicarious liability

The concept of vicarious liability has traditionally been applied to impose liability on the employer for torts committed by its own employees. To a large extent, the rationale of the traditional concept of vicarious liability is that it is the employer who is capable of controlling the way in which the workplace is organized and how the work of the employees is carried out. It is not a requirement that the employer exercise actual control. It is sufficient to establish vicarious liability that the employer has a right to do so. "Subordination" has been used as a keyword to describe the basis for this kind of vicarious liability.[31] In this sense, the concept of control with regard to vicarious liability is a formal requirement. This is what – at the outset - distinguishes the concept of control with regard to vicarious liability from the concept of control with regard to direct (fault-based) liability of the chain leader/parent company, as described previously.

It is also this concept of control that forms the basis for the rule that there is (usually) no vicarious liability for independent contractors (whom the employer normally does not have the right to control).[32] However, making the distinction between employees and independent contractors has become increasingly difficult. In addition, even if the tortfeasor is found to be an independent contractor, certain exceptions to the non–liability rule do exist.[33]

3.2 The concept of relationships "akin to employment" and the relaxation of the control test

It is generally recognized that vicarious liability extends to relationships that are not based on a formal contract of employment. Furthermore, the requirement of control has been relaxed so that other criteria are also relevant when considering whether a relationship is "akin" to employment. This development has been ongoing for a long period of time.

For many years, the control test stood unchallenged but developments on the labour market since (roughly) the beginning of the second half of the 20th century, including the specialization of the workforce and the diversification of the production of goods, posed certain problems in the application of it. Thus, in many cases the courts were presented with questions of vicarious liability, which could not be answered readily on the basis of the control test. For example, the

31 European Group on Tort Law, *Principles of European Tort Law: Text and Commentary* (1st edn, Springer 2005) 116, para 5.

32 S Galand-Carval, 'Comparative Report on Liability for Damage Caused by Others' in J Spier (ed), *Unification of Tort Law: Liability for Damage Caused by Others* (Kluwer Law International 2003) 306, para 64; European Group on Tort Law (n 31) 117, para 9.

33 Furthermore, it is worth noting that some European legal systems (Poland and the Netherlands) apply a general rule of vicarious liability for independent contractors; Galand-Carval (n 32) 306, para 64.

courts had doubts as to how professionals with a particular skill should be handled because in such cases the employer (e.g. an accounting firm or a hospital) had no real way of telling the employee (e.g. a highly specialized accountant or doctor) what to do in specific situations. Moreover, since employees began working more outside the workplace (geographically speaking), it became increasingly difficult to determine when and where the employee in question should be considered to be at work. Also, the fact that enterprises began borrowing employees from other enterprises caused problems in determining whom the employee should be said to be working for when causing the damage in question.[34]

Today, the leading case in English law is the Supreme Court case *Catholic Child Welfare Society and others v. Various Claimants*, [35] concerning the possible vicarious liability of a religious order for the acts of a 'brother'. In this case, Lord Phillips introduced a two-step test to be applied when evaluating whether vicarious liability can be imposed on the basis that a relationship is "akin" to employment. In order to make this assessment, the court must look at five factors:

a a) Is the "employer" more likely to have the means to compensate than the independent contractor (insurance)?
b b) Was the tort committed as a result of the work undertaken for the "employer"?
c c) Is the activity likely to be part of the business activity of the "employer"?
d d) Has the "employer", by employing the "employee" to carry out the activity, created a risk of the tort committed by the "employee"?
e e) Has the "employee", to a greater or lesser extent, been under the control of the employer?

Second, it must be evaluated whether the tort was sufficiently closely related to the employment or quasi employment relationship.[36] As will be apparent, the test contains the criterion "right to control" but adds a number of others. The same is the case in the US, where a "multifactor test" is often used to decide whether a relationship is "akin" to that of employee/employer.[37] Also in other legal systems, the control test has been relaxed and supplemented by other criteria.[38]

Cases evolving around the criterion "akin to employment" typically concern individuals as employees. However, it has been argued that the rationale could

34 See further P Giliker, *Vicarious Liability in Tort – A Comparative Perspective* (Cambridge University Press 2010) 83–93.
35 [2012] UKSC 56.
36 The test has most recently been applied in the case *Various Claimants v. Barclays Bank PLC* (2017) EWHC 1929 (QB) to determine whether a doctor who had been carrying out medical assessments and examinations on behalf of the bank could be regarded an employee of the bank.
37 See D N Conn 'When Contract Should Preempt Tort Remedies: Limits on Vicarious liability for Acts of Independent Contractors' (2009) 15 Fordham Journal of Corporate & Financial Law 179, 185–186.
38 Ibid., Giliker (n 34) 66–68 on German and French law.

also be applied when the independent contractor is a (large) legal entity.[39] In English law, this view does not seem to hold much support following the latest Supreme Court decision for *Cox v. Ministry of Justice*.[40] Here it was expressly underlined that the two-step test

> results in an extension of the scope of vicarious liability beyond the responsibility of an employment, but not to the extent of imposing such liability where a tortfeasor's activities are entirely attributable to the conduct of a recognizably independent business of his own or of a third party.[41]

The court seems to make clear that the criterion "akin to employment" can only be applied to individuals, not to a legal entity that constitutes an independent business. Consequently, it must be presumed that under English law the relationship between the supplier and the chain leader cannot be regarded as akin to an employment relationship.[42]

3.3 Classification of the supplier

Quite clearly, the supplier is not an employee of the chain leader. Furthermore, at least in English law, it seems clear that supply companies also cannot be considered as being akin to employees. This raises the question of whether the supplier can instead be classified as an independent contractor.[43] In tort law, an independent contractor can be defined as someone to whom a task is "outsourced". In other words, an independent contractor is someone who performs tasks that would have otherwise been performed by the employer itself. In line with this, the term "independent contractor" has traditionally been applied to contractors who sell services, as opposed to products. Thus, in the US Second Restatement of Agency, Section 2(3) a general contractor is defined as:

> [A] person who contracts with another [party] to something for [the other party] but who is not controlled by the other nor subject to the other's right to control with respect to his physical conduct in the performance of the undertaking.

Even clearer is the distinction between services and products in the following description of an independent contractor from 1956:

39 Ibid., Terwindt, Leader, Yilmaz-Vastardis, Wright (n 3) 290.
40 [2016] UKSC 10.
41 *Cox* (n 40), para 29
42 On US law and the criterion of "retention of control" see later in the chapter. The following analysis is partly based on a previously published work by the authors: V Ulfbeck & A Ehlers, 'Tort Law, Corporate Groups and Supply Chain Liability for Worker's Injuries: The Concept of Vicarious Liability' (2016) 5 European Company Law 167.
43 A third option would be that the supplier is a contractual partner that is to be considered neither an employee, nor akin to an employee nor an independent contractor.

> [A]n independent contractor may be defined . . . as any person, other than a servant, who is employed to do work. The definition includes such diverse persons as a builder, a road construction engineer, an electrician, a dentist or doctor attending a private patient, a shoe-repairer, a launderer, a dressmaker, a barber, an airline company, a taxi-driver, a copy-typist, an advisory expert, and a charwoman if not a servant. But a vendor is clearly not a contractor for this purpose.[44]

Notably, according to this definition, the seller is clearly not an independent contractor. Consequently, it could be argued that the rules regarding vicarious liability for independent contractors are of no relevance to the question of supply chain liability. This was argued in *Doe v. Wal-mart*, [45] where the buyer claimed that the category of independent contractors did not extend to buyers. However, no authority was cited for this proposition and the court did not address the issue.[46]

Today, it seems that the distinction between independent contractors and sellers can be challenged. In a traditional sales arrangement between two parties, there is no basis for regarding the seller as someone to whom the buyer has outsourced the task of producing (or providing) the product that is being bought by the buyer. Consequently, there would be no basis for imposing vicarious liability on the buyer according to one of the exceptions described as follows, should it turn out that the seller negligently caused damage to something or somebody while producing the product. Clearly, no such vicarious liability arises if the buyer simply buys a product that is in stock from the seller in a market with several sellers to choose among. The situation would likely be the same if a buyer places a onetime order with a seller, buying several of its products.

However, the way modern supply chains work gives rise to the question of whether the situation – in certain circumstances – may be comparable to that of engaging an independent contractor. Thus, modern supply chains are often based on long-term contracts between the parties, reflecting a deliberate decision on the part of the company to "outsource" the production of certain products to entities abroad. In such situations, it is the company that decides what type of products should be produced and the company abroad is entrusted with the task of producing these products. In these situations, it could be argued that the seller should be regarded an independent contractor.

This line of thought seems to have been recognized in US case law. In *Read v. Scott Fetzer Co.*,[47] a manufacturer/distributor was regarded as an independent contractor. Likewise, in the case *Lavazzi v. Mc Donald's Corp*,[48] the term "independent contractor" was applied in the context of a restaurant (the buyer) and its food supplier.

44 G Williams, 'Liability for Independent Contractors' (1956) The Cambridge Law Journal 180.
45 *Doe v. Wal-mart Stores, Inc.*, No. 05-CV-7307 AG (MANx), 2007 U.S. Dist. LEXIS 98102 (C.D.Cal. 30 March 2007).
46 See also Phillips and Lim (n 20) 364.
47 990 S.W 2d.732 (Tex 1998).
48 606 N.E. 2d 845, 850–852 (III. App.Ct. 1992)

Against this background, it is not unlikely that a supplier could be labelled an "independent contractor".[49] This makes it interesting to take a closer look at situations where an enterprise (the "employer") can be held vicariously liable for the acts of an independent contractor.

3.4 Exceptions to the general rule of no liability for independent contractors

3.4.1 The recognition of exceptions

In most legal systems it is recognized that a number of exceptions apply to the general rule that there is no vicarious liability for independent contractors.[50] The most well-established include the doctrines of "retention of control",[51] "non-delegable duties" and the "peculiar risks doctrine". The following contains an analysis of the applicability of these doctrines to work injuries and environmental damage respectively.

3.4.2 Retention of control

Although the requirement of control has been relaxed and is no longer a necessary condition for establishing vicarious liability in certain relations, it still seems to be generally recognized that if the employer, in fact, has retained the right to control, then this can be a sufficient basis for establishing vicarious liability.[52] Several legal systems seem to accept this line of reasoning.[53]

However, it is unclear whether the rule on "retention of control" is in reality a rule on vicarious liability (focusing on the right to control) or of direct liability (focusing on actual control). For example, in US law, the rule is formulated in the following way in the Restatement (second) of Torts § 414:

49 See also Phillips and Lim (n 20), 364 reaching the same conclusion and Terwindt, Leader, Yilmaz-Vastardis, Wright (n 3) 291.

50 For a comparative overview, see Galand-Carval (n 32) 307.

51 Whether "retention of control" should in fact be regarded as a category of vicarious liability, see later in this chapter.

52 When applied to individuals, the retention of control test may not always be distinguishable from the argument that there is a relationship "akin" to employment; see DN Coon (n 37) 195 on US law and G Caval (n 32) 306, note 86 on European law, making the distinction between employees in workplaces where several employers are involved and "truly independent contractors" and others.

53 This seems to be the position in German law; see J Fedtke and U Magnus, 'Liability for Damage Caused by Others under German Law' in J Spier (ed), *Unification of Tort Law: Liability for Damage Caused by Others* (Kluwer Law International 2003) 120, 128. The same line of thought is recognized in Spanish law; see M M Casals and J S Feliu, 'Liability for Damage Caused by Others under Spanish Law' in J Spier (ed), *Unification of Tort Law: Liability for Damage Caused by Others* (Kluwer Law International 2003) 249, 249–250. For the example of "disguised employees" in English law, see B Douglas, *Enterprise Liability and the Common Law* (Cambridge University Press 2010) 161. For US law, see also D N Conn (n 37) 194, criticizing this as a separate category for vicarious liability. See also Phillips and Lim (n 20) 364.

> One who entrusts work to an independent contractor, but who retains control of any part of the work, is subject to liability for physical harm to others for whose safety the employer owes a duty to exercise reasonable care, which is caused by his failure to exercise his control with reasonable care.

Since liability under the rule ultimately is based on the failure of the "employer" to exercise his control with reasonable care, it could be argued that the rule is in fact about direct liability. This has also been held in a recent Illinois Supreme Court decision.[54]

The theory of retention of control has also been brought into play in a supply chain context in the US case *Abdur Rahaman v. J.C. Penny Corporation, Inc.* [55], which was decided according to Delaware law. The case concerned liability for injuries suffered by the supplier's workers but the theory of retention of control could also be applied with regard to environmental liability.

In this case, the court considered whether Jenny Penny could be held liable under the "general contractors theory", according to which – under Delaware law – a general contractor may be held liable towards the employees of the independent contractor under three exceptional circumstances: 1) the general contractor actively controls the manner and method of performing the contract work; 2) the general contractor voluntarily undertakes the responsibility for implementing safety measures; and 3) the general contractor retains possessory control over the premises during work. The court found that none of these conditions was fulfilled.[56] Consequently, and due to the fact that the claims were time barred, the plaintiffs did not succeed with their claim.[57]

Also, this case illustrates the difficulties in drawing the distinction between direct liability and vicarious liability. The focus on "active control" and "undertaking of responsibility" makes it arguable that the Delaware rule rightly be categorized as a rule concerning direct liability rather than vicarious liability.[58]

In sum, it seems unclear to what extent an "employer" can be held liable for the acts and omissions of the independent contractor solely on the basis that the employer retained the right to control an independent contractor. Consequently, it is also unclear whether a chain leader can be held liable for the acts or omissions of the supplier solely on the basis that it retained the right to control the supplier.

3.4.3 Non-delegable duties and workers' injuries

The concept of "non-delegable duties" is to some extent applied in Anglo-American legal systems. The essence of the concept is that some duties cannot be

54 *Carney v. Union Pacific Railroad Company*, 2016 III.118984, 77 N.E. 3rd 1 [2017].
55 C.A. No. N15C-07-174 MMJ [2016].
56 Ibid., *Abdur Rahaman v. J.C. Penny , Inc* (n 55) 24–25.
57 For an interesting analysis of the potential of applying the theory of general contractors in a supply chain context, see Phillips and Lim (n 20) 363 ff.
58 Other court decisions also seem to be unclear on whether the focus is on actual control or the right to control; see Phillips and Lim (n 20) 364–367, citing court practice that makes reference to both criteria and the concept of "assumption of a duty of care".

delegated and if they are, the person delegating may incur liability.[59] It is difficult to find common characteristics of the circumstances falling under this heading. One explanation is that non-delegable duties are duties that are so important that they cannot be delegated.[60] Another explanation is that non-delegable duties are of a personal nature and for that reason cannot be performed by others.[61]

The concept also seems to cover several different situations under US law. In legal theory, it has been claimed that the concept of non-delegable duties can be used merely as a label when, for policy reasons, it has been decided by a court that an independent contractor should be held liable. This has been formulated particularly clearly by Schwartz: 'Under certain circumstances, the party hiring that contractor is vicariously liable for the independent contractor's negligence. In these circumstances, the party's "duty" is regarded as "non-delegable"'.[62] However, according to a more recent interpretation, non-delegable duties are duties that are said to be owed to the public generally, such as, for instance, duties following from statute to provide certain safeguards.[63]

Applying this understanding, non-delegable duties could exist both with regard to the working environment and the environment at large.

However, in case law, the concept of non-delegable duties has primarily been discussed with regard to workers' injuries. This is reflected in English law in the general rule that the employer's duty to take reasonable care for the safety of

59 In English law, non-delegable duties are not seen as establishing vicarious liability. Rather, non-delegable duties are seen as describing cases in which the duty of the person delegating extends 'beyond being careful, to procuring the careful performance of work, delegated to others', Lord Sumption in Woodland 3. See also P Morgan, 'Recasting Vicarious Liability' (2012) 71(3) The Cambridge Law Journal 640: 'Non-delegable duties are often resorted to and adopted as a response to perceived inadequacies in vicarious liability'. See also Giliker (n 34) 108 ff.

60 E Henderson, 'Liability to Employees of Independent Contractors Engaged in Inherently Dangerous Work: A Workable Workers' Compensation Proposal'(1980) 48(6) Fordham Law Review 1165, fn. 3.

61 In English law, it has recently been stated that non-delegable duties are characterized by the fact that 'there is nearly always an affirmative duty for which the defendant has assumed responsibility', M Jones, A M Dugdale, & M Simpson, *Clerk & Lindsell on Torts* (21st edn, Sweet & Maxwell 2015) 6–63. As a recent example from English law of the application of this principle, one could perhaps mention the case *Woodland v. Swimming Teachers Association* [2013] UKSC 66; [2014] A.C. 537, establishing the vicarious liability of the local authority, which had outsourced the provision of swimming lessons and lifeguard services to an independent contractor. Lord Sumption found that the case was one of non-delegable duties, since there was an 'antecedent relationship' between the parties and the defendant had 'assumed liability' towards the plaintiff. For a critique of the line of reasoning in this case, see J Morgan, 'Liability for Independent Contractors in Contract and Tort: Duties to Ensure That Care is Taken' (2015) 74(1) The Cambridge Law Journal 99–139.

62 G T Schwartz 'Liability for Damage Caused by Others under US Law' in J Spier (ed) *Unification of Tort Law: Liability for Damage Caused by Others* (Kluwer Law International 2003) 284.

63 Ibid., Conn (n 37) 193.

employees cannot be delegated.[64] In other words, the employer cannot transfer his liability for the safety of the workplace to somebody else, neither to an employee nor to an independent contractor. Consequently, if – nevertheless – the task of securing the workplace is outsourced to an independent contractor, the employer remains responsible and will be liable for injuries to the employees (industrial injuries) caused by the negligence of the independent contractor.

The question is whether the doctrine could be relevant in the supply chain context. This seems less likely. Firstly, in the supply chain situation, it is the task of producing a product that is being outsourced, not the responsibility for the safety at the workplace. Secondly, the product is not being produced by the employees of the chain leader (the employer) but by employees of the supplier (the independent contractor). Consequently, it must be assumed that the doctrine cannot be used as a basis for imposing liability on the chain leader for the negligence of the supplier in securing the workplace. However, since it could be argued that in reality the effect of the supply chain setup is precisely to outsource issues of safety at the workplace to somebody else, the fairness of the law in this regard has been questioned in legal theory. Thus, Brodie states,

> [A]s matters stand the employer cannot delegate the provision and operation of a safe system of work in respect of those directly employed. Why should it be permitted to do so in respect of other workers who are hired to further the aims of the enterprise?[65]

3.4.4 The peculiar risk doctrine and environmental damage

It is a general legal principle in many legal systems that it should not be possible for an employer to avoid liability for inherently dangerous work by delegating it to an independent contractor. On the face of it, the doctrine would seem to be applicable both with regard to the working environment and the environment at large. Most clearly, the doctrine has been formulated in the US in Restatement (Third) of Torts, Sections 58 and 59:

> Section 59. An actor who hires an independent contractor for an activity that the actor knows or should know poses a peculiar risk is subject to vicarious liability for physical harm when the independent contractor is negligent as to the peculiar risk and the negligence is a factual cause of any such harm within the scope of liability.
>
> Section 58. An actor who hires an independent contractor to do work that the actor knows or should know involves an abnormally dangerous activity is

64 Ibid., Jones, Dugdale and Simpson (n 61) 6–73. The principle was established in the case *Wilson and Clyde Coal Co. v. English* (1937) 3 All ER 628 to modify the consequences of the doctrine of common employment; see also D Brodie, *Enterprise Liability and the Common Law* (1st edn, Cambridge University Press 2014) 152.

65 Ibid., Brodie (n 64) 164.

> subject to vicarious liability for physical harm when the abnormally dangerous activity is a factual cause of any such harm within the scope of liability.[66]

This principle has also been recognized in English law.[67] One of the early, leading cases was *Bower v. Peate.* [68] Here the court found that an employer who hires someone to perform work

> [f]rom which in the natural course of things, injurious consequences . . . must be expected to arise . . . is bound to see to the doing of that which is necessary to prevent the mischief, and cannot relieve himself of his responsibility by employing someone else.[69]

Also in Scandinavia, it is recognized that it is not possible to avoid liability by outsourcing particularly risky tasks to an independent contractor.[70] The principle has been used to impose liability on employers for personal injury or property damage caused in connection with the performance of such tasks.[71] Whereas the principle clearly applies in cases concerning damage caused to *third parties*, such as, for instance, environmental damage, it is less clear whether it also applies to work injuries suffered by the *employee* of the independent contractor. The question has been addressed in US case law. Here, there seems to be no clear rule.[72] However, several decisions that deny protection for the employee do so by arguing that the employee is covered by a workers' compensation scheme.[73]

In the supply chain context, the question was recently addressed in the US case of *Abdur Rahaman v. J.C. Penny Corporation, Inc.* [74] A question before the court was whether Jenny Penny, as the chain leader, could be held liable for the acts of

66 On the US doctrine of peculiar risk, see, for instance, Conn (n 37) 194.
67 W V Horton Rogers 'Liability for Damage Caused by Others under English Law' in J Spier (ed), *Unification of Tort Law: Liability for Damage Caused by Others* (Kluwer Law International 2003) 76, but compare R Stevens 'Non-Delegable Duties and Vicarious Liability' in J W Neyers, E Chamberlain, & S G A Pitel (eds) *Emerging Issues in Tort Law* (Hart Publishing 2007) 343–344, arguing that the basis for this doctrine has disappeared after a special rule of strict liability for extra hazardous activity was rejected by the House of Lords in 1947.
68 [1896] 1 QBD, 326 (Cockburn CJ).
69 Another leading case was *Honeywill and Stein Ltd v. Larkin Bros Ltd* [1949] 1 K.B. 191. Today, the doctrine is believed to enjoy only a 'very limited sphere of operation', Ibid., Jones, Dugdale and Simpson (n 61) 6–71.
70 V Hagstrøm & A Stenvik, *Erstatningsrett* (1st edn, Universitetsforlaget 2015) 249.
71 See, e.g., the decision by the Danish High Court (Western division) of 10 March 1981 (published in the Weekly Law Report at 564), concerning environmental liability.
72 E Henderson, 'Liability to Employees of Independent Contractors Engaged in Inherently Dangerous Work: A Workable Workers' Compensation Proposal' (1980) 48(6) Fordham Law Review 1165–1198.
73 Ibid., 1180.
74 Ibid., *Abdur Rahaman v. J.C. Penny, Inc* (n 55).

their supplier under various theories of vicarious liability.[75] One of the theories brought forward was the "peculiar risk theory". However, the peculiar risk theory was rejected as a basis for a claim, inter alia, because the doctrine was understood as providing protection for "bystanders" only, not for employees. Moreover, the plaintiffs had failed to identify a risk that was peculiar to the garment industry.[76]

This case confirms that the peculiar risk theory can only be applied under US law when the injured party is an innocent bystander and not employees. Consequently, this theory seems to apply better to cases concerning environmental damage (rather than industrial injuries) caused by the supplier. In order to succeed with a claim it must be shown that the task that has been outsourced gives rise to a "peculiar risk" that is inherently dangerous. Of course, it could be argued that the collapse of a building, which caused the injuries in the Rana Plaza disaster, was not a risk peculiar to the garment industry; rather it could happen in any industry in which employees work in factories. Moreover, the task of producing garments is not "inherently" dangerous but only became dangerous because of the way in which it was carried out. However, depending on the nature of the task that has been outsourced to the supply chain, it may be possible to argue that the task was inherently dangerous and that consequently, vicarious liability should be imposed. However, the theory seems to be primarily applicable in situations where third parties (i.e. not employees) are injured by the negligent activities of the supplier.

4 Conclusion

The analysis has shown that the concept of supply chain liability may be developing along two different lines of argument.

One is direct liability. Here, it is clear that litigants, courts and legal literature have been inspired by the liability standard developed in the case *Chandler v. Cape* with regard to the liability of parent companies for their subsidiaries. Consequently, arguably, liability can be based not only on "actual control" but also on the concept of reasonable expectations. It has been argued that – for several reasons – it is more difficult to succeed with claims concerning environmental damage than workers' injuries.

The other line of argument is vicarious liability. It is argued that a supplier must be regarded as an independent contractor. This means that as a starting point, the chain leader cannot be held vicariously liable for the acts and omissions of the supplier. However, several exceptions apply to this rule. Notably, the rule on non-delegable duties has been applied with regard to issues of workplace safety but it does not seem applicable in a supply chain context. Conversely, the rule regarding the creation of "peculiar risks" has been applied with regard to certain types of environmental liability and might also be applicable in a supply chain context. Finally, the rule on retention of control must be presumed to be equally applicable in work injury cases and environmental damage cases. However, it is unclear

75 On the theory of retention of control, see Section 3.4.2.
76 *Abdur Rahaman v. J.C. Penny, Inc* (n 55) 22–23.

whether this is in fact a rule on vicarious liability (potential control) or direct liability (actual control). Moreover, in practice it may be difficult to distinguish between actual control and potential control. This blurs the lines between direct and vicarious liability. Furthermore, one might raise the question of whether the tendency to relax the requirement of control with regard to vicarious liability for individuals may have a "spillover" effect on the rule on retention of control with regard to companies as independent contractors, making it possible to apply a more flexible standard for determining whether vicarious liability should be imposed. Such a development of the law could be seen as a step in the direction of adopting the broader concept of "enterprise liability".

Bibliography

Anker-Sørensen L, 'Parental Liability for Externalities of Subsidiaries: Domestic and Extraterritorial Approaches' (2014) *The Dovenschmidt Quaterly* 102.

Brodie D, *Enterprise Liability and the Common Law* (1st edn, Cambridge University Press 2010).

Bullimore T, 'Sins of the Father, Sins of the Son' (2012) 28 *Professional Negligence* 212.

Casals M M & FeliuJ S, 'Liability for Damage Caused by Others under Spanish Law' in SpierJ (ed), *Unification of Tort Law: Liability for Damage Caused by Others* (Kluwer Law International 2003) 249.

Conn D N, 'When Contract Should Preempt Tort Remedies: Limits on Vicarious Liability for Acts of Independent Contractors' (2009) 15 *Fordham Journal of Corporate & Financial Law* 179.

Dugdale A, *Clerk and Lindsell on Torts* (Sweet & Maxwell2005).

Enneking L, Giesen I, & Lennarts L, *Foreign Direct Liability and Beyond: Exploring the Role of Tort Law in Promoting International Corporate Social Responsibility and Accountability* (Eleven International Publishing 2005).

European Group on Tort Law, *Principles of European Tort Law: Text and Commentary* (1st edn, Springer 2005).

Fedtke J & Magnus U, 'Liability for Damage Caused by Others under German Law' in Spier J (ed), *Unification of Tort Law: Liability for Damage Caused by Others* (Kluwer Law International 2003) 120.

Galand-Carval S, 'Comparative Report on Liability for Damage Caused by Others' in SpierJ (ed), *Unification of Tort Law: Liability for Damage Caused by Others* (Kluwer Law International 2003) 307.

Giliker P, *Vicarious Liability in Tort – A Comparative Perspective* (Cambridge University Press 2010).

Hagstrøm V & Stenvik A, *Erstatningsrett* (1st edn, Universitetsforlaget 2015).

Henderson E, 'Liability to Employees of Independent Contractors Engaged in Inherently Dangerous Work: A Workable Workers' Compensation Proposal' (1980) 48(6) *Fordham Law Review* 1165–1198.

Jones M, Dugdale A M, & Simpson M, *Clerk & Lindsell on Torts* (21st edn, Sweet & Maxwell 2015).

Morgan J, 'Liability for Independent Contractors in Contract and Tort: Duties to Ensure that Care is Taken' (2015) 74(1) *The Cambridge Law Journal* 99.

Morgan P, 'Recasting Vicarious Liability' (2012) 71(3) *The Cambridge Law Journal* 615.

Neyers J W, ChamberlainE, & PitelS G A, *Emerging Issues in Tort Law* (Hart Publishing 2007).

Phillips J, 'Their Brothers' Keeper: Global Buyers and the Legal Duty to Protect Suppliers' Employees' (2009) 63(1645) *Rutgers Law Review* 364.

Revak H, 'Corporate Codes of Conduct: Binding Contract or Ideal Publicity?' (2012) 63 (6) *Hastings Law Journal* 1645–1670.

Rott P & Ulfbeck V, 'Supply Chain Liability of Multinational Corporations?' (2015) 3 *European Review of Private Law* 432.

Sanger A, 'Crossing the Corporate Veil: The Duty of Care Owed by a Parent Company to the Employees of Its Subsidiary' (2012) 71(3) *The Cambridge Law Journal* 480.

Terwindt C, LeaderS, Yilmaz-VastardisA, & WrightJ, 'Supply Chain Liability: Pushing the Boundaries of the Common Law?' (2018) 8(3) *Journal of European Tort Law* 261.

Ulfbeck V, 'Supply Chain Liability of the Public Buyer?' (2017) 12(3) *European Procurement & Public Private Partnership Law Review* 325.

Ulfbeck V, 'Supply Chain Liability for Workers' Injuries – Lessons to be learned from Products Liability?' (2018) 9(3) *Journal of European Tort Law* 12–15.

Ulfbeck V & Ehlers A, 'Tort Law, Corporate Groups and Supply Chain Liability for Worker's Injuries: The Concept of Vicarious Liability' (2016) 5 *European Company Law* 167.

Williams G, 'Liability for Independent Contractors' (1956) *The Cambridge Law Journal* 180.

6 Liability for "greenwashing"?

On unfair commercial practices, the legal duty to be transparent and the case for a "safe harbor"

*Louise A. Vytopil**

1 Introduction

Over the past few decades, Volkswagen has attempted to create a "green" image for itself. The company publicly spoke of reaching ambitious environmental goals and presented itself as a frontrunner in the field of corporate social responsibility (CSR) and the revolution of "green cars". But after the first irregularities were discovered in respect to its diesel cars in 2014, in 2015 it became clear that around 11 million Volkswagen cars contained fraudulent software that could circumvent diesel emission tests. In the media, Volkswagen was criticized for "greenwashing";[1] the carmaker claimed to be "green", while at the same time not really pursuing environmentally responsible policies. Shortly thereafter, the Dow Jones Sustainability Index Committee decided to remove Volkswagen from the Index. More importantly, the diesel scandal led to both criminal investigation and civil litigation in, inter alia, Europe and the United States. In the fall of 2016, a record settlement in the amount of USD 14.6 billion was reached in one of the American class action procedures.[2] Although the aforementioned settlement was unprecedented in terms of the amount, it is not uncommon nowadays for companies to pretend that they are (more) environmentally friendly or socially responsible than they actually are.[3] Companies increasingly communicate in respect to their responsible and/or environmentally friendly policies and use these policies as a

* This chapter was written in private capacity and does not represent the views of the author's institutions.

1 Merriam-Webster's Dictionary defines "greenwashing" as 'expressions of environmentalist concerns especially as a cover for products, policies, or activities'.

2 'U.S. Judge Approves $ 14.7 Billion Settlement in VW Diesel Scandal' (26 October 2016) *Fortune Magazine*.

3 See the decision by Advertising Code Commission (*Reclame Code Commissie*) in respect to Zeeman, 24 December 2015 dossier no.: 2015/01079.

part of their advertising towards consumers. Yet, if a company incorrectly informs its consumers of its social and environmental practices, the question could arise as to whether this company may be held liable by consumers who have made their purchasing decision (partly) on the basis of the "green" information provided by the company.[4] The risk of a company providing incorrect information in respect to its business conduct practices is particularly poignant when it comes to their supply chain practices; companies are typically less in control of their supply chains, and the business practices throughout supply chains are simultaneously fairly non-transparent.

Although any claim from a consumer is likely to be limited in terms of the damages,[5] the reputational damage that could result from such a procedure is high.[6] The question as to whether a company can be held liable based on the officially published CSR information is becoming increasingly important, now that companies are more and more required to disclose "non-financial" information (both pertaining to their own operations and to their supply chains).

In this chapter, I will discuss under which circumstances companies that disclose CSR information can be held liable by consumers for unfair commercial practices in connection with such information on the basis of the EU Directive on Unfair Commercial Practices[7](UCP) and the EU Guidance[8] in respect to this Directive, and whether this is desirable.[9]

4 Some examples of recent US consumer law procedures are the following: *Ruiz v. Darigold, Inc.*, No. C14–1283 RSL (W.D. Wash. 3 November 2014); *Barber v. Nestle USA, Inc.*, No. 15-cv-01364 (C. Cal. 9 December 2015, see infra); *Hodson v. Mars, Inc.*, No. 15-cv-0440 (N.D. Cal. 17 February 2016), *Wirth v. Mars, Inc.*, No. 15-cv-1470 (Calc. Co. 5 February 2016); and *NCL v. Wal-Mart, JC Penney and The Children's Place*, No. 2015 CA 007731 B (D.C. Super initiated 8 October 2015).

5 It should be noted that the Volkswagen scenario would likely not easily translate into an unfair business practice, seeing that consumers generally purchase cars from dealerships rather than from Volkswagen directly.

6 The degree of reputational damage will – in practice – depend on various factors, including the company's "past performance" in the CSR and business sectors. See, among others, J McGuire, A Sundgren & T Schneeweis, 'Corporate Social Responsibility and Firm Financial Performance'(1988) 31(4) Academy of Management Journal 854; B Kytle & J Ruggie, 'Corporate Social Responsibility as Risk Management: A Model for Multinationals' (2005) Corporate Social Responsibility Initiative Working Paper No. 10/2005 <https://sites.hks.harvard.edu/m-rcbg/CSRI/publications/workingpaper_10_kytle_ruggie.pdf> accessed 10 April 2018. In the case of Volkswagen, the reputational damage did not lead to a decline in consumers sales; 'VW Manages Record 2016 Sales Despite Dieselgate Crisis', Reuters, 10 January 2017, <www.reuters.com/article/us-volkswagen-vehiclerregistrations-idUSKBN14U1G0> accessed May 2018.

7 Directive 2005/29/EC of the European Parliament and of the Council of 11 May 2005 concerning unfair business-to-consumer commercial practices in the internal market.

8 Guidance on the implementation/application of Directive 2005/29EC on Unfair Commercial Practises.

9 The Directive, in respect to unfair commercial practices, is a maximum harmonization directive; as a result, the law is identical or highly similar in each EU Member State

I start this chapter in Section 2, with an overview of the existing legislation obliging companies active in the EU to publish CSR-related information. The legislation includes the Directive 2014/95/EU 'Non-Financial Information Directive' (NFI-Directive),[10] as well as transparency legislation with an extra-territorial scope, such as the UK Modern Slavery Act 2015 (MSA) and the California Transparency in Supply Chains Act (CTSCA). In the third section, I will review which legal requirements must be met in order for a consumer to hold a company liable on the basis of misleading advertising in the sense of the Unfair Commercial Practices Directive.[11] In the fourth section, I will analyze how CSR information ties in with liability for unfair commercial practices and when a company's CSR statements can form a basis for liability towards consumers. Finally, in the fifth section I will conclude that if a company publishes CSR information (whether on the basis of a legal obligation to do so or on its own accord), any such information may be used to hold the company liable for misleading advertising, should it turn out the published information is not (entirely) correct. The question then arises whether companies should find a safe harbor if they publish certain CSR information pursuant to a legal obligation to do so, so that they do not have to fear liability based on unfair commercial practices if they offer openness about CSR. In my conclusion, I will argue that the current position taken in the Guidance in respect to the Unfair Commercial Practices Directive is untenable with a view to increased transparency requirements for companies and, rather, a safe harbor should be created in order to reach the full potential of transparency legislation such as the NFI Directive.

2 The duty to be transparent: legal obligations to publish CSR information

Over the past years, multinational corporations have greatly increased the amount of non-financial information[12] they publish. Whereas in 2000 John

and most of the observations made in this contribution will hold in each EU Member State. Note that in this contribution, I do not extensively address the liability for the signing of, and failure to comply with, a code of conduct as referred to in Article 6: 193c, para. 2 (b) Dutch Civil Code. Although it is not inconceivable that a CSR code can lead to consumer liability as referred to in this article, such a discussion goes beyond the scope of this publication, as it will strongly depend on the terms of the code of conduct and the manner in which the CSR policy at hand has been implemented.

10 Directive 2014/95/EU of the European Parliament and of the Council of the 22 October 2014 amending Directive 2013/34/EU as regards disclosure of non-financial and diversity information by certain large undertakings and groups, OJ L 330/1. This Directive is not based on maximum harmonization; regional variations among Member States will therefore arise.

11 Again, the same criteria hold throughout the European Union, as a result of the fact that this Directive is based on maximum harmonization.

12 Non-financial information relates to non-financial aspects of the company's performance and the way in which the company operates: the way in which the company

Ruggie reported that less than 100 of the 80.000 multinationals worldwide reported in respect of their human rights and environmental performance, CSR reporting – especially among large companies – has now become so common that in 2015 more than 90 per cent of the 250 largest companies worldwide reported on CSR.[13]

This increase in the publication of non-financial information has been encouraged by the adoption of transparency legislation. Many listed companies are now legally obligated to publish certain non-financial information, for instance, as part of their annual report or as an independent CSR or modern slavery statement. Additionally, semi-legal instruments such as the Dutch Corporate Governance Code now stipulate that companies that fall within the scope of the Code are to not only take into account environmental, social and human rights issues, but also to draft policies on such issues.[14] Multinational corporations that enter the United Kingdom or California consumer markets must comply with even more extensive obligations in respect to human rights. Both the UK MSA and the California Transparency in Supply Chains Act apply extraterritorially: they also provide for transparency obligations for companies that do not have their corporate seat or headquarters in (respectively) the United Kingdom or California. The obligations that stem from these acts thus also apply, for instance, to Dutch or French companies that meet the criteria.[15] In the next sections, I will describe the NFI Directive, the UK MSA and the CTSCA; I will conclude this section by describing current legal developments in the field of transparency legislation.

2.1 EU Non-Financial Information Directive

In 2014, the European Parliament adopted the NFI Directive. On the basis of this Directive, "large" undertakings[16] that qualify as public-interest entities in the

deals with environmental, social, human rights and other aspects (such as anti-bribery and corruption) of its business.

13 KPMG Report 'Currents of Change, The KPMG Survey of Corporate Responsibility Reporting 2015', available at <https://assets.kpmg.com/content/dam/kpmg/pdf/2015/11/kpmg-international-survey-of-corporate-responsibility-reporting-2015.pdf> accessed 10 April 2018.

14 Based on Principles 1.1 and 1.1.3 of the Dutch Corporate Governance Code version December 2016, the Board and the Supervisory Board are required to take into account on long-term value creation. Based on Principle 1.1.1.vi, the corporate strategy should focus on 'other business-related aspects of the company and its related business, such as environment, social and human affairs, the chain in which the company operates, respect for Human rights and the fight against corruption and bribery'; see the Dutch Corporate Governance Code, December 2016.

15 Article 54, Part 6 UK Modern Slavery Act; Section 3 California Transparency in Supply Chains Act 2010 (Senate Bill No. 657).

16 An undertaking qualifies as "large" in the sense of Directive 2013/34/EU if it exceeds on the balance sheet dates at least two of the three following criteria: (a) balance sheet total: EUR 20.000 000; (b) net turnover: EUR 40.000 000; (c) average number of employees during the financial year: 250. The threshold posed by the NFI Directive is higher: a company must have 500 employees for the Directive to apply.

sense of Directive 2006/43/EC[17] are required to include a non-financial statement in their directors' report if they employ more than 500 employees on average during that financial year. The non-financial statement must – as a minimum – contain information on environmental, social and employee matters, with respect to human rights, anti-corruption and bribery matters, including:

a a brief description of the undertaking's business model;
b a description of the policies pursued by the undertaking in relation to those matters, including due diligence processes implemented;
c the outcome of those policies;
d the principal risks related to those matters linked to the undertaking's operations, including, where relevant and proportionate, its business relationships, products or services that are likely to cause adverse impacts in those areas, and how the undertaking manages those risks;
e non-financial key performance indicators relevant to the particular business.

If the company does not pursue a policy in respect to these matters, it is required to explain why it does not do so. The Directive consists of a mix of minimum- and maximum-harmonization clauses. As a result, Member States are permitted to decide on stricter measures than what is provided by the Directive in respect of a number of matters, including whether or not to require that the published information is verified by an independent assurance services provider.[18] Each Member State was able to make a different choice in respect to the involvement of the auditor. For instance, upon much deliberation, the Netherlands finally decided to stipulate that the non-financial information published is subject to the same assurance as the director's report. Denmark opted for an auditor's check in respect to the presence of the non-financial statement, as well as a consistency check of disclosures.[19]

17 Public-interest entities are defined in Article 2(13) of Directive 2006/43/EC on statutory audits of annual accounts and consolidated accounts: '"Public-interest entities" means entities governed by the law of a Member State whose transferable securities are admitted to trading on a regulated market of any Member State . . . , credit institutions . . . and insurance undertakings . . . . Member States may also designate other entities as public-interest entities, for instance entities that are of significant public relevance because of the nature of their business, their size or the number of their employees'.

18 The Directive does not address who qualifies as an "independent assurance services provider"; this is a matter of national law. In the Netherlands, only registered accountants and statutory auditors qualify as such. It is believed that if the information provided is verified by an external party, this would make the statement "fairer and more accurate" (Commission Guidelines on Non-Financial Reporting C 215/7, para. 3.2).

19 The GRI-report "Member State Implementation of Directive 2014/95/EU" provides a nice graphic overview of the choices made in each Member State <www.globalreporting.org/resourcelibrary/NFRpublication%20online_version.pdf> accessed 10 April 2018.

Another choice left to Member States relates to the question of whether companies are permitted to exclude certain non-financial information if

> the disclosure of such information would be seriously prejudicial to the commercial position of the undertaking, provided that such omission does not prevent a fair and balanced understanding of the undertaking's development, performance, position and impact of its activity.[20]

The NFI Directive applies in respect of financial years starting after 31 December 2016; as a result, the first non-financial reports were expected during the course of 2017. The European Commission has estimated that throughout the EU, 18,000 companies will fall within the scope of the NFI Directive.[21] In the meantime, many (European) multinationals not only have to comply with the NFI Directive, but also with other legislation that is national in nature but has an extraterritorial effect. A number of examples of such acts of legislation will be discussed in the next sections.

2.2 UK Modern Slavery Act 2015

In 2015, the MSA was adopted in the United Kingdom.[22] The MSA does not only apply to companies that have their registered offices in the United Kingdom; provided that a company meets the criteria set out in Part 6 of the MSA, a foreign company can also fall within the scope of the MSA. This is the case if a company qualifies as: (1) a commercial organization, which (2) supplies goods or services, (3) has a total turnover of at least GBP 36 million and (4) complies with the criterion of 'carr[ying] on a business, or part of a business' in the United Kingdom. These criteria are more easily met than it would seem. The turnover criterion is not restricted to sales in the United Kingdom but instead pertains to *global* annual sales; as a result, not only do the largest Dutch companies, such as Shell and Ahold, meet the criteria, but so do many smaller companies, such as Bugaboo and Grolsch.[23]

Article 54 of the MSA contains the core of the obligation to publish certain information. This article provides that companies that fall within the scope of the MSA each year are to publish an annual transparency statement. In their statement, companies must indicate which measures they take to ensure that slavery and human trafficking do not occur within their company and their company's supply chains (ideally going beyond the first tier of the supply chain). As with the

20 Article 1, NFI Directive, Amending Article 19a Directive 2013/34/EU.
21 Proposal for a Directive, COM (2013) 207 final 16 April 2013, 7.
22 For a comprehensive overview of the MSA and the obligations for Dutch companies, see L Vytopil & J Butijn, 'UK Modern Slavery Act 2015' (2016) Tijdschrift voor Sanctierecht & Onderneming 132.
23 This follows from the public annual report of the listed companies for the financial years 2014 and 2015, which describes how high the turnover is and in which countries they are active.

NFI Directive, the MSA is based on the comply-or-explain principle.[24] The MSA does not require companies to take actual, concrete steps to combat modern slavery. It only requires that the company states whether it has any slavery and human trafficking policies in place and if so, what the effects of these policies are.

So which subjects should be addressed in a MSA statement by a company in order to meet the criteria posed by the MSA? Article 54 (5) MSA contains a (non-exhaustive) list of six issues that can be included in the statement: (1) the organization's structure, its business and its supply chains (ideally beyond the first tier of its supply chain); (2) its policies in relation to slavery and human trafficking; (3) which due diligence processes it has in place in relation to slavery and human trafficking in its business and supply chains; (4) which parts of its business and supply chains contain a risk of slavery and human trafficking taking place, and the steps the company has taken to assess and manage that risk; (6) to what extent the company is effective in ensuring that slavery and human trafficking are not taking place in its business or supply chains, measured against such performance indicators as it considers appropriate and finally, (7) whether it provides its staff with training about slavery and human trafficking.

The board of directors of the company must approve the statement.[25] The Home Office Guidance provides that the statement is to be published in English; it may additionally be published in another language when relevant to the company's business and supply chains.[26] The company's transparency statement must then be published on the company's website, either by means of a clear link or through a dropdown menu on the homepage. In the absence of a website, the company must provide a copy of the statement to anyone requesting it within 30 days. The company should thus be transparent about the measures it will take to prevent modern slavery in the supply chain.

2.3 California Transparency in Supply Chains Act[27]

A second example of relevant transparency legislation with an extraterritorial scope is the CTSCA, effective as of 1 January 2012. The CTSCA has as its goal increased transparency for consumers in respect of products tainted with human trafficking and slavery, thereby encouraging them to purchase responsibly, and

24 The company does not need to mention why it does not conduct policies as defined in the MSA.

25 Article 54, para. 6 MSA stipulates who is to sign the statement. Since the MSA is a UK act of legislation, its starting point is UK legal persons, which should be applied by analogy to foreign companies. In the case of limited liability companies, it would be the board of such a company that should sign the statement.

26 The Home Office Guidance states that the Statement is "public-facing"; it should therefore be written in simple language to ensure that everyone understands the statement. There are no direct sanctions for non-compliance with the MSA; therefore there are no sanctions for non-compliance with the language requirements.

27 Parts of this paragraph appeared before in my dissertation, A L Vytopil, *Contractual Control in the Supply Chain: Corporate Social Responsibility, Codes of Conduct, Contracts and (Avoiding) Liability* (Eleven Publishing 2015).

improving the lives of victims of human trafficking and slavery Section 2 (h)–(j) CTSCA.[28] The CTSCA applies to retail sellers and manufacturers doing business in the State of California, regardless of the country of their incorporation, and that have a gross revenue of over US 100 million dollars in annual worldwide gross receipts. Each year, the Franchise Tax Board makes a list of these companies available to the attorney general. It therefore covers only companies that offer tangible products for sale within the State of California, not service providers. If companies fall within the scope of the CTSCA, they must disclose – at a minimum – the company's efforts to eradicate slavery and human trafficking from its direct supply chain (top-tier) for tangible goods offered for sale.

Specifically, and at a minimum, companies are to disclose on their website, with a conspicuous and easily understood link on their homepage, what they do in respect to each of the following: First of all, they must state whether they engage in the verification of product supply chains to evaluate and address risks of human trafficking and slavery. Companies must specify whether their verification was conducted by a third party. Second, they must indicate whether they conduct audits of suppliers to evaluate supplier compliance with the company's standards for trafficking and slavery in supply chains. This disclosure must specify if the verification was not an independent, unannounced audit. Third, following the CTSCA, companies must clarify whether they require that direct suppliers certify that materials incorporated into the product comply with the laws regarding slavery and human trafficking of the country or countries in which they are doing business. Fourth, companies must announce to what extent they maintain internal accountability standards and procedures for employees or contractors failing to meet the company's standards regarding slavery and trafficking. Finally, the company must indicate if it provides relevant company employees and management with training on human trafficking and slavery, particularly with respect to mitigating risks within the supply chains of its products.

Similar to the MSA, companies are not required to solve any problems they encounter in respect to human trafficking and slavery; they are only required to provide transparency on such issues. If companies do not meet the transparency requirements set out in the CTSCA, the attorney general may bring an action for injunctive relief. At the moment, as of May 2018, no such action has yet been brought by the attorney general. Nonetheless, the Act expressly states that

28 The resource guide on the CTSCA that is issued by the California Department of Justice provides the following: 'In recent years, California consumers have demanded that producers provide greater transparency about goods brought to market. Consumers utilize this additional information to drive their purchasing decisions, and various indicators suggest that Californians are not alone. A recent survey of western consumers revealed that people would be willing to pay extra for products they could identify as being made under good working conditions. A recent law in California is poised to help California consumers make better and more informed purchasing choices. The California Transparency in Supply Chains Act provides consumers with critical information about the efforts that companies are undertaking to prevent and root out human trafficking and slavery in their product supply chains – whether here or overseas' (7).

nothing in the section shall limit the remedies available for a violation of any other state or federal law. Alternative legal actions (such as a consumer's claim of misleading advertising statements) therefore remain possible.

The MSA and the CTSCA are not the only examples,[29] but they are considered among the earliest transparency laws (in particular, in relation to the supply chain) that apply extraterritorially.[30] As a result of such legislation, foreign companies that fall within the scope of that legislation will have to publish more information on their CSR policy. This information is partly for the benefit of investors (as is the case with the NFI Directive) and partly for the benefit of consumers (as with MSA and CTSCA). In either case, the question will arise as to whether that information will also be used to influence (directly or indirectly) consumers' purchase decisions and, if so, how that information would play a part in a claim for damages based on misleading advertising.

3 Liability towards consumers on the basis of unfair commercial practices

Next, the question arises of when the CSR statements published by the company (whether or not based on the legislation referred to in the previous section) could lead to liability of the company. A consumer could possibly initiate an action based on unfair commercial practices consisting of deception.[31] This section sets out the

29 For example, in the Netherlands, the aforementioned Corporate Governance Code 2016 deserves a mention. This code (which applies to stock exchange listed companies) emphasizes long-term value creation and risk management (relating not simply to financial risks but *all* identifiable material risks). In the United States, Article 1502 of the Dodd-Frank Act provides another ground for corporate transparency; on the basis of this provision (and the related Conflict Minerals Rule), companies must file a conflict minerals report with the Securities and Exchange Commission (SEC) if they use the "conflict" minerals tin, tantalum, tungsten or gold, which originate from the Democratic Republic of Congo and surrounding countries. The status of this last act of legislation is somewhat unclear as a result of the Trump's administration's plans to revoke the Dodd-Frank Act.

30 In this context, note the Dutch bill proposed by Van Laar/Kuiken in relation to a duty of care in respect of child labor. This bill was adopted by the Lower House on February 6, 2017 and is still under debate by the Senate. On the basis of this bill, from 2020, Dutch companies would be required to declare that they take appropriate care to prevent that their goods or services are created using child labor. In other words, this bill would create a statutory duty of care in respect to child labor for Dutch companies. The penalty for non-compliance would be not only an administrative sanction but also criminal prosecution. Initiative proposal-Kuiken Wet zorgplicht kinderwerk, Kamerstukken II 2016/17, 34506, A, <www.eerstekamer.nl/wetsvoorstel/34506_initiatiefvoorstel_van_laar> accessed 10 April 2018.

31 It is noted that the company could also be addressed on other grounds as a result of (omitting) a CSR statement it published. Incorrect CSR information could also trigger an action by default on the part of the company. For example, it is also conceivable that shareholders request the Enterprise Chamber of the Court of Appeals in Amsterdam to provide the company with instructions on the establishment of the board report when the report does not comply with the provisions of Title 9 of Book

conditions under which consumers can initiate such a process (with the prospect of success).

The core article on which liability for unfair trade practices is based is Article 4 of the UCP Directive.[32] If the requirements have been met, a consumer claiming that he/she had been misled by a company may be compensated for his damages. Such a consumer could argue that, had he/she known the true nature of the CSR practices of the multinational corporation (MNC), he/she would not have purchased a product manufactured by the MNC. "Commercial practices" are defined as 'any act, omission, course of conduct or representation, commercial communication including advertising and marketing, by a trader, directly connected with the promotion, sale or supply of a product to consumers'. A trader ('a natural or legal person acting in commercial practices for purposes relating to his trade, business, craft or profession') acts unlawfully in respect to a consumer ('a natural person, acting for purposes outside his trade, business, craft or possession') if he/she conducts trade practices that are unfair. Commercial practices qualify as unfair if they are 'contrary to the requirements of professional diligence' and if they 'materially distort' decision-making behavior in respect to a product for the average consumers reached or addressed.[33]

A company's CSR practices therefore only fall within the scope of the UCP Directive if they communicate with consumers (rather than businesses) in a commercial manner. Business-to-business advertising is excluded from the scope of the UCP Directive. Moreover, the UCP Directive only applies to 'commercial practices' that are 'directly connected' with the promotion, sale or supply of a product. The question is what falls within the scope of such a "direct connection".[34] Preamble 7 to the UCP Directive indicates that the Directive 'does not address commercial practices carried out primarily for other purposes, including for example commercial communication aimed at investors, such as annual reports and corporate promotional literature'.[35] The exclusion of corporate communications will therefore be an important limitation in practice, although the most

2 of the Dutch Civil Code and may, on the basis of Article 2:139 and 2:249 Dutch Civil Code, hold the management of the company liable for the damage caused by the misleading representation of the business.

32 Directive 2005/29/EC of the European Parliament and of the Council of 11 May 2005 concerning unfair business-to-consumer commercial practices in the internal market and amending Council Directive 84/450/EEC, Directives 97/7/EC, 98/27/EC and 2002/65/EC of the European Parliament and of the Council and Regulation (EC) No 2006/2004 of the European Parliament and of the Council.

33 Directive 2005/29/EC of the European Parliament and of the Council of 11 May 2005 concerning unfair business-to-consumer commercial practices in the internal market and amending Council Directive 84/450/EEC, Directives 97/7/EC, 98/27/EC and 2002/65/EC of the European Parliament and of the Council and Regulation (EC) No 2006/2004 of the European Parliament and of the Council ('Unfair Commercial Practices Directive'), Article 3, para. 1 and 2.

34 Also see A Rühmkorf, *Corporate Social Responsibility, Private Law and Global Supply Chains* (Edward Elgar 2015) 131–141.

35 Directive 2005/29/EC of the European Parliament and of the Council of 11 May 2005.

recent guidance on the UCP Directive (on which there is more in the paragraphs that follow) seems to expand this application.

A commercial practice is said to be unfair if it materially distorts or is likely to materially distort the ability of the average consumer to take an informed decision, as a result of which the average consumer does take or may take a decision in respect of an agreement that he/she otherwise would not have.[36]

Four requirements flow from these phrases: professional diligence, an informed decision about an agreement, the average consumer and a material distortion. The first requirement – professional diligence – is defined in Article 2(h) of the UCP Directive as 'the standard of special skill and care that a trader may reasonably be expected to exercise towards consumers, commensurate with honest market practice and/or the general principle of good faith in the trader's field of activity'.

Articles 6–9 of the UCP Directive provide examples of such unfair commercial practices, because they are misleading or aggressive. The consumer's ability to take an informed decision must have been materially distorted. The first question is what falls within the scope of the term 'informed decision about an agreement'. Article 2(k) of the UCP Directive defines a transactional decision as

> any decision taken by a consumer concerning whether, how and on what terms to purchase, make payment in whole or in part for, retain or dispose of a product or to exercise a contractual right in relation to the product, whether the consumer decides to act or to refrain from acting.

A socially conscious consumer may base his/her decision to purchase a product on a label attached to the product in an attempt to find out more about its origins. Was it made in Bangladesh or in the Netherlands? How was it produced? Are there claims about the extent to which CSR norms were met – for instance because it was produced as part of the "conscious collection" from H&M? CSR considerations must therefore have been included in the decision whether or not to purchase in order for a consumer to be able to make a claim under this section.

A second important notion is that of the "average consumer". This criterion is not defined in the Directive; the Court of Justice of the European Union defines the "average consumer" as a consumer 'who is reasonably well-informed and reasonably observant and circumspect'.[37] The assumption is therefore not that one may, without question, rely on a company's claims in advertisements. Social, cultural and language factors are taken into account as well. The question then becomes what assumptions, in respect to a company's corporate social performance, the "average consumer" could have made. Would the average consumer

36 Directive 2005/29/EC of the European Parliament and of the Council of 11 May 2005, Article 5(2).

37 First defined as such by the Court of Justice for the European Union on 16 July 1998 in *Gut Springenheide GmbH and Others v. Oberkreisdirektor des Kreises Steinfurt Ä Amt für Lebensmittelüberwachung*, Case C-210/96. See also B Duivenvoorde, *The Consumer Benchmarks in the Unfair Commercial Practices Directive* (Springer 2014) 20–23.

be required to be circumspect with regard to a company's marketing claims in respect of CSR? Vranken suggests that the consumer is under a certain duty to investigate. Verkade, too, argues that consumers must realize that they do not know everything, and that they should not accept every claim that is laid before them.[38] I nonetheless believe that, considering the opaque nature of CSR practices in supply chains in general, it is hard even for experienced professionals to get a proper grasp of the circumstances under which a product is made, let alone that it can be expected of the average consumer that he/she has an accurate notion of the conditions under which a product is made.

Finally, the decision-making process must have been "materially distorted", as required by Article 2(e) of the UCP Directive. In other words, the consumer's decision-making ability must have been altered in such a way that it changed the decisions that he/she would have otherwise made. A consumer would therefore need to argue that, had he/she known of the true CSR practices of a company, he/she would have chosen another, more sustainable product instead.

Articles 6 and 7 of the UCP Directive pertain to misleading acts and omissions and are the most relevant for unfair CSR practices. In respect to misleading practices, the requirement of "professional diligence" is no longer required. The other requirements, of the material distortion of the ability of the average consumer to make an informed decision about an agreement, must still be met. The unfair commercial practice must have been a (co-)decisive factor for the consumer's decision. Article 6(1) of the UCP Directive sets out that a trade practice qualifies as misleading if

> it contains false information and is therefore untruthful or in any way . . . deceives or is likely to deceive the average consumer [and it] causes or is likely to cause him to take a transactional decision that he would not have taken otherwise.

The first relevant example of such false information, provided in para. 1 sub. b, relates to 'the main characteristics of the product, such as its . . . method or date of manufacture or provision'. If a company, therefore, claims that a product was made in Europe under socially responsible conditions whereas it was actually made in Bangladesh under irresponsible conditions, it would fall within the scope of this article. Claims about the ethical conditions under which a product was made could also give rise to liability under this section (provided the other requirements have also been met), assuming that these ethical claims are factually inaccurate rather than incorporating broad, opinion-based claims about the product. The second category relevant to this research is provided in para. 2 sub. b, if a company's statement contains

38 See the note of J B M. Vranken at HR 30 mei 2008 LJN BD2820 NJ 2010/622 (De Boer c.s./TMF), sub 2, and the note of D W F Verkade at Gut Springenheide NJ 2000/375, sub 3.

> non-compliance by the trader with commitments contained in codes of conduct by which the trader has undertaken to be bound, where (i) the commitment is not aspirational but is firm and is capable of being verified, and, (ii) the trader indicates in a commercial practice that he is bound by the code.

The term 'code of conduct' relates to both agreements and sets of rules not imposed by an authority that define the behavior of traders that have undertaken to be bound. Those who have undertaken to be bound by a code of conduct are defined as 'code owners'.[39]

Article 12 of the UCP Directive contains a clause relating to the burden of proof in respect of the question whether the misleading information was in fact provided by the trader to the consumer. The burden of proof is on the trader with respect to the material accuracy and completeness of the information provided, considering the circumstances of the case at hand and the interests of the trader and other parties involved in the procedure. The consumer therefore still has the burden of proof in respect to the misleading or factually inaccurate character of the commercial practice. The consumer who files a claim against a company must therefore still prove that – for instance – the labor conditions under which the suppliers of the company produced a good were not in line with the claims by the company. In order to prove such facts, the consumer will likely need to rely on reports and investigations by the media or NGOs, since he/she will have insufficient verifiable information to prove these facts him/herself.

4 CSR statements as a source of liability for unfair commercial practices

In order to fall within the scope of the UCP Directive, any CSR information provided by a company must qualify as a 'commercial practice' in the sense of Article 2(d) of the UCP Directive. This requires that the relevant information concerns a presentation of business or commercial communication directly related to sales promotion, sale or delivery of a product to consumers. The question is whether information resulting from a CSR statement is covered. In June 2016, the European Commission published a revised version of its Guidance on the Implementation/Application of Directive 2005/29/EC on Unfair Commercial Practices (Guidance).[40] The Guidance states that it is intended to facilitate the

39 A company can therefore be held liable if it has publicly assumed a code of conduct that contains firm commitments that are verifiable, but it does not live up to the contents of said code. Examples of such codes are, for instance, those adopted by an entire business sector, such as the Dutch Advertising Code (*Nederlandse Reclame Code*), but codes only used by one company could fall within its scope. Whether these practices could create an actionable cause will depend much on the factual practices of a company, as well as the wording used in the code of conduct. I will not describe these actions in further detail within the scope of this chapter.

40 Commission Staff Working Document, Guidance on the Implementation/Application of Directive 2005/29/EC on Unfair Commercial Practices, COM (2016) 320,

implementation of Directive 2005/29/EC on unfair commercial practices, but that it is 'itself not legally binding'.[41] That means that the Guidance does not bind either Member States or the European Union Court of Justice (CJEU). The Guidance serves as a "living handbook", which is – in due time – to adapt to social developments. It will ultimately be for the CJEU to determine how the UCP Directive is to be explained and whether it will follow the Guidance in this respect. Until the CJEU rules in this respect, the Guidance will serve as a guide to interpretation of the UCP Directive in a particular case. Using a number of cases, I will be using the Guidance to see what the consequences of its interpretation of the UCP Directive would mean for companies that communicate about their CSR practices.

4.1 Form of CSR statements and the criterion of "commercial practice"

When will CSR communications qualify as commercial practice under the UCP Directive? This will depend on a number of factors; most important is the form in which the information is presented to the consumer. If CSR information is employed in advertising, it will generally qualify as such. An example of this is found in the Dutch chocolate company Tony's Chocolonely chocolate. Tony's Factory launched its chocolate brand in 2005 and used the slogan '100% guaranteed slave-free'.[42] Competitor Bellissimo believed that Tony's Factory misled its consumers by using this slogan, since it could not guarantee that the chocolate was produced without any slave labor. In summary proceedings, the District Court of Amsterdam ruled that Tony's Factory made it sufficiently plausible that it traced its cocoa. As a result, the cocoa used by the company would be kept separate from any non-slave-free cocoa.[43] The use of any "CSR slogans" on packaging material will therefore generally qualify as a commercial practice within the meaning of the UCP Directive.

However, in most cases, it will not be so clear-cut whether CSR information qualifies as such. The UCP Directive does not provide any concrete direction. However, the recently published Guidance does address the question under which circumstances CSR statements could qualify as commercial practice.

> Corporate social responsibility refers to companies taking responsibility for their impact on society by having in place a process to integrate social,

available at <http://ec.europa.eu.proxy.library.uu.nl/justice/consumer-marketing/files/ucp_guidance_en.pdf>.

41 Guidance, p. 5.

42 Note that this case fell within the scope of Directive 2006/114/EC concerning misleading and comparative advertising, rather than within the scope of the UCP Directive.

43 Amsterdam District Court, 6 February 2007, ECLI:NL:RBAMS:2007:AZ7870. Nevertheless, the slogan "100% guaranteed slave-free" is no longer used; in the meantime, the chocolate is brought to the market using the slogan "Together we make chocolate 100% slave free" – a significantly less hard commitment towards the consumer, in short.

> environmental, ethical and consumer concerns into their business operations and core strategy. This has become a marketing tool used to meet the growing concern of consumers that traders comply with ethical standards. . . . This may have an impact on the transactional decision of a consumer who has to choose between two competing products of similar quality and price. For this reason, such initiatives will, in most cases, be 'directly connected with the promotion, sale or supply of a product' and therefore qualify as a commercial practice within the meaning of the UCPD.[44]

The Guidance therefore generally considers CSR communications a marketing tool towards consumers. The Guidance does not specify when CSR statements (by way of exception) would *not* qualify as "commercial practices" within the meaning of the UCP Directive. As a result, the Commission generally considers CSR statements as meeting the criterion of 'commercial practice' in the sense of the UCP Directive. Simultaneously, preamble 7 of the UCP Directive stipulates that the Directive does not apply to commercial practices that are intended for other purposes, such as communications aimed at investors (including annual reports and promotional materials).

The Commission's decision to view CSR primarily as a marketing tool is a remarkable and perhaps an ill-considered choice. After all, the Commission does not seem to take into account the development described as follows, which increasingly requires companies to communicate on non-financial aspects to both investors and consumers.

In spite of the fact that a non-financial or CSR statement is primarily aimed at (potential) shareholders, one CSR statement will often play a role in a company's marketing instruments. Especially when a company publishes only one CSR statement in order to meet all applicable national and international transparency regulations, and it also makes this statement available to consumers on a dedicated "sustainability website", such a statement will form a liability risk to the company, since it will, in the opinion of the European Commission, fall within the scope of the UCP Directive. This is especially the case if this statement is also accessible through a link on the (commercial) consumer website, such as a webshop. Only if a CSR statement is exclusively made available to investors on a dedicated website would such a statement perhaps be beyond the scope of the term "commercial practice".[45] Either way, the company could argue that that statement is not 'directly related to the sale promotion, sale or delivery of a product to consumers' as referred to in Article 2(d) of the UCP Directive.

This issue is easily illustrated by the case of the clothing manufacturer H&M. H&M sells 600 million garments per year. H&M, inter alia, sells its products in an

44 Guidance, 63.

45 This also includes Preamble 7 of the UCP Directive, which provides as follows: 'This Directive does not apply to commercial practices that are principally intended for other purposes, such as commercial communication aimed at investors, such as annual reports and promotional material on companies.'

online store, through www.hm.com.[46] If a consumer needs information about the origin and CSR conditions under which products are made, that consumer will likely click on the "Sustainability" link in the online store, thereby accessing H&M's sustainability website at http://sustainability.hm.com. At the sustainability website, inter alia, H&M's sustainability report, as well as financial statements, annual reports and CSR codes for H&M suppliers, can be found. The available information does not clearly communicate that this information is *not* aimed at consumers. Although these statements are not primarily designed to provide consumers with more information, they will influence the purchasing decision of the "careful and critical consumer" who is looking for information about the circumstances under which a piece of clothing is manufactured.

If the information published by H&M would later prove to be incorrect and misleading – for example, because it becomes clear that the factories that produce clothing for H&M use forced labor – this could lead to an action based on misleading advertising in the sense of the UCP Directive. If companies provide more (factual) information about CSR circumstances (rather than communicating on general aims and wishes, such as "the company is committed to preventing human rights violations"), they increase their chances of providing information that later turns out to be incorrect or inaccurate.[47] The risk of being held liable on the basis of unfair or misleading commercial practices then also increases.

4.2 Content of CSR statements: when does "greenwashing" qualify as "misleading"?

If a company publishes only one CSR statement in order to comply with all applicable national and international legislation, and they also make this statement available to consumers through a dedicated sustainability website, such a statement will soon comply with the criterion of "commercial practice" in the sense of the UCP Directive. This raises the question of to what extent any possible "greenwashing" would qualify as misleading in the sense of the UCP Directive.[48] In the

46 Most European H&M websites use the following path to access sustainability information. In the online store at <www.hm.com>, sustainability information can be found at the bottom of the page under "Sustainability" (or an equivalent term in the local language). Although this link is placed below a header that reads "CORPORATE INFO", this is the only manner of accessing sustainability information from H&M. This link directs consumers to the H&M Group Sustainability website (<http://about.hm.com/en/sustainability.html>), with another link to the sustainability website, which holds the sustainability report (at <http://sustainability.hm.com>).

47 See also Vytopil (n 27) 246–249.

48 Several European governments have adopted specific guidelines for the use of "green" advertising. I refer to the Danish Consumer Guidance on the use of environmental and other claims in marketing, from the Danish Consumer Ombudsman; The UK Green Claims Guidance of the Department of Environment, Food and Rural Affairs, available at <www.gov.uk/government/uploads/system/uploads/attachment_data/file/69301/pb13453-green-claims-guidance.pdf>, and finally the French Practical Guide to Environmental Claims for traders and consumers from the Ministry for

Guidance, the European Commission indicates that if a product is marketed using unverifiable or incorrect claims pertaining to, for example, environmental friendliness or labor conditions under which the product was produced, this qualifies as "greenwashing". Practices may qualify as misleading if they center on vague and general notions such as being "environmentally friendly" or "green". If a consumer uses such notions as a ground for their purchasing decision, and are consequently misled, the "greenwashed" claim may fall within the scope of the UCP Directive. It is therefore sensible for companies to be both balanced and realistic in their CSR statements. Once they use claims that are (too) optimistic or vague, they may be held liable on the basis of misleading advertising in the sense of the UCP Directive once it turns out their claims are unfounded.

A complete and transparent CSR statement that is both realistic and perhaps indicates where the company sees room for improvement will be less likely to trigger a claim for misleading advertising towards consumers.[49] Dutch company Tony's Chocolonely now no longer uses the slogan '100% guaranteed slave-free', but rather promotes its products on the basis of the slogan 'Together we make chocolate 100% slave free'. A significant step down from its "slave-free guarantee", it is a much more conservative and perhaps more realistic approach.

5 CSR statements: a "safe harbor" for the company?

The Guidance provided by the European Commission in respect to sustainability statements results in a low threshold for consumers wishing to hold a company liable on the basis of misleading advertising. This raises the question of whether the approach chosen by the European Commission may be counterproductive. It could lead to companies using a "minimum information" strategy in order to avoid being held liable. After all, no company will have complete information at all times, and any inaccuracies could give rise to a claim. It could be argued that companies should be able to live up to the spirit of transparency legislation, rather than just the letter of such legislation, and be truly transparent without the risk of being held liable. I therefore find that it should be considered that companies be

Ecology, Sustainable Development, Transport and Housing and the Ministry for Commerce, Trades, Small and Medium-sized Enterprises, Tourism and Consumer Affairs, available at <www.economie.gouv.fr/files/files/directions_services/cnc/docs/the_practical_guide_to_environmental_claims_2012.pdf>.

49 In the *Barber v. Nestlé* case described here, the Californian judge ruled that 'no reasonable consumer who reads the four documents Plaintiffs identify in context could conclude that Nestlé's suppliers comply with Nestlé's requirements in all circumstances. On the contrary, Nestlé seems to anticipate a certain level of non-compliance. It is not shy about identifying for consumers the rules and expectations for its suppliers, but it does not mislead them into thinking that its suppliers abide by those rules and meet those expectations in every instance'. Barber's claim on the basis of misleading advertising was thus rejected. *Melanie Barber et al. v. Nestle USA Inc.*, District Court for the Central District of California et al., case number: 8:15-cv-01364, 13.

granted a safe harbor[50] when they publish transparency statements as required by law.

5.1 Safe harbor

The doctrine of a "safe harbor" originates from American law. It means that courts may rule that a certain behavior or a particular act will be deemed not to violate any rules.[51] As a result, a person or organization engaging in such behavior cannot be held liable. In *Cel-Tech Comms., Inc. v. L.A. Cellular Tel. Co.*, the California Supreme Court explained the doctrine as cases in which 'the legislature has allowed certain conduct or considered a situation and concluded no action should lie'.[52] This doctrine is also applied to unfair commercial practices cases.

In 2015, *Barber v. Nestlé*, the California first instance court ruled on this matter in respect of a company's omission in a transparency statement on the basis of the CTSCA.[53] The California court applied the safe harbor doctrine to Nestlé's CSR statement. The question was whether Nestlé was guilty of deception under the California Unfair Competition Law, since Nestlé had not stated in its CTSCA statement that the fish used in Purina Cat Food was captured using forced labor. Barber argued that Nestlé had stated in its CSR statements and policies that it 'expects the Supplier to adhere to all applicable laws and regulations . . . and strives to comply with international and industry standards and best practices' and that 'the Supplier must under no circumstances use, or in any other way benefit, from forced labor'. It argued that these statements were misleading, since forced labor was found in Nestlé's supply chain. Barber argued that they would not have purchased the relevant products if it had known of the actual working conditions in Nestlé's supply chain.

The California district court ruled that Nestlé found a safe harbor. Nestlé was under no obligation to state more than what was required on the basis of the CTSCA. Moreover, the court held that the statements published by Nestlé were clearly "aspirational" in nature: there were no hard commitments or warranties. As a result, it should have been clear to Barber and other consumers that Nestlé did not provide any guarantees. In this chapter, I would argue that EU companies,

50 See also E Brown, 'No Good Deeds Goes Unpunished: Is There a Need for a Safe Harbor for Aspirational Corporate Codes of Conduct?' (2007) 26(2) Yale Law & Policy Review 267.

51 Not to be confused with the privacy-law term "safe harbor" as described in, for example, the Commission Decision of 26 July 2000 pursuant to Directive 95/46 / EC of the European Parliament and of the Council concerning the suitability of protection By the Safe Harbor Principles for the Protection of Privacy and the Related Frequently Asked Questions published by the United States Department of Commerce (notified under document number C (2000) 2441).

52 *Cel-Tech Comms., Inc. v. L.A. Cellular Tel. Co.*, 20 Cal. 4th, 163, 182 (Cal. 1999).

53 M Barber et al., Nestle USA Inc et al., U.S. District Court for the Central District of California, case number: 8: 15-cv-01364, available at <www.csrandthelaw.com/wp-content/Uploads/sites/2/2016/01/Nestle-dismissal.pdf>. Barber et al. have appealed this decision.

too, should be able to find a safe harbor in respect to CSR statements and policies. This should hold, in particular, if said CSR policies and practices have been published pursuant to a legal obligation to be transparent. Companies should be able to find a safe harbor in respect to these statements and should not be held liable on the basis of unfair commercial practices, provided that certain basic requirements have been met.

5.2 A safe harbor for EU companies?

I believe that it would be sensible for the CJEU to rule that companies should be able to find a safe harbor in respect to their CSR statements under the UCP Directive. After all, transparency legislation is on the increase. Companies are increasingly required to produce certain non-financial, CSR, Environmental, Social and Governance (ESG) or sustainability information. The NFI Directive aims to increase the relevance, consistency and comparability of the non-financial information reported by companies. The CTSCA aims to provide better information services for consumers, as well as highlighting efforts by companies towards the eradication of slavery. Finally, Article 54 of the MSA aims to increase corporate transparency. These pieces of legislation do not aim to prescribe certain CSR policies that are to be adopted by companies, but instead aim to increase transparency in respect to these areas.

If companies are subsequently punished because their statements are believed to be incomplete or palaverous (even when transparency laws do not pose any particular requirements in this respect) and the European Commission sees the concept of "commercial communications" as being so broad that CSR statements generally fall within their scope, this would create a legally undesirable situation. In that case, it could be argued that the goal of transparency legislation (i.e. providing "better" CSR information and more relevant information for both consumers and investors) cannot possibly be met. After all, companies are then punished for publishing information that meets legal transparency requirements.

I believe that the notion of a safe harbor could be incorporated into EU law if the CJEU (or the national courts) were to declare that certain CSR statements, codes of conduct or policies cannot lead to liability on the basis of the UCP Directive, as long as they comply with relevant transparency law requirements. This would be consistent with Preamble 7 of the UCP Directive, which states that 'this Directive does not apply to commercial practices that are principally intended for other purposes, such as commercial communication aimed at investors, such as annual reports and promotional material on companies'. It would, however, effectively require that the current approach taken under the Guidance be abandoned by the European Commission. After all, the current approach under the Guidance means that virtually all CSR statements (whether mandatory or not) fall under the scope of "commercial practices". This stance does not provide a workable perspective if considered in line with other relevant CSR legislation. This is particularly risky for those companies with multilevel supply chains (as is the case with most large companies). For those companies, it is often impossible to know what is going on at each individual layer in the supply chain. As a result, companies may be the last to know of any malpractices in the supply chain. Companies may decide to comply with transparency legislation by publishing the most minimal CSR statement possible: one that complies with the bare minimum requirements, but does not offer any true insights to consumers. Although this minimizes the risk of liability towards consumers, this cannot possibly be in the spirit of such transparency legislation.

If legislators want to avoid companies' publishing very minimal CSR statements, they should determine that companies have a safe harbor for those transparency obligations under the UCP Directive. They should be able to publish CSR information without the risk of being held liable as a result. In the absence of such a safe harbor, there is a risk that companies will limit themselves to an extremely minimal CSR statement to minimize the risk of liability. That is not in line with the spirit of transparency legislation. Indeed, transparency legislation aims at providing consumers and investors with realistic information so that consumers and investors alike can make considerate purchase or investment decisions. If CSR statements only aim to meet minimal legal requirements, instead of instigating an open dialogue, it may be that the letter but not the spirit of transparency legislation is met. I therefore believe that companies should be permitted to paint a realistic and simultaneously open picture by means of their CSR transparency statements. This would increase transparency vis-à-vis consumers as well as investors, thereby meeting the objectives of the transparency legislation.

6 Conclusion

It is clear that companies increasingly publish CSR information. Inter alia, the NFI Directive, the UK MSA and the California Transparency in Supply Chains Act require that companies publish information about their CSR policy and the measures they take to address certain human rights violations. At the same time, last year, the European Commission published its revised Guidelines on the UCP Directive, which conclude that CSR statements will generally qualify as commercial practices within the meaning of that Directive. Because of that broad interpretation of the understanding of commercial practices, companies run the risk of being held liable on the basis of unfair commercial practices if their statements turn out to be inaccurate. This broad interpretation of the term "commercial practice" with the resultant possible liability may have unintended consequences. It is likely that companies will suffice with very limited CSR statements, which comply with the letter of transparency legislation, but not the spirit thereof. I believe this would not be a desirable development. I believe that (European) courts should create a safe harbor for CSR statements. When CSR statements comply with applicable legislation, they should not serve as grounds for liability under the UCP Directive. Until that time, it would be sensible for companies to provide factually correct, but not too "aspirational" CSR statements, as they are preferable to "green" but potentially misleading CSR statements.

Bibliography

Brown E, 'No Good Deed Goes Unpunished: Is There a Need for a Safe Harbor for Aspirational Corporate Codes of Conduct?' (2007) 26(2) *Yale Law & Policy Review*.

Gates G, 'How Volkswagen Has Grappled with its Diesel Scandal' (11 January 2017) *The New York Times*.

Kytle B & Ruggie J, 'Corporate Social Responsibility as Risk Management: A Model for Multinationals' (2005) Corporate Social Responsibility Initiative Working Paper No. 10/2005.

McGuire J, Sundgren A, & Schneeweis T, 'Corporate Social Responsibility and Firm Financial Performance' (1988) 31(4) *Academy of Management Journal* 854–872.

Rühmkorf A, *Corporate Social Responsibility, Private Law and Global Supply Chains* (Edward Elgar Publishing 2015).

Vytopil L, *Contractual Control in the Supply Chain: On Corporate Social Responsibility, Codes of Conduct, Contracts and (Avoiding) Liability* (Eleven International Publishing 2015).

Vytopil L & Butijn J, UK Modern Slavery Act 2015 (2016) 4 *Tijdschrift voor Sanctierecht & Onderneming*: 132.

Part III

INTERPLAY AND OVERLAP OF CONTRACT AND TORT LAW

7 Interplay between contract and tort in the supply chain

Vibe Ulfbeck and Ole Hansen

1 Introduction

The preceding chapters have analyzed supply chain liability separately in contract law and tort law. However, contract law and tort law also interact in situations concerning supply chain liability. One of the reasons for this is that each supply chain is composed of a series of contracts that tie the actors in the chain together and define their roles (the contract law aspect) but at the same time these relationships between the actors may produce side effects on third parties that are protected by tort law (the tort law aspect).

The topic of the connection between contract law and tort law at the general level has been studied from various angles. Several studies concern the *overlap* between contract and tort, i.e. situations in which a contractual breach also gives rise to tortious liability, either towards the other party to the contract or towards third parties, so that an injured party can choose either a contract law or a tort law claim to protect his or her interests (concurrency of actions).[1] The subject of this chapter is different.[2] It focuses on situations where tort triggers the application of a contract law regime or vice versa.[3] For example, it is well known that an injury incurred by a tortious act may activate an insurance contract. In this way tort law generates contract law effects. Conversely, a contract may also establish a factual situation that triggers tort law rules. For example, an employment contract will establish a legal relation between the employer and the employee which brings into play tort law rules on vicarious liability for the acts of the employee.

1 Classical studies on this include, in German law, P Schlechtriem, *Vertragsordnung und Ausservertragliche Haftung* (Metzner 1972), and Georgiades, *Die Anspruchskonkurrenz im Zivilrecht und Zivilprozessrecht* (Beck 1967); in French Law, G Viney, *Introduction a la Responsibility* (1995); in Scandinavian law, B Gomard, *Forholdet mellem erstatningsregler i og udenfor kontrakt* (1958). For a recent, comparative overview, see R De Graaff 'Concurrent Claims in Contract and Tort: A Comparative Perspective' (2017) 4(25) European Review of Private Law 701.

2 For a focus on overlap between contract and tort in the supply chain, see Chapter 8.

3 A more recent study concerning the interaction of contract and tort is C von Bar and U Drobning, *The Interaction between Contract and Tort and Property Law in Europe* (Sellier European Law Publishers 2004).

In the supply chain context, the interaction between the two legal regimes takes place in various ways. So far, this interaction has not been subject of much attention in legal literature. In the following, Section 2 examines whether tort law may affect the extent to which CSR clauses in contracts are enforced by parties. In Section 3, it is examined whether the effects of contracts, including CSR obligations, may also reflect back on tort law and impact on the extent to which it is possible to establish tort law liability in a given situation. Finally, Section 4 examines the extent to which the interactions between the two systems create dilemmas with regard to the possible liability of the chain leader as well as the possible liability of the supplier.

2 Tort law as a generator of contractual enforcement

As described in Chapters 3 and 4, often it is difficult to enforce CSR clauses on the basis of contract law. Some obstacles are legal obstacles. First, CSR obligations are often found in codes of conduct and it is not always clear that these codes are part of the contract at all. Second, to the extent that clauses are written in vague and imprecise language, they may be difficult to enforce. Third, CSR obligations often concern third party interests but third-party beneficiary law will most often not allow the injured third party to rely on the contract to raise a claim for damages against a non-complying supplier. Basically, this means that although contracts seem to be used as a tool for achieving CSR goals, traditional (classical) contract law faces difficulties in serving as a tool for the enforcement of CSR commitments. Another reason why CSR clauses are not always enforced is that the parties to a contract may lack incentives to take effective control of CSR issues in the contract. Thus, although parties in a supply chain based on long-term contracts may be concerned with the general reputation of a brand connected to (typically) the chain leader's products, the parties' main interest will often be the commercial terms of the contract[4] and ensuring long-term collaboration within the chain. This can mean that compliance with codes of conduct concerning third party interests will be pushed into the background of the commercial realities of the transactions.[5]

4 For further elaboration of this argument, see Chapter 4, Section 2 of this book.
5 In legal theory, relational contract law theories have pointed to the conflict between the fundamental principles of contract law and such socio-economical norms establishing a relational understanding of contracts. For further consideration on the impact of the relational character of contracts in the supply chain, see Chapter 3 in this volume and cf. in general, e.g., I R Macneil, 'Contracts: Adjustment of Long-Term Economic Relations under Classical, Neoclassical, and Relational Contract Law' (1978) 72(6) Northwestern University Law Review 854–905; and O E Williamson, 'Transaction-Cost Economics: The Governance of Contractual Relations' (1979) 22 (2) Journal of Law & Economics 233–262. The work of Macneil and Williamson still plays a role in modern contract law theory; see, e.g., N M Davidson, 'Relational Contracts in the Privatization of Social Welfare: The Case of Housing' (2006) 24(2) Yale Law & Policy Review 263–316, F Gomez, 'Cooperation, Long-Term Relationships and Open-Endedness in Contractual Networks' in F Caffagi (ed), *Contractual*

However, as shown in Chapter 5, regardless of the effects of contracts between the parties in a supply chain, tort law may in some cases provide an independent basis for liability. Thus, protected interests under tort law are, for instance, "life", "personal integrity" and "the environment". Notably the *Chandler* case[6] may provide a basis for arguing that tort law can serve as a basis for bringing claims for personal injuries, loss of life or environmental damage based on reasonable expectations on the part of the injured parties, generated by a variety of different factors, such as some degree of actual control on the part of the chain leader with the supply chain and the superior knowledge on the part of the chain leader as compared to the supplier.[7]

As described in Chapter 5, as of December 2018 only few cases have concerned supply chain liability but in the longer run, the role played by tort law may also have consequences on the contractual side. Thus, the risk of encountering a tort lawsuit and the media attention that such a suit would involve may create incentives for the parties to use the contract as a (real) tool for controlling the supply chain so as to avoid negative incidences and connected liability.[8] In other words, the threat of lawsuits on the basis of tort law may lead parties to draft CSR clauses in such way that they are more easily enforceable and may be used as an effective tool for the achievement of CSR goals.[9] In this way, tort law actions may bring into play contracts and contract law.

Whereas tort law may generate incentives for the use of contracts as a steering tool in order to avoid tort liability, it is at the same time clear that the use of more clearly formulated CSR clauses and/or CSR policies may also reflect back on tort law and the possibility of imposing tort law liability. The following section gives some examples of this.

3 Contract law reflecting back on tort law

3.1 The basis of liability

3.1.1 Self-regulation in contracts and the standard of care in tort law

As explained in Chapter 2, a number of soft law norms regarding the responsibility of the enterprise today exist. Examples include the UN Global

Networks, Inter-Firm Cooperation and Economic Growth (Edward Elgar 2011) 21–38; E M Weitzenboeck, *A Legal Framework For Emerging Business Models – Dynamic Networks as Collaborative Contracts* (Edward Elgar Publishing 2012) 167–171; and O Hansen, 'Public Law by Contract: The Reluctant Creation of Private Markets for Welfare Service' (2017) 25(3) European Review of Private Law 619–649.

6 *Chandler v. Cape* (2012)EWCA Civ 525

7 For a fuller explanation of these criteria, see Chapter 5 in this volume.

8 In Chapter 4, Section 3 of this book, the parallel argument is made with regard to the recognition of third parties as third-party beneficiaries to the contract.

9 On the connection between media attention and companies' CSR reporting, see J Haddock-Fraser & L Fraser, 'Assessing Corporate Environmental Reporting Motivations: Differences Between "Close-to-Market" and Business-to Business" Companies' (2008) 15(3) Corporate Social Responsibility and Environmental Management 140.

Compact,[10] the UN Guiding principles[11] and the OECD guidelines for Multinational Enterprises.[12] The extent to which such soft law norms can be directly "absorbed" by tort law and influence the standard of care is uncertain. The reason for this is that the direct adoption of such norms would, in reality, mean regarding ethical norms as equal to legal norms.[13] However, the soft law norms can influence tort law indirectly. Thus, as also explained in Chapters 2 and 3, international soft law norms are widely adopted in supply chain contracts. The soft law norms may also be incorporated into agreements between industries and NGOs. The incorporation of such standards into contracts of various kinds may support a development that eventually turns living up to the standards into an *industry practice*. It is widely accepted that industry practices may be relevant when determining the standard of care in tort law.[14] In this way, the contractual standard may be transformed into a more general standard, which can also be relevant in tort law liability cases that concern other parties than the parties to the original contract.

10 See UN Global Compact, available at <www.unglobalcompact.org/>.

11 J Ruggie, 'Guiding Principles on Business and Human Rights: Implementing the United Nations "Protect, Respect and Remedy Framework"', <www.ohchr.org/Documents/Issues/Business/A-HRC-17-31_AEV.pdf> accessed 15 August 2018.

12 OECD Guidelines for Multinational Enterprises, available at <www.oecd.org/investment/mne/1922428.pdf>.

13 It is normally accepted that ethical norms and legal norms represent two different norm systems in the sense that what is legally permitted may not always be seen as ethically correct. Consequently, applying ethical norms as legal norms will most often mean not just "specifying" in more detail what is the standard of care; rather, it will mean *raising* the bar with regard to the legally required standard of care. This should not be done unintentionally; see V Ulfbeck, *Erstatningsretlige Grænseområder* (Jurist- og Økonomforbundet 2010) 33–34. In favour of direct 'norm adoption' by tort law, M Torrance, 'Persuasive Authority Beyond the State: A Theoretical Analysis of Transnational Corporate Social Responsibility Norms as Legal Reasons within Positive Legal Systems' (2011) 12(8) German Law Journal 1573, 1603.

14 See, for instance, C Glinski, 'The Ruggie Framework, Business Human Rights, Self-Regulation and Tort Law: Increasing Standards through Mutual Impact and Learning' (2017) 35(1) Nordic Journal of Human Rights 15, 28; C Witting, *Liability for Negligent Misstatements* (Oxford University Press 2004) 252 on how professional bodies may have power to determine industry practice for a given profession. The situation can be compared to the concept of trade usage in contract law; see, for instance, the United Nations Convention on Contracts for the International Sale of Goods, art. 9 (2). Related literature includes I Schwenzer and B Leisinger, 'Ethical Values and International Sales Contracts' in R Cranston, J Ramberg, & J Ziegel (eds), *Commercial Law Challenges in the 21st Century: Jan Hellmer in Memoriam* (Stockholm Centre for Commercial Law, Juridiska Instituionem, 2007) 249, 264–265; C Poncibò, "The Contractualisation of Environmental Sustainability' (2016) 12 European Review of Contract Law 335–355, 342–344; C Ramberg, 'Emotional Non-Conformity in the International Sale of Goods, Particularly in Relation to CSR-Policies and Codes of Conduct', in I Schwenzer and L Spagnolo (eds) *Boundaries and Intersections: 5th Annual MAA Schlechtriem CISG Conference* (Eleven International Publishing 2015) 71; K Peterkova Mitkidis, *Sustainability Clauses in International Business Contracts* (Eleven International Publishing 2015) 163–166.

Another question is whether *individually adopted norms* may also influence the liability of a particular enterprise that has adopted the norms, for instance, in a code of conduct. It is generally accepted that the tort law standard of care may vary for different groups of defendants.[15] For instance, it is the general rule that professionals are subject to a stricter liability standard than others.[16] In addition, professional liability standards may vary depending on the type of profession. This differentiated approach raises the question of the extent to which liability standards can be individual and whether a particular enterprise can be subject to a particular standard that only applies to that enterprise. In legal literature, there is some support for the view that such "individual self-regulation" can be accepted as forming tort law duties.[17] With regard to supply chains the relevant question is whether a code of conduct that has been adopted as company policy by a chain leader may influence the tort law liability standard applicable to this specific chain leader. One way of arguing is by making use of contractual thinking. Thus, a code of conduct could be seen as evidence that a company has *voluntarily assumed* responsibility for the parties mentioned in the code.[18] In the previously mentioned *Chandler* case a central part of the reasoning was that the common code of conduct (together with other facts) reflected a voluntary assumption of responsibility towards the employees of the subsidiary.[19]

3.1.2 Tort liability for interference with third-party beneficiary rights and protection of incidental third parties through tort law

As explained in Chapter 2 of this book, codes of conduct may be incorporated into the contract between the chain leader and a supplier. In legal literature it has

15 See, for instance, European Groupon Tort Law, *Principles of European Tort Law, Text and Commentary* (Springer 2005) 76, C Glinski (n 14) 27 'Standardization nevertheless allows for differentiated responsibilities, for example through a fine-tuned classification of different "peer groups"'. For Scandinavian law, see V Ulfbeck (n 13) 30.

16 European Groupon Tort Law, *Principles of European Tort Law, Text and Commentary* (Springer 2005) 76.

17 Glinski (n 14) 27; A Beckers, *Enforcing Corporate Social Responsibility Codes. On Global Self-Regulation and National Private Law* (Hart Publishing 2015) 177 with further references. Some cases support this view; see *Toussaint v. Blue Cross & Blue Shield*, 408 Mich.579, 614 f. 292 N.W.2d 880, 892 (1980), and from Scandinavian law, see the Danish decision U 2008.70 Ø (Court of Appeal).

18 See Beckers (n 17), 177. This argument was made but rejected in the case *Doe v. Wal-Mart* due to the concrete wording of the code of conduct; see *Doe v. Wal-Mart*, No. 08–55706 (9th Cir. 2009), para. 8623.

19 In US legal theory, this line of thought has been combined with the doctrine of the Good Samaritan, under which someone who provides a voluntarily gratuitous service is obliged to do so with reasonable care so as to prevent causing harm to others. It has been argued that this doctrine could also be applicable with regard to codes of conduct; see J Phillips and S-J Lim, 'Their Brother's Keeper: Global Buyers and The Legal Duty to Protect Supplier's Employees' (2009) 61(2) Rutgers Law Review 350 ff.

been argued that a breach of such an incorporated code by the supplier may give rise not only to liability in contract law but also in tort law against third parties.[20]

The first category of cases concerns a situation in which it has been established that the contract between the chain leader and the supplier constitutes a third-party beneficiary contract.[21] The argument is that if a contract is a third-party beneficiary contract, which establishes an obligation on the part of the supplier to observe a code of conduct vis-à-vis a third party, then a breach of the code by the supplier may in reality have been brought about by the chain leader and therefore also lead to the liability of the chain leader. The liability could be labelled liability for tortious interference with third party-beneficiary rights.[22] For instance, the chain leader may impose a production schedule on the supplier that makes compliance with the commercial part of the contract so burdensome that it is impossible for the supplier to also observe the CSR obligations in the contract. In an empirical study carried out by J Phillips and S-J Lim, a supplier is quoted as having said,

> Sometimes buyers put us in an impossible situation. When a certain item is selling well, buyers ask us to produce beyond our capacity. To fulfill the buyer's sudden demand surge, we ask our employees to work longer than the legal overtime. Unless the buyers are willing to compromise production, the factories cannot meet code standards.[23]

It could be argued that the chain leader in this way causes the supplier to neglect the obligations in the code of conduct towards third parties or the environment and that, consequently, not only the supplier but also the chain leader should be liable for the resulting damage.[24] This line of reasoning was applied in the decision *Noel v. Pizza Hut*, [25] which concerned a third-party beneficiary contract. The court found that 'If . . . [t]he promisor of the third-party agreement is responsible for the breach, jointly or alone, there is no legal theory that protects the promisee from liability for the breach'.[26] Thus, the theory provides a basis for suing not only the supplier but also the chain leader.

The second category of cases concerns situations where it is not possible to establish that the contract between the chain leader and the supplier constitutes a third-party beneficiary contract. Here the argument is that, although it may not be

20 Beckers (n 17) 150 mentions that this topic has been largely unexplored in legal theory. See also Phillips and Lim (n 19) 333, 372.
21 On this topic, see Chapter 4 of this book.
22 On liability for tortious interference with contract in general, see inter alia H.S Perlman, 'Interference with Contract and other Economic Expectancies: A Clash of Tort and Contract Doctrine' (1982) The University of Chicago Law Review 61.
23 Phillips and Lim (n 19) 333, 372.
24 Phillips and Lim (n 19) 333, 372.
25 805 P 2d.1244, 1251 (Kan. Ct. App 1991), accessible at <https://law.justia.com/cases/kansas/court-of-appeals/1991/65-019.html> accessed September 2018.
26 805 P 2d.1244, 1251 (Kan. Ct. App 1991), accessible at <https://law.justia.com/cases/kansas/court-of-appeals/1991/65-019.html> accessed September 2018.

possible to establish that the injured party is an intended third-party beneficiary of the contract that incorporates the code of conduct, it may still be possible to argue that the third party is an incidental (factual) beneficiary to this contract.[27] Whereas an incidental beneficiary does not have the right to enforce the contract,[28] it could be argued that the beneficiary is protected by tort law to the extent that the beneficiary has suffered loss by relying on the proper performance of the contract. In German law the concept of the contract with protective effects for third parties may provide a legal basis for a similar result. In English law there is case law supporting this line of thinking.[29] Transferred to the supply chain setting, this would mean that, for instance, a supplier's employee who has relied on the supplier to live up to CSR obligations under the contract between the supplier and the buyer and has suffered loss (for instance work injuries) as a consequence, would be able to make a claim in tort against the supplier.[30]

3.1.3 Tort liability on the basis of contractual control

Also in other ways, the pursuance of CSR goals by means of contract may reflect back on tort law. As explained in Chapter 5, showing the exercise of "control" of the supply chain by the chain leader is an essential element in establishing a third-party tort law claim for damages. This will often be the case both with regard to direct and vicarious liability. Put briefly, it could be stated that "the more contractual control, the more potential tort law liability". The following section focuses on contractual control as a means of establishing direct liability according to the *Chandler* criteria.

As explained in Chapter 5, in the *Chandler* case, the court found that liability could be based inter alia on "reliance" on the parent company by the employees of the subsidiary. Moreover, the reliance was generated by the parent company's having some degree of control over the subsidiary, reflected in different ways, including the parent company's intervention in business decisions and by the code of conduct made applicable to all entities in the enterprise.

In the supply chain context, it can be argued that the necessary control can be established on the basis of contract by including certain terms in the contract. It is common to distinguish between, on the one hand, the commercial terms of the contract – i.e. terms containing requirements with regard to product requirements, including technical requirements – and on the other hand, CSR terms, sometimes called the regulatory terms of the contract.[31] With regard to the

27 See also Chapter 4 in this book.
28 Following the general principle of privity of contract, see in general V Ulfbeck, *Kontrakters Relativitet* (Gad Forlag 2000).
29 See Beckers (n 17) 150 ff analyzing the German concept of contracts with protective effects towards third parties and English equivalents.
30 On the importance of "reliance" in tort law claims under the *Chandler* criteria, see Chapter 5 and later on in this chapter.
31 F Cafaggi, 'The Regulatory Functions of Transnational Commercial Contracts: New Architectures' (2013) Fordham International Law Journal 1558, 1558.

commercial part of the contract, a basic element of control on the part of the chain leader often consists of the fact that the content of the contracts between the suppliers will depend on the content of the contract between the chain leader and the first-tier supplier (the main contractor). This can be said to follow from the nature of the supply chain. Often control on the part of the chain leader is reinforced by provisions in the contract between the chain leader and the main contractor that the chain leader has a right to make unilateral changes and the main contractor is under an obligation to transfer such changes "upstream".[32]

In addition, a more elaborate system of control will often be established by the chain leader to oversee the supplier's compliance with the commercial terms of the contract. Thus, the contract between the chain leader and the supplier may require the supplier to report back to the chain leader on various aspects concerning deliveries. The kind of control needed with a supplier's fulfilment of the commercial terms of the contract will depend upon the nature of the supplier's performance. If the supplier's performance is of a rather non-specific or generic nature, the chain leader's need for control may be reduced to a regular overview of production numbers and speed, in-stock status and – if necessary – also the quality of performance.

For example, a supplier's production of plastic components for packaging may not demand much control effort from the chain leader once the pattern and quality are fixed.

In these types of transactions, a shift in the chain leader's needs during the contract period may be reflected in unit price clauses coupled with estimated, or perhaps guaranteed, minimum orders. However, the more specific and complex the nature of performance, the more chain leaders will have to rely on the specific supplier's ability to perform. Because of the higher transaction costs and commercial dependence,[33] cooperation and long-term relation to the supplier becomes important.[34] Chain leaders will often reserve the right to unilaterally vary the content of the supplier's performance not only with respect to amounts, but also with respect to the quality and kinds of products and services involved.[35] Further, such highly complex and specific performances will often create an incentive for the chain leader to implement advanced control systems into the chain and demand that suppliers accept an intense overview of the supplier's performance.[36] Such contract-based systems may involve, e.g., continuous surveillance of the supplier's production, its business conditions and even its financial position.[37]

32 Ibid., 1570.
33 Cf. Williamson (n 5) 259–260 and in Chapter 3, Section 5 on relational contract theory.
34 Cf. e.g. F Gomez (n 5) 21; and G Gereffi, J Humphrey, & T Sturgeon, 'The Governance of Global Value Chains' (2005) 12(1) Review of International Political Economy 78–104.
35 Cf. e.g. Macneil (n 5) 854–905; R Halson, *Contract Law* (2nd edn, Longman 2013) 325; Hansen (n 5) 633–634.
36 See T Dietz, *Global Order Beyond Law* (Hart Publishing 2016) 84–88, 168.
37 See, e.g., P Kajüter & H I Kulmala, 'Open-Book Accounting in Networks – Potential Achievements and Reasons for Failures' (2005) 16(2) Management Accounting Research 179–204.

If a software component for the steering system of an airplane is manufactured for the chain leader by a supplier in India, the contract may only be entered into after due diligence – like pre-contractual investigations into the supplier's business and production conditions. Accordingly, to anticipate costly interruptions and problems with supply, during the contract period, the chain leader will follow the production and business conditions closely.

Generally, the digitalization of transactions in almost all sectors of the economy has radically expanded the chain leader's ability within a manageable budget to surveil practically all aspects of an even-distantly located supplier's business. The effect of "big data" on business models and supply systems can hardly yet be estimated, but the potential for combining contractually based transactions between legally independent contractors with day-to-day or even real time surveillance or control is immense and multi-facetted.[38]

Obviously, such systems can be applied not only with regard to the commercial terms of the contract, but also with regard to CSR requirements.[39] To some extent control and surveillance systems, with regard to the CSR parts of the contract, exist today in supply chains.[40] Control and surveillance based on the contract may generate reliance on the part of the supplier's employees that the chain leader has assumed responsibility for the working conditions in the supply chain and the extent to which the contract is carried out in accordance with the code of conduct. In this way, the terms of the contract may become relevant for establishing direct tort liability based on actual control and reliance (the *Chandler* criteria) in the supply chain. However, as will be explained in the following, there might not be an incentive on the supply chain leader to control adherence to CSR goals at all.

4 Dilemmas created by the interplay between contract and tort

4.1. The dilemma of control

It seems clear from the previous discussion that the concept of "control" is central in a liability context with regard to supply chain liability. However, the problem of basing liability on actual control is obvious: To the extent that control of the working environment or other sustainability objectives may lead to liability, chain leaders may refrain from controlling these matters. If including a code of conduct in the contracts and attempting to control the extent to which it is implemented,

38 See T Dietz, 'Relational Contracts 2.0: Efficiency and Power' in A C Cutler and T Dietz (eds), *The Politics of Private Transnational Governance by Contract* (Routledge 2017) 113–129 and e.g. A Lyall, P Mercier, & S Gestettner, 'The Death of Supply Chain Management', Harvard Business Review Blog, available at <https://hbr.org/2018/06/the-death-of-supply-chain-management> accessed September 2018.

39 See, e.g., G Distelhorst, J Hainmueller, & R M Locke, 'Does Lean Improve Labor Standards? Capability Building and Social Performance in the Nike Supply Chain' (2016) 63(3) Management Science 707–728.

40 Cafaggi (n 31) 1573 ff.

in the end may lead to liability for the company for not having succeeded in its endeavours, this may discourage the companies from taking control. This, of course, is undesirable if the aim is to achieve sustainability goals. Thus, the application of the criterion of actual control may be said to create a dilemma. On the one hand, actual control may form the basis for the imposition of liability; on the other hand, the risk of liability will create incentives to avoid control.

The dilemma is already reflected in case law. Thus, in the *Das* case[41] described in Chapter 5, part of the policy argument for not imposing liability was that imposing a duty of care would 'encourage undesirable, defensive tactics' that would make the situation 'worse, not better' for the defendants.[42] Similarly in the *Okpabi* case,[43] the court expressed the view that

> the issuing of mandatory policies plainly cannot mean that a parent has taken control of the operations of a subsidiary . . . such as to give rise to a duty of care in favour of any person or class of persons affected by the policies.[44]

In other words, applying the criterion of "actual control" is not without problems, in terms of the incentives it creates.[45]

However, it could be argued that even if chain leaders may refrain from assuming control of the CSR parts of the contract in order to avoid exposing themselves to liability towards third parties on the basis of CSR infringements somewhere in the supply chain, the technological and commercial realities of global business structures might invoke liability of the chain leader in any case.

As mentioned in Section 3.1.3, dependent upon the nature of performance, the chain leader may have considerable control over and insight into the supplier's performance of the commercial parts of the contract. Already today, the use of "big data" is used as a contract management tool in supply chains. Digital surveillance forms the basis for the use of both monetary incentives and "punishments" in the shape of bonuses and contractual fines (penalties) or "taxes". Even if the aim of the control system is (primarily) to oversee the supplier's compliance with the commercial terms of the contract, including the technical specifications, information gained from such intense surveillance will often also – incidentally or indirectly – include information on CSR performances and thereby establish the element of "control", which can form a basis for liability, for example, for workplace conditions. In other words, intense surveillance of the supplier's performance according to the commercial terms of the contract may indirectly bring about knowledge of and control over compliance with CSR commitments.

41 *Das v. George Weston Limited* (2017) ONSC 4129.
42 *Das* (n 41), para 536.
43 *Okpabi and others v. Royal Dutch Shell Plc* (2018) EWCA Civ 191.
44 *Okpabi* (n 43) 89.
45 The same problem is discussed in Chapter 6 of this book with regard to liability towards consumers. Here, it is suggested that the solution to the problem is the creation of a 'safe harbor' for chain leaders so that they cannot incur liability as long as they live up to their CSR policies.

Another and more difficult question is whether the technological development and the possibilities embedded in modern digital communication in itself may affect the legal position of a chain leader even if the chain leader chooses not to use these means of control. Thus, even if the chain leader does not wish to control the supply chain at all it can be asked, whether the mere technological possibility (without considerable expenses) of establishing an efficient control system will affect the assessment of the chain leader's possible liability towards third parties. In other words, from at tort law perspective it seems highly questionable to what extent a chain leader can avoid liability by choosing not to take control and to "look the other way" when the possibility of control exists and the exercise of control becomes still more easy.

4.2 The dilemma of the liability of the supplier: strict or mild?

At the more general level, coordinating the liability rules applicable in the supply chain may pose a challenge.

As explained in Chapter 3, in the contractual relationship between a chain leader and a supplier, the supplier will often be the weaker party, in need of protection against far-reaching and unfair contract terms and practices. Courts may to some extent be inclined to protect the supplier as the weaker party in the contractual relationship with the chain leader.

At the same time however, wide-reaching protection of the supplier through relief of liability may reduce the possibilities of injured third parties obtaining compensation from the supplier. Thus, the third party, in making a claim against the supplier, may have to rely on the contractual obligations undertaken by the supplier vis-à-vis the chain leader in arguing that he/she is a third-party beneficiary of this contract. However, if the contract between the supplier and the chain leader is deemed invalid due to unfairness, the third party will have no basis for a compensatory claim in the contract between the chain leader and the supplier. This, of course, does not rule out the possibility that the employee may have a claim based on its own contract with the supplier (as employer), but standards in this contract may not be as high as the ones demanded in the contract with the chain leader. Moreover, if the contract between the chain leader and the supplier is deemed invalid, the employee will not be able to use this contract as a tool for requiring proper conditions in its employment contract with the supplier.

This problem is particularly clear when third parties seek to rely on the contract between the chain leader and the supplier under third-party beneficiary law. However, the *Das* case[46] illustrates that contractual requirements may also be relevant with regard to a tort law claim in establishing the relevant duty on the part of the defendant. The *Das* case, amongst other things, concerned the possible liability of the private certification body Bureau Veritas for the collapse of the building at Rana Plaza in Bangladesh, leading to death and personal injuries for a large number of workers. Bureau Veritas had been hired by the chain leader to

46 *Das* (n 41).

carry out social auditing with regard to the Bangladesh supplier and had certified the supplier. According to the contract, Bureau Veritas was under a duty to investigate the extent to which the supplier lived up to CSR standards. In contrast, Bureau Veritas was under no obligation to inspect the building in which the employees were working for "structural integrity". Consequently, the court reached the conclusion that Bureau Veritas could not be held liable towards the injured third parties.[47] Interestingly, the decision thereby acknowledged the relevance of the contract in defining the scope of the certifier's task and thereby, the scope of liability under tort law towards third parties.

5 Conclusion

The previous examples show that there is room for considerable interaction between contract and tort with regard to establishing supply chain liability. This interaction, and the possible dilemmas that it creates in the supply chain, has attracted limited attention in legal literature. Presumably, one of the reasons for this is that scholars and practicing lawyers often define themselves as being in the field of either contract law or tort law. However, as shown in this chapter, in order to be able to deal with the complex legal problems connected to supply chain management, a unifying approach seems necessary.

Bibliography

Davidson N M, 'Relational Contracts in the Privatization of Social Welfare: The Case of Housing' (2006) 24(2) *Yale Law & Policy Review* 263–316.

De Graaff R, 'Concurrent Claims in Contract and Tort: A Comparative Perspective' (2017) 4(25) *European Review of Private Law* 701–726.

Dietz T, *Global Order Beyond Law* (Hart Publishing 2016) 84–88, 168.

Dietz T, 'Relational Contracts 2.0: Efficiency and Power' in Cutler A C & Dietz T (eds), *The Politics of Private Transnational Governance by Contract* (Routledge 2017) 113–129.

Distelhorst G, Hainmueller J, & Locke R-M, 'Does Lean Improve Labor Standards? Capability Building and Social Performance in the Nike Supply Chain' (2016) 63(3) *Management Science* 707–728.

European Group on Tort Law, *Principles of European Tort Law, Text and Commentary* (Springer 2005).

Georgiades A, *Die Anspruchskonkurrenz im Zivilrecht und Zivilprozessrecht* (Beck 1967).

Gereffi G, HumphreyJ, & SturgeonT, 'The Governance of Global Value Chains' (2005) 12 (1) *Review of International Political Economy* 78–104.

Glinski C, 'The Ruggie Framework, Business Human Rights, Self-Regulation and Tort Law: Increasing Standards through Mutual Impact and Learning' (2017) 35(1) *Nordic Journal of Human Rights* 15–34.

Gomard B, *Forholdet mellem erstatningsregler i og udenfor kontrakt* (GadJura 1958).

47 In this respect, the court also considered whether a special relationship had been created between Bureau Veritas and the employees based on 'reasonable reliance ' on the part of the employees. The court found this not to be the case; see *Das* (n 41), para. 535.

Gomez F, 'Cooperation, Long-Term Relationships and Open-Endedness in Contractual Networks' in Caffagi F (ed), *Contractual Networks, Inter-Firm Cooperation and Economic Growth* (Edward Elgar 2011) 21–38.

Haddock-Fraser J & Fraser L, 'Assessing Corporate Environmental Reporting Motivations: Differences Between "Close-to-Market" and Business-to Business" Companies' (2008) 15(3) *Corporate Social Responsibility and Environmental Management* 140.

Halson R, *Contract Law* (2nd edn, Longman 2013).

Hansen O, 'Public Law by Contract: The Reluctant Creation of Private Markets for Welfare Service' (2017) 25(3) *European Review of Private Law* 619–649.

Kajüter P & Kulmala H I, 'Open-Book Accounting in Networks – Potential Achievements and Reasons for Failures' (2005) 16(2) *Management Accounting Research* 179–204.

Lyall A, Mercier P, & Gestettner S, 'The Death of Supply Chain Management' (June 15, 2018) *Harvard Business Review Blog* <https://hbr.org/2018/06/the-death-of-supply-chain-management> accessed September 6, 2018.

Macneil I R, 'Contracts: Adjustment of Long-Term Economic Relations under Classical, Neoclassical, and Relational Contract Law' (1978) 72(6) *Northwestern University Law Review* 854–905.

Peterkova Mitkidis K, *Sustainability Clauses in International Business Contracts* (Eleven International Publishing 2015) 163–166.

Phillips J & Lim S-K, 'Their Brother's Keeper: Global Buyers and The Legal Duty to Protect Supplier's Employees' (2009) 61(2) *Rutgers Law Review*.

Poncibò C, 'The Contractualisation of Environmental Sustainability' (2016) 12 *European Review of Contract Law*.

Ramberg C, 'Emotional Non-Conformity in the International Sale of Goods, Particularly in Relation to CSR-Policies and Codes of Conduct' in Schwenzer I & Spagnolo L (eds), *Boundaries and Intersections: 5th Annual MAA Schlechtriem CISG Conference* (Eleven International Publishing 2015).

Schlechtriem P, *Vertragsordnung und Ausservertragliche Haftung* (Metzner 1972).

Schwenzer I & Leisinger B, 'Ethical Values and International Sales Contracts' in Cranston R, Ramberg J, & Ziegel J (eds), *Commercial Law Challenges in the 21st Century: Jan Hellmer in Memoriam* (Stockholm Centre for Commercial Law, Juridiska Instituionem 2007).

Torrance M, 'Persuasive Authority beyond the State: A Theoretical Analysis of Transnational Corporate Social Responsibility Norms as Legal Reasons within Positive Legal Systems' (2011) 12(8) *German Law Journal* 1573.

Ulfbeck V, *Kontrakters Relativitet* (Gad Forlag 2000).

Ulfbeck V, *Erstatningsretlige Grænseområder* (Jurist-og Økonomforbundet2010) 33–34.

Viney G, Traité de civil in *Introduction a la Responsibility* (LGDJ 1995).

Von Bar C & Drobning U, *The Interaction between Contract and Tort and Property Law in Europe* (Sellier European Law Publishers 2004).

Weitzenboeck E M, *A Legal Framework for Emerging Business Models – Dynamic Networks as Collaborative Contracts* (Edward Elgar Publishing 2012) 167–171.

Williamson O E, 'Transaction-Cost Economics: The Governance of Contractual Relations' (1979) 22(2) *Journal of Law & Economics* 233–262.

Witting C, *Liability for Negligent Misstatements* (Oxford University Press 2004) 252.

8 Developing supply chain liability

A necessary marriage of contract and tort?

Jaakko Salminen and Vibe Ulfbeck

1 Introduction and mission

Law mirrors societal change by responding to perceived injustices. This takes place through both legislation and court-led doctrinal development. At the same time, law also shapes the possible future paths of societal development: law grants specific forms of governance benefits and deficits, the cumulative sum of which steers actors in their choice of which mechanisms to use to govern their activities. Take the fragmentation of production into multinational groups of companies and contractually organized global supply chains as an example. The root causes of fragmentation are factors external to the law. First, by the end of the 19th century, advanced transportation technologies enabled the efficient dispersion of manufactured goods, which, coupled with then-reigning ideas of centralization for bureaucratic efficiency, gave impetus to centralized mass production and globally fragmented distribution chains.[1] Then, during the 20th century, advanced communication technologies enabled the efficient dispersion of production, which, coupled with new ideas of outsourcing for increased efficiency, have given rise to globally fragmented production chains.[2] What has received much less focus is that

1 For the role of transport technologies, see generally R Baldwin and P Martin, 'Two Waves of Globalization: Superficial Similarities, Fundamental Differences' (1999) The National Bureau of Economic Research Working Paper No. 6904; R Baldwin, 'Trade and Industrialisation after Globalisation's 2nd Unbundling: How Building and Joining a Supply Chain Are Different and Why it Matters' (2011) The National Bureau of Economic Research Working Paper No. 17716. For the role of bureaucratic efficiency, see generally the classic texts of industrial organization from Coase to Williamson and beyond, arguing, for example, that bounded rationality and opportunism lead to vertical integration, with many of these texts neatly summed up in W W Powell, 'Neither Market nor Hierarchy: Network Forms of Organization' (1990) 12 Research in Organizational Behavior 295.

2 For the role of communication technologies, see generally Baldwin (n 1); Baldwin and Martin (n 1). For the management-oriented focus on fragmenting and outsourcing less value-producing production processes, see C K Prahalad and G Hamel, 'The Core Competence of the Corporation' (1990) 68 Harvard Business Review 79. For one approach to conceptualizing the new forms of production, see, e.g., G Gereffi, 'Global Value Chains in a Post-Washington Consensus World' (2014) 21(1) Review of International Political Economy 9.

the *organizational form* chosen to govern fragmented production is dependent on governance structures allowed by law.[3]

A key factor in how law enables different forms of governance and organization is by setting the parameters of liability regimes related to private ordering. Private law allows for two primary forms of organization: contract and corporation. During the late 19th and early 20th centuries, both became extremely effective means of limiting liability. This liability-limiting effect can even be compounded, so that instead of an individual company or a contract, as in Coase's classic text from 1933,[4] focus has shifted towards groups of companies and, more recently, contractually organized supply chains. While also applicable within individual jurisdictions, the liability-limiting effect of private ordering through corporate or contractual structures is particularly visible when production is spread over several jurisdictions. Companies that outsource production to third countries are not easily held liable for the production-related contingencies of their subsidiaries or suppliers on the basis of private law,[5] and in many countries the natural alternatives – i.e. local labour, human rights, environmental, and economic regulation, and the enforcement of such regulation – are not adequate to guarantee decent working conditions, protection of human rights, a clean environment, or sufficient economic base.[6]

There has been discussion over international instruments to resolve or at least alleviate such problems, but at least for the short term these face considerable political challenges.[7] In particular, three alternatives have sprouted up. One has been to argue that because of the political challenges of international regulation, transnational governance could be the domain of private actors.[8] This means that private actors, such as companies and NGOs, perhaps to some extent together with international organizations or state actors, would cooperate to govern

3 IGLP Law and Global Production Working Group, 'The role of law in global value chains: a research manifesto' (2016) 4 London Review of International Law 57.

4 R Coase, 'The Nature of the Firm' (1937) 4(16) Economica 386.

5 See Chapters 2–5 in this volume.

6 E.g. L A Pratt, 'Decreasing Dirty Dumping? A Reevaluation of Toxic Waste Colonialism and the Global Management of Transboundary Hazardous Waste' (2011) 35(2) William and Mary Environmental Law and Policy Review 581; R M Locke, *The Promise and Limits of Private Power: Promoting Labor Standards in a Global Economy* (Cambridge University Press 2013); D Quentin, 'Corporate Tax Reform and "Value Creation": Towards Unfettered Diagonal Re-Allocation across the Global Inequality Chain' (2016) 7(1) Accounting, Economics, and Law 1.

7 With regard to an international treaty on business and human rights, see O De Schutter, 'Towards a New Treaty on Business and Human Rights' (2016) 1(1) Business and Human Rights Journal 41. With regard to the thematically more limited (and thus simpler in terms of reaching political consensus) Paris Agreement under the United Nations Framework Convention on Climate Change, one need only follow current political debate in the US, which is in the process of denouncing the agreement.

8 K Abbott and D Snidal, 'Strengthening International Regulation Through Transnational New Governance: Overcoming the Orchestration Deficit' (2009) 42(501) Vanderbilt Journal of Transnational Law 501.

production-related contingencies.[9] As a consequence, private governance mechanisms, such as labour or environmental standards and special forms of contractual governance, have developed rapidly, in particular under the umbrella of corporate social responsibility (CSR).[10] Despite these developments, however, private governance seems persistently inadequate to prevent human rights, labour, environmental, and economic problems, and in several cases developments in this regard are more a response to global media outrages than pre-emptive governance.[11]

Second, the perceived failures of both international regulation and private governance have resulted in a recent drive towards more local laws aimed at regulating transnational production, both in the form of soft law instruments, such as those of the OECD,[12] and local hard laws, such as those sprouting up in Europe and the United States.[13] However, such regulation is still in its infancy. It is comparatively rare and often focused on particular issues such as bribery or sourcing minerals from specific conflict zones, while also being mired in political compromise and the many theoretical and practical questions of how transnational supply chains can and should be regulated.[14]

Private law liability, under general doctrines of tort or contract, provides a third alternative that could counter the deficits of both private governance and existing

9 E.g. S L Schwarcz, 'Private Ordering' (2002) 97(1) Northwest University Law Review 319; D Wielsch, 'Global Law's Toolbox: Private Regulation by Standards' (2012) 60(4) American Journal of Comparative Law 1075; G Sarfaty, 'Regulating Through Numbers: A Case Study of Corporate Sustainability Reporting' (2013) 53 Virginia Journal of International Law 575.

10 For recent developments in private governance, see, e.g., Locke (n 6); K H Eller, 'Private Governance of Global Value Chains from Within: Lessons from and for Transnational Law' (2017) 8(3) Transnational Legal Theory 296; J Salminen, 'The Accord on Fire and Building Safety in Bangladesh: A New Paradigm for Limiting Buyers' Liability in Global Supply Chains?' (2018) 66(2) American Journal of Comparative Law 411–451, available open access at <https://doi.org/10.1093/ajcl/avy030>.

11 The mechanisms that sprouted up post-Rana Plaza provide just one example. Salminen (n 10). More generally, Locke (n 6).

12 For the OECD Guidelines for Multinational Enterprises and its various sector-specific guidances, see <http://www.oecd.org/corporate/mne/>.

13 Examples might include the 1977 US Foreign Corrupt Practices Act (15 U.S.C. § 78dd-1 et seq.), the 2010 Californian Transparency in Supply Chains Act (Cal. Civ. Code § 1714–43), the 2012 US Dodd-Frank Act Section 1502 on conflict minerals, the 2014 EU Directive 2014/95/EU of the European Parliament and of the Council of 22 October 2014 amending Directive 2013/34/EU as regards disclosure of non-financial and diversity information by certain large undertakings and groups ('Non-Financial Reporting Directive'), and the 2017 French law on a corporate duty of care (Loi n° 2017–399 du 27 mars 2017 relative au devoir de vigilance des sociétés mères et des entreprises donneuses d'ordre, J.O. March 28, 2017, p. 0074).

14 For some examples, see G A Sarfaty, 'Shining Light on Global Supply Chains' (2015) 56(2) Harvard International Law Journal 419; A S Chilton and G A Sarfaty, 'The Limitations of Supply Chain Disclosure Regimes' (2017) 53 Stanford Journal of International Law 1.

transnational regulation by placing on lead firms a general duty to adequately govern their supply chains. However, in several high-profile cases courts have been hesitant to find lead firms liable for the inadequate governance of their supply chains.[15] We focus on this hesitation by arguing that there is historical precedent for the court-led development of private law liability for production-related contingencies. This precedent comes in the form of product liability law, spanning over a century of cases in multiple jurisdictions, such as the tort-focused *Donoghue v Stevenson*[16] and the contractual *Henningsen v Bloomfield Motors*[17] and beyond.[18] Prior to the development of product liability, existing legal safeguards could not counter the liability deficits caused by the fragmentation of distribution chains that, from the perspective of law, separated users from manufacturers. This led to several dogmatic innovations to overcome this separation, such as the common law tort of negligence and novel contractual causes of action. These developments eventually led to the rise of a product liability tort cause of action that was essentially a marriage of contract and tort made to overcome the inherent limitations of both.

In this chapter, we explore product liability law, i.e. liability for defective production practices towards users of products, as a model for developing supply chain liability, or liability for defective production practices in relation to social, environmental, and economic contingencies. We first chart the societal and dogmatic developments leading to product liability in jurisdictions such as the United States, England, Germany, France, and the European Union (EU) (Section 2). We then compare the contextual differences and similarities of product liability and supply chain liability. In particular, we focus on the coordination of different kinds of fragmented production by lead firms, concluding that there are enough similarities to merit discussion over whether doctrinal developments similar to those that took place in relation to product liability could also take place in relation to supply chain liability (Section 3). Finally, we look at current approaches to using contract and tort to establish supply chain liability. We conclude that a similar marriage of these two forms of action as that which took place in relation to product liability law could alleviate many of the problems currently related to supply chain liability (Section 4). We end this chapter with a brief concluding section.

2 The rise of product liability law

The rise of product liability, or liability for defective production practices towards users injured by produced goods, is related to several 19th-century developments in production and consumption. These are the proliferation of novel and complex

15 G Holly, L Smit, and R McCorquodale, 'Making Sense of Managing Human Rights Issues in Supply Chains' (2018) Report of the British Institute of International and Comparative Law 13–21.
16 [1932] UKHL 100, [1932] AC 562 (appeal taken from Scot.)
17 161 A.2d 69 (N.J. 1960)
18 See Sections 2, 3, and 4.

products not appraisable by traditional standards, the increasing complexity of relationships between the diverse actors involved in the production of goods, and the increasingly global nature of actors involved in production. Together, all these developments displaced existing non-legal (e.g. local reputational mechanisms)[19] and legal (e.g. classical ideas of contract and tort law) safeguards intended to enable commerce and production. As a consequence, it became clear that there was a mismatch between existing paradigms of law and societal expectations of right and wrong. Due to political difficulties, this mismatch was in many cases resolved by a primarily court-led development of local paradigms of contract and tort, with ultimately similar results in several jurisdictions.[20]

First, the proliferation of increasingly *complex products* made it difficult for buyers and users to appraise goods or the way in which the goods were produced. Such products range from canned foods to medicines and automobiles.[21] In short, buyers could no longer be expected to understand and appraise the products they were buying to the same extent as earlier – canned goods are more difficult to appraise than ham from the local butcher, an automobile is much more complex than a plough, and medicines are beyond the understanding of most of their users. This reality resonated in both contract and tort doctrine with a number of paradigmatic changes for both.

In relation to contract law, earlier *caveat emptor* doctrines were mitigated through implied warranties[22] and, later on, explicit limitations of liability were also made dependent on specific conditions.[23] In relation to tort law, most famously under the common law, new torts were fashioned, first in relation to specific categories of dangerous goods and then more generally in relation to *all* goods under the guise of a new tortious duty of care resulting in liability for an open category of negligent acts (i.e. the tort of negligence).[24] Existing and new tortious duties of care, however, ran the problem of placing potentially strenuous burdens of proof on claimants who could have little or no access to showing what and where exactly was negligent in the acts of defendant conglomerates. This resulted in a focus on contractual forms of recourse, because there, the burden of proof lay more on defendants, at least until courts were brave enough to put in place stricter forms of tort liability.[25]

19 These were increasingly replaced by a focus on *brands* instead of products itself, in part contributing to ideas that brand owners should be held liable for their products.
20 Compare, for example, historical developments in England, the United States, Germany, France, and the European Union: J Stapleton, *Product Liability* (Butterworths 1994); S Whittaker (ed), *The Development of Product Liability* (Cambridge University Press 2010).
21 E.g. C C Regier, 'The Struggle for Federal Food and Drugs Legislation' (1933) 1(1) Law and Contemporary Problems 3.
22 S Whittaker, 'The Development of Product Liability in England' in S Whittaker (ed), *The Development of Product Liability* (Cambridge University Press 2010); Jean-Sébastien Borghetti, 'The Development of Product Liability in France' in S Whittaker (ed), *The Development of Product Liability* (Cambridge University Press 2010).
23 Stapleton (n 20); Borghetti (n 22).
24 Whittaker (n 22).
25 Stapleton (n 20).

Second, production became more complex, not only through the proliferation of more complex goods and production practices, but *the number of actors* involved in production and distribution also multiplied. Goods were increasingly bought from various middle-actors, upsetting the idea of classical contractual theories being limited only to direct relationships between the manufacturers and users of goods. At the same time, the economic efficiency-related debate between the centralization and fragmentation of production resulted in different combinations of actors with different amounts of power to influence and organize the rest of the chain. And finally, while, for example, family members could occasionally be included in claims raised by heads of families, in many situations mere users who had no connection to the chain of sales were left without recourse, in part because of the very existence of the contractual chain of sales itself.[26]

The crux of the liability problem here was that the different private law mechanisms used to control the relationships of actors in many cases could no longer capture all relevant actors under their scope. While contractual causes of action between a buyer and a non-manufacturing seller might not have any relationship to the actor responsible for manufacturing a defective good, mere users separate from the chain of sales might have no cause of action. Also, as manufacturers burgeoned into bigger conglomerates, apportioning liability within such an actor proved problematic. These questions were resolved not only by – as described previously – developing new causes of action, such as the common law tort of negligence, which could create legally meaningful relationships even beyond contractual and corporate boundaries, but also by testing new forms of organizational liability such as the *Organisationspflicht* ultimately embedded in German delict law,[27] and in particular by developing contractual liability mechanisms towards a similar objective, i.e. to enable the use of contractual causes of action beyond privity.[28] Examples include third-party beneficiary law, contracts with protective effects for third parties, the law of agency, and implied warranties that could be relied upon by third parties.[29]

Third, with the advent of new transport and communication mechanisms, the different physical locations related to production could be widely dispersed. Coupled with the diverse state territories where production and use of produced goods take place, this results, from a legal perspective, in the problem of *conflicting jurisdictions*. In a much simplified form, this problem could be spelled out as which production related actor to sue, in which jurisdiction, under which procedural rules, and under which substantive law. Should, for example, the injured user of an automobile in California sue the Californian retailer, the US-based importer, the Japanese manufacturer, or a Korean

26 Whittaker 2010 (n. 22); V Palmer, 'Why Privity Entered Tort – An Historical Reexamination of Winterbottom v Wright' (1983) 27(1) American Journal of Legal History 85.

27 G Wagner, 'The Development of Product Liability in Germany' in S Whittaker (ed), *The Development of Product Liability* (Cambridge University Press 2010).

28 Stapleton (1994), n 20; Whittaker (ed.) (2010), n 22.

29 See Chapters 3 and 4 in this volume.

component manufacturer, in the user's own jurisdiction or the respective defendant's jurisdiction, and under which laws?[30]

In many cases, the parameters of private international law in relation to such questions are complex and uncertain. To ease litigation, one approach has been to limit the scope of a product liability regime to *within* a jurisdiction. For example, when a manufacturer is located outside a jurisdiction, product liability laws may allow an injured party to sue the actor that imported the good instead, thus identifying a local defendant and avoiding difficult questions of private international law. This is the approach adopted by the EU in its Council Directive (85/374/EEC) of 25 July 1985 on the approximation of the laws, regulations, and administrative provisions of the Member States concerning liability for defective products ('Product Liability Directive').[31] Similarly, local procedural rules may allow private users to resort to local courts. The EU's Regulation (EU) 1215/2012 of the European Parliament and of the Council of 12 December 2012 on jurisdiction and the recognition and enforcement of judgments in civil and commercial matters ('EU Brussels Regulation Recast') is one example, allowing consumers and users more generally in many cases to sue at their own domicile.[32]

In sum, courts responded to changes in how products are made and sold by developing the general principles of contract and tort law, taking into account the diverse parameters of private international law. Of course, these developments did not take place in a vacuum. The societal changes brought about much political debate and legislative discussion. For one example, over several decades the US debates over food and drug safety in the late 19th and early 20th centuries captured the imaginations of a global audience in the form of Upton Sinclair's 1906 novel, *The Jungle*, and eventually resulted in several regulatory improvements and new controls, such as the establishment of the US Food and Drug Administration in 1906.[33] For another example, unlike in Germany, France, and the US, in England court-led developments of product liability law did not proceed much further than the tort of negligence for political reasons and regulatory action was necessary instead.[34] Nonetheless, from a private law perspective the ultimate development of the basic private law instruments of contract and tort liability were undertaken by the courts, with legislators providing an encouraging backdrop and, eventually at least in the EU, a more efficient dissemination and harmonization of the diverse national approaches to product liability law.[35]

The outcome of these markedly judicial developments was the enabling of legal claims by injured users towards those actors who were seen to be responsible for injuries caused by defective production practices. The justifications for these claims were at least partly founded in the new realities of exchange, e.g. the changed

30 For one example, see *World-Wide Volkswagen Corporation v Woodson*, 444 US 286 (1980).
31 85/374/EEC, OJ L 210/29, August 7, 1985.
32 Regulation (EU) 1215/2012, OJ L 351/1, December 20, 2012.
33 Regier (n 21).
34 Whittaker (n 22); Stapleton (n 20).
35 Whittaker (n 22); Stapleton (n 20).

perception of manufacturing as represented by brands and brand control rather than by the actor from whom a defective product was directly bought or otherwise received.[36] Justifying the imposition of liability on the manufacturer rather than on the immediate seller were also notions of the manufacturer as the cheapest cost avoider and as the actor in the best position to insure and spread the loss.[37] Prior to these judicial developments, in some cases claims for injuries caused by defective products would not have been possible at all without new causes of action, such as the tort of negligence.[38] In other cases, claims could have been possible but were severely hindered by, for example, burdens of proof, in the case of available tort claims,[39] or lack of access to a meaningful actor to sue under contract claims.[40]

At the same time, debate started on how far-ranging the changes in general paradigms of law should be.[41] For example, the question of whether the new product liability cause of action should sound in contract or tort was crucial to the question of to what extent contractual actions in the US could generally be seen to override privity. In many cases the outcome was that the new product liability cause of action was seen to sound in tort instead of contract *but* in a stricter form than normal tort claims. In practice the end result in many jurisdictions was a tort cause of action with a contractually derived burden of proof. At the same time this new form of liability was infused with select defences, which ultimately made the cause of action stricter than normal tort but not strict *per se*.[42] At the EU level, the Product Liability Directive, inspired by the US Restatement (second) of Torts, finally made clear that the liability standard in consumer cases is stricter than under general tort law and based on the notion of legitimate expectations of the consumer. Both this stricter liability and the notion of legitimate expectations are concepts that are well-known in contract law. At the same time, the liability standard is combined with the protection of not only contractual parties but also third parties as known in tort law.

Thus, whatever the current legal classification of product liability, it is clear that contract and tort theories became necessarily intertwined in its development. To what extent this was more a forced marriage or more one of convenience is up for debate. In the next two sections we discuss whether similar developments could be possible in another context related to defective production practices, i.e. supply chain liability. First, in Section 3, we will highlight the contextual parallels and differences between product liability and supply chain liability. Then, in Section 4, we will look in more detail at the current dogmatic problems of supply chain liability to see whether similar legal developments as took place in relation to product liability could be possible.

36 See, e.g., cases such as *Henningsen v Bloomfield Motors*.
37 Generally, on justifications, see Stapleton (n 20), Part Two.
38 E.g. prior to *Donoghue v Stevenson*, [1932] UKHL 100, [1932] AC 562 (appeal taken from Scot.) in England.
39 E.g. post-*Donoghue v Stevenson* in England, even despite discussion of using doctrines such as *res ipsa loquitur* to counter this, for see which Whittaker 2010 (n 22)
40 E.g. in case the actor with which one was in privity with, such as a retailer, was insolvent or protected by contractual limitations of liability.
41 Stapleton (n 20) 29–36.
42 Ibid., 96–98.

3 Structural parallels and differences between product liability and supply chain liability

In this section we argue that the current situation with regard to supply chain liability (and more generally, production liability, which includes both supply chain liability and foreign direct liability) is in many ways comparable to the situation of product liability a hundred or so years ago in the US and Europe. At that point in the history of product liability law, courts were being increasingly requested to protect users from goods manufactured through defective production practices, even if it was very much unclear what kind of cause of action could be used to do so in an effective and balanced fashion.[43] Right now, courts are being requested to protect those suffering from defective production practices, such as harm caused to employees or the environment by foreign subsidiaries or suppliers, without a clear idea of what kind of a cause of action (if any?) should be used for a balanced and effective response.[44]

The time thus seems ripe for initiating a comparison between product liability and supply chain liability. Therefore, in this section we look into the parallels and differences of the two. We cover a) the current general state of development of supply chain liability (Subsection 3.1); b) the organizational structure of production (Subsection 3.2); c) differences in protected actors (Subsection 3.3); d) practical and theoretical justifications of liability (Subsection 3.4); and e) the question of jurisdictional conflicts (Subsection 3.5).

3.1 Supply chain liability and foreign direct liability, two subcategories of production liability

With supply chain liability, we understand a company's liability for the effects of its decision to structure production through contractual suppliers in a way that harms third parties, such as supplier or sub-supplier employees, the environment, or the economic interests of a state. There is an important structural difference between

43 For just two examples from the US, see the classic cases of *Mazetti v Armour & Co*, 135 P 633 (Washington 1913) and *Macpherson v Buick*, 111 N.E. 1050 (1916). More generally for the rise in case law, see William Prosser's two papers W Prosser, 'The Assault Upon the Citadel (Strict Liability to the Consumer)' (1960) 69 Yale Law Journal 1099, and W Prosser, 'The Fall of the Citadel (Strict Liability to the Consumer)' (1966) 50 Minnesota Law Review 791. Of course, it is difficult to pinpoint any exact point in time. Another possible starting point might be provided by the late 19th century common law developments related to torts for dangerous things, for which see Whittaker (n 22).

44 For supplier employees, see, e.g., *Doe v Wal-mart*, 572 F.3d 677 (9th Cir. 2009); *Das v George Weston, Ltd.*, 2017 ONSC 4129 (appeal pending), *Rahaman v J.C. Penney Corp.*, C.A. No. N15C-07–174 MMJ, (Del. Super. Ct. May 4, 2016); *Jabir v KiK Textilien und Non-Food GmbH*, Landgericht Dortmund [Dortmund Regional Court], 7 O 95/15 (Ger., on trial). For environmental interests, see, e.g., *Arica Victims KB v Boliden Minerals AB*, Skellefteå Tingsrätt [Skellefteå District Court] 2018-02-07 T 1012–13 (Swed.) (appeal pending); *Trafigura*, for which see L Enneking, *Foreign Direct Liability and Beyond* (Eleven International Publishing 2012), 102–104.

supply chain liability and foreign direct liability, another form of liability in production structures.[45] Whereas supply chain liability focuses on contractually organized supply chains, i.e. governance through contract, foreign direct liability focuses on the relationships of parent companies to their subsidiaries, i.e. corporate group governance.[46] A focus on multinational enterprises has highlighted foreign direct liability over the last few decades, while supply chain liability has remained in a comparative shadow until recent high-profile cases, such as those related to the Rana Plaza disaster.[47]

Both supply chain liability and foreign direct liability could be seen as subcategories of a more general concept of production liability. Arguably the two are interrelated, so that a regulative focus on multinational corporate groups may drive interest in contractual supply chains as a means of regulatory avoidance.[48] Therefore any focus on the one necessarily also needs to account for the other: to guarantee a level playing field any private law regulatory techniques, such as the use of the tort of negligence to govern one mode of production, should extend to the other.[49] This sets an important preliminary parameter to any discussion of supply chain liability. It may also help explain why there has been so little focus to date on the similarities between product liability, which aimed at overcoming contractual boundaries of production, and production liability. The reason may simply be that, to date, the debate over production liability has focused on multinational groups of companies, which were not a similarly focal issue in relation to earlier debates of product liability. With the rise of global supply chains, however, the legal–structural context of production has shifted from subsidiary structures to contractual supply chains, making comparison to product liability more natural, as many of the key questions of product liability focused on the relationship of actors to a chain of contracts.

It is under debate to what extent supply chain liability or foreign direct liability exist and in what form. Several cases have tried to impinge on brand companies

45 Foreign direct liability see Enneking (n 44).

46 For one typology of differences between the two, compare, e.g., the mechanisms of corporate governance described in D Szabó and K Sørensen, 'Non-financial Reporting, CSR Frameworks and Groups of Undertakings: Application and Consequences' (2017) 17(1) Journal of Corporate Law Studies 137 with the typology of governance through contract described in J Salminen, 'Contract-Boundary-Spanning Governance Mechanisms: Conceptualizing Fragmented and Globalized Production as Collectively Governed Entities' (2016) 23(2) Indiana Journal of Global Legal Studies 709.

47 For the earlier focus on corporate groups, see, e.g., P Muchlinski, 'The Changing Face of Transnational Business Governance: Private Corporate Law Liability and Accountability of Transnational Groups in a Post-Financial Crisis World' (2011) 18(2) *Indiana Journal of Global Legal Studies*, 665. For some recent examples of supply chain liability, see Salminen (n 10).

48 See, e.g., J Salminen, 'Sustainability and the Move from Corporate Governance to Governance Through Contract' in B Sjåfjell and C Brunner (eds), *Cambridge Handbook on Corporate Governance, Regulation, and Sustainability* (Cambridge University Press, forthcoming 2019).

49 Thus, for example, Ulfbeck and Rott have proposed that the company law-related scenario in *Chandler v Cape Industries Plc*, [2012] EWCA Civ 525, should be transferrable to a supply chain perspective. P Rott and V Ulfbeck, 'Supply Chain Liability of Multinational Corporations?' (2015) 23(3) European Review of Private Law 415.

liability for their outsourced production, e.g. on the grounds that they have knowingly outsourced production to places where poor working conditions or environmental disregard are widespread,[50] or on the grounds that companies have taken it upon themselves to control their supply chains, e.g. by codes of conduct, monitoring, or even more invasive mechanisms of control, such as capability building,[51] and combinations of these criteria.[52] Currently, it seems possible that liability exists; however, this possibility of liability is greatly marred by uncertainties such as debate over what exactly tortious duties of care cover, whether contractual claims are possible at all, and what the relevant parameters of private international law are in relation to transnational claims, to say nothing of practical matters such as showing a corporate defendant's negligence without easy access to a corporation's inner workings.[53]

3.2 Organizational structure

Historically and structurally, a key similarity between the development of product liability law and supply chain liability is the problem posed by the fragmentation of the way production and distribution are organized into contractual chains of actors.[54] With regard to product liability law, the central characteristic was the fragmentation of *distribution*. Thus, the initial focus was on the separation of manufacturers from users via contractual chains of distributors, retailers, and the like. Within these chains, some actors, "lead firms" is one term,[55] were more implicated in the governance of production than mere retailers, thus serving as natural outlets for claims, at least from a non-legal perspective. For example, manufacturing companies and companies that controlled the brands and

50 E.g. *Das v George Weston, Ltd.*, 2017 ONSC 4129 (appeal pending) with regard to the Rana Plaza disaster, and the *Trafigura* affair, for which see Enneking (n 44) 102–104.
51 E.g. *Doe v Wal-mart*, 572 F.3d 677 (9th Cir. 2009) and the arbitrations related to the Bangladesh Accord, for which see Holly, Smit, and McCorquodale (n 15), 20.
52 E.g. *Chandler v Cape Industries Plc*, [2012] EWCA Civ 525, where both knowledge *and* control were required for liability.
53 See Chapters 2–5.
54 Baldwin and Martin (n 1); Baldwin (n 1).
55 A "lead firm" is a focal actor in a supply chain from an organizational perspective and often also the actor associated with a specific brand. For one typology, lead firms can be seen as more buyer-oriented (e.g., clothing brands) in that they focuses on design and marketing and outsource other aspects of production to suppliers, more producer-oriented (e.g. auto-manufacturers) in that they undertake key aspects of production in-house, e.g., for R&D reasons, but nonetheless outsource various less focal aspects of production to suppliers, or intermediaries (e.g. internet-based shopping or mobility platforms) that provide platforms for connecting users and suppliers. See, e.g., G Gereffi, 'Shifting Governance Structures in Global Commodity Chains, With Special Reference to the Internet' (2001) 44(10) American Behavioral Scientist 1616; G Gereffi, J Humphrey and T Sturgeon, 'The Governance of Global Value Chains' (2005) 12(1) Review of International Political Economy 78. One, perhaps similar, term is focal company, for which see S Seuring and M Müller, 'From a Literature Review to a Conceptual Framework for Sustainable Supply Chain Management' (2008) 16(15) Journal of Cleaner Production 1699.

advertising that consumers thought they were buying into were naturally seen by users as liable parties instead of middle-actors such as retailers. Classic cases in point include the *Donoghue v Stevenson* case, where a user (not a buyer) raised a claim against the manufacturer of an allegedly defective bottle of lemonade instead of the restaurant that sold the bottle, *Mazetti v Armour*, where a claim was raised by a customer against the manufacturer of canned food instead of the restaurant that served it, or *Macpherson v Buick*, where a claim was raised by a buyer against the manufacturer of the automobile rather than its retailer.[56]

A similar development lies behind supply chain liability. Here, however, instead of the fragmentation of distribution chains, the focus is on the fragmentation of *production* itself. Company law and contract law enable production to be fragmented in two different ways, through subsidiary companies or contractual suppliers. The rise of new communication technologies made fragmentation practically feasible, as control could be extended "just-in-time" to other production-related actors around the globe.[57] This is coupled with a management focus on higher-value producing "core competences", such as design and marketing, leading to the outsourcing of lower-value producing aspects of production, such as manufacturing.[58] At the same time, the current focus on governing multinational corporate groups may leave contractual supply chains out of the picture to a large extent, helping to drive actors towards contractual organization.[59] In sum, different aspects of production are increasingly outsourced to extensive multi-tiered chains of short- to long-term suppliers and contractors. From a user's perspective, however, it remains clear that it is the same global brand that is organizing the production often *through* strong buyers (lead firms), and these lead firms may be seen as the natural liable parties rather than the intermediary suppliers.

Thus, from a legal–structural perspective, both product liability and supply chain liability focus on overcoming a liability deficit caused by changes in production practices. These changes are based on similar patterns of fragmentation of distribution and production that existing contract and tort paradigms enable by not being able to account for the contingencies of organizing production through them.

3.3 Protected parties

At first sight, the difference between which actors are protected by product liability and which by supply chain liability would seem considerable because the former focuses on actors suffering from the *use* of negligently produced goods and the latter on actors suffering more directly from negligent production practices and not by way

56 *Mazetti v Armour & Co*, 135 P 633 (Washington 1913); *Macpherson v Buick*, 111 N. E. 1050 (1916); *Donoghue v Stevenson*, [1932] AC 562. Similarly, from a contemporary perspective, see H Street, *The Law of Torts First Edition* (Stevens 1955), 176–177, also quoted at Whittaker (n 22) 73.

57 Baldwin (n 1).

58 Prahalad and Hamel (n 2).

59 Salminen (n 48).

of the produced good itself. However, with regard to actors protected by product liability regimes, it can be emphasized that product liability claims can be raised not only by consumer users but also more generally, such as by different enterprises operating within a supply chain.[60] And taken more broadly, in both cases the protected parties are explicitly in need of protection because of negligent production practices. Thus, from the perspective of interests such as the environment and supplier employees, the current situation regarding lead firm liability is in many ways comparable to the situation of users and consumers *prior* to the rise of product liability law.

First, supplier employees could be compared to buyers of defective products in that supplier employees, like buyers, are part of the chain of contracts comprising the production and resale of a good. Supplier employees could thus sue their closest contractual partner: their local employer. However, in many cases it would arguably be better to sue the actor that is in control of both profits and brand risks and can choose where and how to organize its production practices. This is typically the lead firm, whether it be an operative parent or buyer company. The lead firm is generally not only financially more stable than its suppliers but also, the brand being its main source of income, more responsive to threats to brand image, such as allegations of unethical production practices. And, in particular, it has made the conscious choice to organize production in a way that may end up harming supplier employees.

Second, local inhabitants injured by, for example, negative environmental impacts of production could be compared to users of defective products not involved in the chain of sales but nonetheless injured by a product, similarly to family members or passers-by in product liability law. They are not directly involved in the chain of contracts and thus typically cannot sue on a contractual basis and are thus comparable to the question of users of products that were not connected to the chain of sales in relation to product liability law. Also similarly to users of products, injured persons and environmental interests are in need of protection from the contingencies of defective production practices that have caused them harm. And again, similarly to supplier employees, there are pressing reasons for those representing injured persons or environmental interests to raise claims not against local suppliers or contractors but against the lead firm, which is in a better financial situation, cares more about its brand image, and has made the conscious choice to organize production in a way that may end up harming local inhabitants and environmental interests.

Thus, both categories of actors in need of protection find analogy in product liability law. There are clear similarities between product liability and supply chain liability from the perspectives of attributing liability within novel structural forms

60 E.g. the US *East River v Transamerica Delaval* 476 U.S. 858 (1986); EU *Alsthom Atlantique SA v Compagnie de construction mécanique Sulzer SA*, ECJ (C-339/89). Though in such situations they are typically replaced by the contractual private ordering of professional actors, as in many legal systems the limitation of such liability is possible *solely* in transactions between professional parties.

of production and the general categorization of injured actors in need of protection, irrespective of whether they are placed *within* or *without* the chain of contracts constituting the production structure. Furthermore, from a practical perspective, users tend to see production as a whole, no matter how fragmented it is, as falling under the umbrella of a particular lead firm.[61] These similarities also make it logical to extend the practical and theoretical justifications provided for product liability law to supply chain liability.

3.4 Practical and moral justifications

From a practical perspective, supply chain liability should not prove too problematic. As already mentioned, it is, first, the choice of the lead firm to outsource production to specific actors, engaging their own risk analysis and decision-making procedures in these production choices. And, second, it is well-documented that lead firms can and do control fragmented production when it is required of them or when it suits their own interests, for example, in order to maintain supply chain wide cost-management or research and development capabilities.[62] In fact, in can be questioned whether the possibility of effective control is more a condition precedent of fragmented production, rather than something that can be developed as an afterthought. Baldwin in particular implies that without the possibility of control enabled by modern communication technologies, production would not fragment as it has done.[63] This same idea is reflected in concepts such as just-in-time production and the shift from centralized manufacturing to a focus on core competences, as already described in Section 3.2.

From the perspective of moral justifications, the main idea behind enterprise liability, one central moral justification for product liability law, is that

61 From the perspective of consumers, all aspects of production are clearly seen as one and centrally controlled by lead firms (see, e.g., cases referred to in n 56). Somewhat similarly, for an interesting perspective on the relationship of contracts between consumers and lead firms to harmed third parties, in particular sweatshop employees, see L T S Len, *Minimum Contract Justice: A Capabilities Perspective on Sweatshops and Consumer Contracts* (Hart 2017).

62 Compare, e.g., the contrasting auto-industry examples of means of control portrayed in P Kajüter and H I Kulmala, 'Open-Book Accounting in Networks – Potential Achievements and Reasons for Failures' (2005) 16(2) Management Accounting Research 179; O Ben-Shahar and J J White, 'Boilerplate and Economic Power in Auto Manufacturing Contracts' (2006) 104 (5) Michigan Law Review 953. For control for ethical reasons, see in particular Locke (n 6). For the extent to which compliance can be required by regulation, see Säteilyturvakeskus, 'Investigation of the Procurement and Supply of the Emergency Diesel Generators (EDG) and Related Auxiliary Systems and Equipment for the Olkiluoto 3 Nuclear Power Plant Unit' (2011). While nuclear power plants are probably the extreme example from a production perspective, in many other fields the requirements for regulatory compliance of production are also high, say, in relation to airliners or developing technologies such as autonomous vehicles.

63 Baldwin and Martin (n 1); Baldwin (n 1).

taking a risk in search of profit should incur on the risk-taker liability for the risk materializing.[64] Enterprises know that profit-seeking activities are generally risky and may fail. Furthermore, they generally know that when searching for profit, harm may be done to other actors – for example, when trying out new and uncertain forms of production that, if they succeed, can save costs or deliver new products but that, if they fail, may instead provide products that harm users in ways that cannot be envisaged without trying them out. Intuitively, this would apply similarly to new production practices consisting of outsourcing production to new and untried producers and the contingencies that may arise as a result.

Balancing between the societal drawbacks of harm and injuries caused by risk-taking and the societal benefits of technological development attributed to risk-taking has become a constant political debate with roots ultimately in conceptions of what, in fact, is the purpose of society and life more broadly. It is probably impossible to provide exact parameters to this question. Nonetheless, product liability again provides a starting point, as it has for several decades focused on balancing these exact same elements. Under product liability regimes the positive and negative aspects of risk-taking in relation to entrepreneurs have been counterbalanced, for example, through the various defences now accompanying product liability law.[65] Other mechanisms are also involved in mitigating the product liability-related risks of lead firms, such as insurance and the availability of advanced mechanisms for monitoring and auditing outsourced production to avoid problems in the first place. All these approaches could also be, and certainly in part already are, used in relation to supply chain liability.[66]

Thus, while providing an exact answer to the question of the parameters of liability under private law is difficult, it is easy to see that any liability would be mitigated by factors ranging from legal defences to liability (both private law and regulatory) to insurance to new private processes of oversight. Both moral theory and everyday production practices would thus similarly affect production in relation to product liability and supply chain liability.

3.5 Jurisdictional issues

A challenging and fundamental problem is posed by transnational situations and is tied to ideas of independence, legitimacy, and participation. Originally, product liability law could in many cases be focused within a jurisdiction, thus to a large extent appearing to avoid questions of jurisdictional interference.[67] However, if supply chain liability is dealing with transnational situations, the question arises to what extent regulators *or* courts in one jurisdiction should tackle with the actions of a local lead firm that will have practical consequences for how production is

64 Stapleton (n 20) 185–217.
65 Such as the development risk defence, which is regarded one of the most important ones. See, e.g., Stapleton (n 20), 225–229, 236–242.
66 For advanced auditing and monitoring mechanisms in contractual supply chains, see, e.g., Locke (n 6).
67 See Section 2.

undertaken in another jurisdiction, thus potentially – it could be argued – infringing on the foreign jurisdiction's independence in deciding what kinds of labour, environmental, or other standards are in place.

To avoid the problem of 'state interference', private governance, for example through compliance mechanisms embedded by lead firms into their supply contracts, has been seen as one solution.[68] Such private governance mechanisms, however, ultimately depend on the benevolence of individual lead firms and are therefore often incapable of adequately solving the problem.[69] A measure of tort liability is therefore required, and the question is to what extent such liability, whether put in place by regulation or the development of national private law, would be considered as unwelcome meddling in the affairs of another state.

Again, this question cannot be debated in full detail here. *But*, first, it is clear that law is not foreign to transnational regulation, as witnessed by numerous existing examples.[70] Second, it is clear that it is exactly this type of regulation that is envisaged by the instruments put in place by nation states to regulate transnational production and concepts such as transnational public policy.[71] Third, there seems to be no practicable alternative to regulating global production through either extensive transnational regulation or by adjusting the core paradigms of private law liability in a way similar to what happened during the development of product liability law.[72] Finally, looking back at product liability it is clear that product liability regimes in practice extend the regulatory power of one jurisdiction into another.[73] Actors in one jurisdiction who intend to market their products in another must ensure that their production practices, wherever they may be physically situated, reflect product liability standards in the target jurisdiction.

3.6 Differences and similarities: a tentative outcome?

This brief outline of some key similarities and differences between product liability and supply chain liability is not conclusive. However, it provides a strong impetus

68 Abbott and Snidal (n 8).
69 See Chapter 2 in this book, on enforcement of CSR clauses in contracts.
70 One classic example is the US Foreign Corrupt Practices Act, for which see, e.g., D Kennedy and D Danielsen, *Busting Bribery: Sustaining the Global Momentum of the Foreign Corrupt Practices Act* (Open Society Foundations 2011).
71 See, e.g., the instruments discussed in Salminen (n 48). For transnational public policy, see *World Duty Free Company Limited v Kenya*, ICSID Case No. ARB/00/7 (2006).
72 Cases in point on the failure of existing approaches include disasters such as *Rana Plaza* and *Trafigura* and the continued use of child labour, for which see, e.g., S Boseley, 'Child Labour Rampant in Tobacco Industry' (25 June 2018) *The Guardian*, <https://www.theguardian.com/world/2018/jun/25/revealed-child-labor-rampant-in-tobacco-industry> accessed 6 September 2018.
73 D Danielsen, 'Local Rules and a Global Economy: An Economic Policy Perspective' (2010) 1(1) Transnational Legal Theory 49.

for comparing product liability and supply chain liability from a legal dogmatic perspective. This impetus is magnified by the use of legal mechanisms developed in the early stages of the history of product liability law, such as the tort of negligence, in contemporary cases focusing on supply chain liability. If, in a product liability context, the tort of negligence was found to be severely inadequate, would it not be similarly so in the comparative scenario of supply chain liability, and would it not eventually be developed towards a similar conclusion as under fully-fledged product liability law?

Therefore, in Section 4, we will look at some of the challenges of both current tort and contract causes of action in regulating transnational production and suggest that a similar marriage of contract and tort as took place in relation to product liability law could provide one workable solution. Of course, the differences between product liability and supply chain liability must also be born in mind, in particular in relation to transnational scenarios of production.

4 Product liability as a model for supply chain liability: taking the leap

We have argued that, first, societal changes in production practices during the 19th and 20th centuries displaced existing modes of liability. Product liability law was the ultimate outcome of manifold legal responses to this liability deficit. Product liability law was developed by courts (with regulatory support) by updating the existing private law paradigms of contract and tort into what ultimately could be seen as a marriage of both to overcome the deficits of either.

Second, we argued that the societal changes in production practices underlying globally fragmented supply chains during the 20th century similarly displaced existing modes of liability. From this perspective, current discussions of supply chain liability are clearly related to product liability law. Even more strikingly, causes of action that were developed for product liability law but proven insufficient are now seen as the starting point for supply chain liability.

This leads to the leap of faith underlying this chapter. Could we draw from product liability law-related developments of contract and tort in order to develop a more functional form of supply chain liability? In the next sections we will, from this supply chain liability perspective, discuss the merits and deficiencies of tort law, contract law, and a potential product liability-inspired marriage of the two.

4.1 The tort of negligence: a "classic" starting point?

In many recent supply chain liability cases the common law tort of negligence, as developed to respond to the question of product liability in *Donoghue v Stevenson* and later case law, provides the starting point.[74] This has to do with global currents of production and private international law. First, in several (but certainly not

74 *Donoghue v Stevenson*, [1932] UKHL 100, [1932] AC 562 [appeal taken from Scotland].

all) recent high-profile cases, the subsidiaries or suppliers in question have been located in former commonwealth countries, such as Pakistan or Bangladesh, that at least ostensibly ascribe to the basic principles of the common law.[75] Second, while instruments such as the EU Brussels Regulation allow European parent companies and employers to be sued in their own domiciles, choice of law statutes and principles regarding tort/delict primarily point towards using the law of the place where damage occurred as the law applicable to the dispute.[76] While there are exceptions to this, the exceptions are limited and unexplored.[77] Furthermore, some practically important issues such as which law to use for calculating damages and costs may be tied to the applicable substantive law. Calculating damages and costs under one country's measure may lead to the costs of a procedure in another country not being coverable by costs that can be reclaimed.[78] Numerous other procedural problems may also arise.[79]

Thus the practical end result in several recent cases where European or North American companies have been sued for inadequate governance of their supply chains has been that European or North American courts have jurisdiction and the applicable law is some variant of the common law. This brings directly into play the English succession of cases debating the extent of duties of care towards third parties that was started in *Donoghue v Stevenson*.[80] The primary gist of these cases is that a duty of care *may* extend from a company towards third-party actors such as subsidiary or supplier employees or the environment. As described in Chapter 5, it can be presumed that the liability standard developed in the *Chandler* case concerning parent liability for the acts of a subsidiary will also be applicable in the

75 E.g. *Jabir v KiK Textilien und Non-Food GmbH*, Landgericht Dortmund, 7 O 95/15 (on trial); *Das v George Weston, Ltd.*, 2017 ONSC 4129 (appeal pending), and *Oguru, Efanga & Milieudefensie v Royal Dutch Shell Plc and Shell Petroleum Development Co Nigeria Ltd*, Gerechtshof den Haag, 18.12.2015 / 200.126.804–01 200.126.834–01. A notable exception is the Swedish *Arica Victims KB v Boliden Minerals AB*, Skellefteå Tingsrätt 2018-02-07 T 1012–13 (appeal pending), concerning a Swedish company that outsourced the treatment of toxic sludge to Chile, thus implicating two civil law jurisdictions. For further cases primarily focusing on common law jurisdictions, see R Meeran, 'Tort Litigation against Multinational Corporations for Violation of Human Rights: An Overview of the Position Outside the United States' (2011) 3 (1) City University of Hong Kong Law Review 1; C van Dam, 'Tort Law and Human Rights: Brothers in Arms on the Role of Tort Law in the Area of Business and Human Rights' (2011) 2 Journal of European Tort Law 221. For some general thoughts on why the common law jurisdictions seem so often implicated in transnational litigation, see Muchlinski (n 47). For whatever reasons, similarly high-profile supply chain liability cases have yet to turn up in, say, China, even if from a production perspective there would seem to be ample possibilities for such, for example, in light of the recent mass of suicides at factories of Apple's Chinese suppliers.

76 van Dam (n 75); Meeran (n 75).

77 E.g. van Dam (n 75).

78 M D Goldhaber, 'Corporate Human Rights Litigation in Non-U.S. Courts: A Comparative Scorecard' (2013) 3 UC Irvine Law Review 127.

79 van Dam (n 75); Meeran (n 75).

80 Generally, e.g., M Lunney and K Oliphant, *Tort Law: Text and Materials* (4th edn, Oxford University Press 2010) 105–149.

supply chain context.[81] As a starting point this means that two central parameters are the extent to which the lead firm had knowledge or ought to have had knowledge of the state of affairs in the supply chain and the extent to which the claimants could reasonably, on the basis of the amount of control exercised by the lead firm, rely on the lead firm to act on their behalf.

While this technically may offer an expectation of a measure of success for litigation, major problems remain, in particular in being able to establish liability under the *Chandler* standard. It is very difficult for outsiders to show what exactly a corporation knows or ought to know when deciding to outsource production to a specific actor or how exactly a corporation exercises control over its subsidiaries or suppliers. Here, a contract-like approach to burdens of proof would no doubt be useful. It is, after all, up to a lead firm to decide how and to which actor it outsources production; thus, it could be argued that the onus of providing this information and justifying its choices should be on the lead firm before the injured actor is required to show anything. An alternative is provided by other avenues of developing presumptions of proof under tortious/delictual liability. One example is the German *Organisationspflicht*, which made a corporation *prima facie* responsible for all aspects of its organization in relation to users of goods.[82]

Much, of course, depends on the system of tort/delict law in place at the location where damage occurred. Some scholars, such as van Dam, have proposed that civil law systems of delict might be more appreciative of supply chain liability claims than the common law tort of negligence.[83] This is because the emphasis in Western European civil law systems of delict is more on victims' rights rather than on defendants' duties of care as under the common law. Whether this would make a difference in practice is, however, difficult to say because of the previously mentioned problems related to applicable law. Again, more of a focus on contracts, as outlined in the next section, might also help in changing the parameters related to applicable law.

A further question relates to the organizational foundation of production in contractual relationships and the interrelationship of two different levels of law: private ordering through contract and public regulation, either directly or through tort/delict. If all are potentially applicable to a dispute, which one prevails: contract, tort, or regulation? The question is complex and multiple answers are possible. Historically, in some legal systems the mere existence of a contract may have been able to prohibit any recourse to tort.[84] Currently the situation is often more nuanced.[85] In any case the general question remains: if a contract contains a specific clause limiting liability, to what extent does this limitation of liability rule out claims rising under tort. The answer depends on

81 See also Rott and Ulfbeck (n 49).
82 See Rott and Ulfbeck (n 49), describing this concept of liability and linking it to the supply chain context.
83 van Dam (n 75) 243–244.
84 Palmer (n 26).
85 E.g. J Stapleton, 'Duty of Care and Economic Loss: A Wider Agenda' (1991) 107 (April) Law Quarterly Review 249.

the public policy and regulatory frameworks of individual jurisdictions. In relation to product liability law, courts and regulators developed jurisdiction specific doctrines that typically allowed claims to override contractual limitations except in cases where both involved actors were professionals.[86] A similar approach would probably be necessary under supply chain liability; otherwise, increasingly advanced contractual governance mechanisms such as the Bangladesh Accord might allow actors to use several contractual defences to shield them from liability.[87]

All these points highlight the question of whether tort law should not be to some extent "contractually aware". Therefore, in the next section we will look at the contractual parameters of governance and consider this in relation to both product and supply chain liability.

4.2 The contractual parameters of governance beyond privity?

An alternative to tortious/delictual liability is provided by contractual liability. At least one recent case has raised this question in a supply chain liability context, namely *Doe v Wal-mart.* [88] Interestingly, the localization of disputes can be very different if focus is on contract instead of tort, again due to both production and private international law-related practices. First, the contracts or contract-like arrangements used by lead firms to govern their production structures are typically situated in a jurisdiction close to the lead firm, if not its own. Second, the applicable law in case of contractual disputes is generally either explicitly chosen in the governance contract or is implicitly found to apply to it – both approaches more closely associated with the lead firm instead of the place where damage occurred. For example, in *Doe v Wal-mart*, the law applicable to the contractual claims raised by foreign supplier employees against Walmart was found to be the law of a US state on the basis of Walmart's contractual arrangements.[89] Under the 2018 reiteration of the Bangladesh Accord, relationships between European brand companies and the Bangladeshi actors covered by the accord are explicitly subject to Dutch law.[90] Thus, instead of applying the general principles of Pakistani or Bangladeshi tort law, a case involving Bangladeshi supplier employees might instead be judged under the contract law of the US state of domicile of a global brand or a selected European jurisdiction.[91]

86 Whittaker (n 22); Borghetti (n 22); Stapleton (n 20).
87 Salminen (n 10).
88 572 F.3d 677 (9th Cir. 2009).
89 Discussed in more detail in the trial court ruling, *Jane Doe v Wal-mart Stores Inc*, California Central District Court Case No. 2:05-cv-07307.
90 Available at <http://bangladeshaccord.org/wp-content/uploads/2018-Accord-full-text.pdf>.
91 For example, this could be the case, where an employee of a supplier relies on a contract between the lead firm and a supplier as a third-party beneficiary to the contract.

Contractual claims generally have a very different kind of distribution of burden of proof than tort claims. Under contract, the onus is typically on the defendant to show that it has fulfilled its obligations. On the other hand, a perceived drawback of contractual causes of action has been that they generally require a more qualified relationship than tortious duties of care, even if this depends on the contractual paradigm in place in a specific jurisdiction. A number of contractual theories may allow the extension of contractual claims beyond privity, as seen in Chapters 2–4.

Among multiple possible contractual theories, one that received particular attraction in the US was the imposition of warranties on manufacturers, which followed the product and thereby extended to all actors in the chain of sales and beyond, thus enabling contractual claims towards manufacturers from beyond privity.[92] Furthermore, this implied warranty could override any limitation clauses in individual contracts of the chain.[93] In the supply chain context, there is no product being passed on from the buyer to the supplier or its employees. Consequently, the theory of a warranty following the product cannot be applied directly. In US law, the theory was eventually also given up in product liability law. Instead, the warranty was considered to be made directly to the consumer.[94] It was a basic element of warranty theory that it required reliance on the warranty on the part of the claimant.

The question is whether in the supply chain context it could also be argued that a lead firm/buyer has undertaken a commitment directly towards the supplier and/or the employees of the supplier expressly or impliedly. A place to look for such (express) commitments could be in the buyer's code of conduct.[95] For instance, if it is stated in a code of conduct that the compliance of suppliers is monitored by the buyer, the question arises whether this statement can be regarded as a unilateral promise directly towards the employees of the supplier and other actors affected by non-compliance with the code.[96]

Several civil law jurisdictions recognize the idea of the unilateral binding promise. This is reflected in instruments such as the PECL Article 2:107 and the DCFR Article 4.301.[97] In parallel to (early) understandings of the concept of a

92 See Prosser, 'The Fall of the Citadel (Strict Liability to the Consumer)' (1966) 50 Minnesota Law Review 800 with references. The following paragraphs are based on V Ulfbeck, 'Supply Chain Liability for Workers' Injuries – Lessons to be Learned from Products Liability?' (2018) 9(3) Journal of European Tort Law 1, 10.

93 Stapleton (n 20). For related contractual doctrines under French and German law that allow causes of action beyond privity, see Borghetti (n 22) and Wagner (n 27).

94 Prosser (n 92) 801.

95 It has also been explored whether a code of conduct can be regarded as a binding contract, see, for instance, A Beckers, *Enforcing Corporate Social Responsibility Codes: On Global Self-Regulation and National Private Law* (Hart 2015), 81 ff., examining whether a code of conduct can be regarded as an offer to the public that is made binding once it is accepted by a member of the public.

96 This is discussed by Beckers (n 95) 98 ff.

97 Possibly also CESL Article 12 could be seen as recognizing the concept.

warranty as placing emphasis on reliance, a unilateral promise can also become binding and enforceable if it is relied upon by the addressed public.[98] National legal systems recognize different versions of this concept. In common law jurisdictions, the concept is expressed in the principle of promissory estoppel.[99] According to the doctrine of promissory estoppel, a promise is binding if it is relied upon by others and there are valid reasons that justify enforcement. In German law, the concept of the unilateral promise is reflected in several specific statutory provisions.[100] At a more general level, the principle can also be seen as reflected in the German concept of *Vertrauenshaftung*, which originally was proposed as a basis for product liability claims in German law, where it was found that 'the marketing and advertising activities of the manufacturer were so intense that they justifiably caused the consumer to rely on the implied message that the product was safe.'[101]

In legal doctrine, there are different opinions as to the extent to which a code of conduct can be considered a unilateral promise. In US legal theory, some scholars seem to embrace the idea (albeit with reservations).[102] In European legal scholarship, the idea has been rejected with regard to both German law and English law as it stands today.[103] In both cases the discussion changes when codes are embedded as parts of contracts, which more clearly puts into play doctrines such as third-party rights, and even more so if lead firms put in place complex and proactive governance mechanisms that either resemble or are explicitly contracts.[104] However, in particular in relation to actors not part of the chain of

98 Beckers (n 95) 98.
99 For US law, see the *Restatement of the Law (Second), Contracts* (1981), § 90.
100 For an overview, see Beckers (n. 95) 102 ff.
101 Wagner (n 27).
102 J Phillips and S-J Lim, 'Their Brother's Keeper: Global Buyers and The Legal Duty to Protect Supplier's Employees' (2009) 61(2) Rutgers Law Review 333, p. 375 ff. See also the case *Duldulao v St. Mary of Nazareth Hospital*, Ctr. 505 N.E. 2d 314 (III 1987). This case concerned a former employee claiming that she had been discharged in violations of an "employee handbook". The court found that, in order for the content of the handbook/a policy to constitute binding obligations on the part of the employer, three criteria had to be fulfilled with regard to the handbook/policy: (1) it must contain a promise that is sufficiently clear that an employee can reasonably believe that an offer has been made; (2) it must have been disseminated to the employee and the employee must have been aware of its contents; and (3) the employee must have accepted the offer by commencing or continuing to work after learning of the policy statement. The test developed in this case has subsequently also been used in cases concerning codes of conduct with regard to the rights of the employees of the company; see, for instance, the case *Weber Shandwick Worldwide v Reid*, No. 05 C 709, 2005 US Dist. LEXIS 14482, at 1–13, 8 (N.D. III May 12, 2005), concerning former employees sued by their former employer. It is worth noticing that the concept of the reasonable expectations of the employee plays a central role.
103 See Beckers (n. 95) 106: ' . . . in both legal systems, the scope of application of these existing categories remains too narrow currently to make use of them in relation to the publicly declared corporate codes'.
104 Salminen (n 46). A case in point is the Bangladesh Accord, a governance contract connecting two ends of a supply chain.

contracts, such as environmental interests, doctrines such as the third-party beneficiary theory may become increasingly strenuous. In addition, a purely contractual approach would create a divide between lead firms that simply outsource *without* any codes of conduct or other governance and lead firms that explicitly govern outsourced production, for example, by way of codes of conduct. Would the first be excused and the second not, with the result that injured parties would be treated differently, or would implicature be developed to cover such situations?[105] While no doubt theoretically feasible, from a practical dogmatic perspective the development of a supply chain liability regime based solely on contractual doctrine seems unreasonable; a more globally translatable approach that is less focused on the intricacies of an individual jurisdiction's conceptualization of contractual causes of action may be necessary in practice.[106] And this leads us to the necessity of a marriage, once again, as already has happened in relation to supply chain liability's elder sister-in-law, product liability.

4.3 A second marriage between contract and tort in the family, with regulatory blessings

Product liability, after all, eventually overcame problems by imposing on *all* manufacturers liability for defective production practices. Thus, in relation to product liability law the causes of action developed under contractual theories in the US were eventually classified as sounding instead in tort, in part in order to maintain conceptual clarity.[107] Similarly, in Germany, scholars proposed the use of contractual claims for a number of reasons, but ultimately the German Federal Supreme Court decided to adopt a delict-based product liability action with contractual features instead of relying on contract per se.[108] With the introduction of the Product Liability Directive, the concept of a defect, and thereby the "reasonable expectations" of the injured party became a central element in the product liability standard. This coincides now with the concept of reasonable expectations of injured employees, according to the *Chandler* criteria. The concept of reasonable expectations may be regarded as originating in contract law, but under both product liability and supply chain liability this contractual concept is merged into a tort law liability standard.

In addition, despite the challenges in applying contractual constructions, it was exactly the contractual foundations of production and the allure of a more

105 For a discussion of the "dilemma of control", see Chapter 7 of this volume.

106 See, e.g., the German concept of contracts with protective effects on third parties, to say nothing of the more innovative uses of traditional third-party beneficiary theories in several legal systems, for which see Chapters 2–4 of this book. One of the main arguments against using contract as a basis for a claim in the supply chain is that it would be more limited in scope than tort unless the paradigms of contract are twisted almost beyond recognition. At the same time, tort law, and in particular the common law tort of negligence, has a wide jurisdictional base for historical reasons.

107 Stapleton (n 20).

108 Wagner (n 27).

claimant-friendly burden of proof that helped push contractual alternatives through in the early years of product liability law. Similarly, in relation to supply chain liability, focus should thus be on the possibility of governance and what this means for liability. Under product liability, the de facto standard is that a lead firm feels confident that it can maintain the regulatory standards of the target market in relation to product defects despite outsourcing production to suppliers in other jurisdictions who may operate under different standards of production and for whom the lead firm is vicariously liable. *Thus the standard of care in relation to production practices, to a considerable degree, is already that of the targeted market, and this degree could be extended on similar grounds.* If a lead firm decides to outsource production, it should similarly aim at standards of employee and environmental protection comparable to those in place in the target market. One could think about it this way: outsourcing production shows that the lead firm is confident that it can guarantee that outsourced production fulfils at least the most basic regulatory requirements of the target market in relation to product quality. Extending this to production-related contingencies would be a comparatively small step. Furthermore, it seems to match the users' (i.e. consumers') expectations – how else could one explain for example fair trade, the uproar over Rana Plaza, and the recent rise of transnational regulation?

To guarantee general applicability, the basis of supply chain liability should be tortious. The justification, however, is clearly based on contractual reality – a company chooses to outsource via contract and can, via its contractual arrangements, guarantee that production fulfils its requirements. It is by quirk of historical development and path dependency that such contractual arrangements have become excellent at limiting liability, as was also the case in relation to product liability law, but law ultimately overcame this. The evolutionary path towards tortious supply chain liability could thus very well be that of product liability in the US or its historically much-condensed variant, that of product liability in Germany. The regulatory road also remains open, but due to today's political economy it is probably as politically hazardous as in Thatcher's England, where only the EU's promise of a level market (and the comparative protection from external actors that stringent product liability regulation enabled) helped motivate the political system to accept modern product liability.

Even if a direct regulatory response to supply chain liability does not materialize, current regulatory debates and initiatives provide yet another historical similarity to the development of product liability. The early years of product liability were besotted by debate over regulatory intervention into production practices, and while they did not directly establish liability, these debates and initiatives supported the court-led development of product liability. The current situation in relation to supply chain liability is markedly similar. While new duties of care are being tested in courts and new mechanisms of private governance are being developed with break-neck speed, several new soft and hard law instruments have recently focused on regulating transnational supply chains. At the very least, these regulatory initiatives should help provide the necessary backdrop and political message to courts to accept that the time has come for introducing a new type of duty of care to respond to the liability deficits inherent in modern supply chains.

5 Conclusion

Contract and tort offer two different perspectives on disputes arising in global supply chains, not only from the perspective of law but also from the perspective of the role of the lead firm in organizing production. To what extent should focus be, via tort law, on the place where damage occurs instead of, via contract law, on the place where the damage-causing activity is directed and organized? Whatever the answer in any individual case and jurisdiction, in relation to product liability law it became clear that those injured in the periphery of supply chains needed a viable means of recourse to the centre-stage, where production was organized. To facilitate the possibility of shifting recourse from the periphery to the centre-stage of production, both contract and tort causes of action intermingled to create what is now the tort of product liability.

Supply chain liability effectively deals with a similar structure as did product liability: geographically fragmented but centrally governed production. Such production is enabled through either of the two classic alternatives for structuring production: contract or corporation. Either contract or company law relationships are thus naturally involved in setting up the scene of how fragmented production is organized. Take either mode of organization: the choice to engage suppliers and subsidiaries is in the hands of a lead firm. Similarly, the content of this relationship is in the hands of a lead firm. Even if not necessarily a paradigmatic contractual or corporate law relationship, there clearly is a *qualified* relationship of governance between a lead firm and its suppliers and subsidiaries, whether or not, for example, mechanisms of corporate social responsibility such as ethical standards and monitoring are put in place.

Whether liability for this governance sounds in contract or tort is ultimately irrelevant. Governance is based on a combination of both and could thus well give rise to a similar marriage of contract and tort as was the case in relation to the qualified relationship between manufacturers and users of products that gave rise to product liability law – contractual parameters for liability and burdens of proof combined with the inclusivity of tort/delict towards actors harmed by defective production practices. Moreover, following the *Chandler* decision, a focus on legitimate expectations as well-known under product liability law has also been introduced into a production governance context. This could be seen as pointing in the direction of a future merging of tort law concepts and contract law concepts also with regard to supply chain liability.

Of course, there are practical questions of where to draw the line: at the first-tier suppliers? At second tiers? Or in the extreme, as in special cases such as nuclear construction, by including the entire value chain, comprising numerous tiers of actors?[109] How is a lead firm defined in the first place? Several alternative parameters are available, but in general , drawing on the example of product liability, a comprehensive approach seems possible.[110] After all, if a company in any case

109 See, e.g., Säteilyturvakeskus (n 62).

110 In relation to product liability law, a key question, for example, in Germany was whether small mom-and-pop enterprises should be excluded from liability because of its being an unfair burden on them. Ultimately the answer was no, for which see

needs to ensure that every nut and bolt in its product fulfils reasonable expectations of users in the target market and does not break down, causing the death of, say, passers-by injured by an automobile breaking down and careening onto a sidewalk at full speed, then they should similarly be able to ensure, as users may expect, that each nut and bolt has also been produced in line with the standards of the target market in relation to labour and the environment. The alternative, of course, would be to outsource within the target market, as generally used to be the case before the rise of globalization.

Corporations are the best experts at knowing their own supply chains, making economic choices based on available information, and, where uncertainty remains, insuring their liabilities. They have decades of experience in developing private governance mechanisms, including CSR mechanisms, to efficiently govern their supply chains. A measure of liability, as is currently increasingly debated at the courts, is not unexpected. It could be coupled with some defences against such liability, perhaps comparable to the development risk defence under product liability law, to balance development and liability. In any case, it seems that developing supply chain liability from today's uncertain state, for example by drawing on the experiences of product liability, would not inhibit the global fragmentation of production but instead replace the current uncertainties related to litigation over production-related contingencies with increased certainty over how exactly companies should govern outsourced production. This should not be a bad thing.

Bibliography

Abbott K W & Snidal D, 'Strengthening International Regulation Through Transnational New Governance: Overcoming the Orchestration Deficit' (2009) 42(501) *Vanderbilt Journal of Transnational Law* 501.

Baldwin R, 'Trade and Industrialisation after Globalisation's 2nd Unbundling: How Building and Joining a Supply Chain Are Different and Why it Matters' (2011) *The National Bureau of Economic Research* Working Paper No. 17716, <http://www.nber.org/papers/w17716.pdf>.

Baldwin R & Martin P, 'Two Waves of Globalization: Superficial Similarities, Fundamental Differences' (1999) *The National Bureau of Economic Research* Working Paper No. 6904.

Beckers A, *Enforcing Corporate Social Responsibility Codes: On Global Self-Regulation and National Private Law* (Hart 2015).

Ben-Shahar O & White J J, 'Boilerplate and Economic Power in Auto Manufacturing Contracts' (2006) 104(5) *Michigan Law Review* 953.

Borghetti J-S, 'The Development of Product Liability in France' in Whittaker S (ed), *The Development of Product Liability* (Cambridge University Press 2010).

Wagner (n 27). While many recent transnational regulations focus on larger firms, probably economic-political reasons, others, such as the UK Bribery Act (2010), the US Foreign Corrupt Practives Act (1977), and the Section 1502 of the US Dodd–Frank Wall Street Reform and Consumer Protection Act (2010), show that more comprehensive approaches are also possible. See, e.g., Salminen (n 48).

Chilton A S & Sarfaty G A, 'The Limitations of Supply Chain Disclosure Regimes' (2017) 53 *Stanford Journal of International Law* 1.

Coase R H, 'The Nature of the Firm' (1937) 4(16) *Economica* 386.

Danielsen D, 'Local Rules and a Global Economy: An Economic Policy Perspective' (2010) 1(1) *Transnational Legal Theory* 49.

De Schutter O, 'Towards a New Treaty on Business and Human Rights' (2016) 1(1) *Business and Human Rights Journal* 41.

Eller K H, 'Private Governance of Global Value Chains from Within: Lessons from and for Transnational Law' (2017) 8(3) *Transnational Legal Theory* 296.

Enneking L, *Foreign Direct Liability and Beyond* (Eleven International Publishing 2012) 102–104.

Gereffi G, 'Shifting Governance Structures in Global Commodity Chains, With Special Reference to the Internet' (2001) 44(10) *American Behavioral Scientist* 1616.

Gereffi G, 'Global Value Chains in a Post-Washington Consensus World' (2014) 21(1) *Review of International Political Economy* 9.

Gereffi G, Humphrey J, & Sturgeon T, 'The Governance of Global Value Chains' (2005) 12(1) *Review of International Political Economy* 78.

Holly G, Smit L, & McCorquodale R, 'Making Sense of Managing Human Rights Issues in Supply Chains', (British Institute of International and Comparative Law 2018) 13–21.

IGLP Law & Global Production Working Group, 'The Role of Law in Global Value Chains: A Research Manifesto' (2016) 4(1) *London Review of International Law* 57.

Kajüter P & Kulmala H I, 'Open-Book Accounting in Networks – Potential Achievements and Reasons for Failures' (2005) 16(2) *Management Accounting Research* 179.

Kennedy D, Danielsen D, & Bribery B, *Busting Bribery: Sustaining the Global Momentum of the Foreign Corrupt Practices Act* (Open Society Foundations 2011).

Locke R M, *The Promise and Limits of Private Power: Promoting Labor Standards in a Global Economy* (Cambridge University Press 2013).

Meeran R, 'Tort Litigation against Multinational Corporations for Violation of Human Rights: An Overview of the Position Outside the United States' (2011) 3(1) *City University of Hong Kong Law Review* 1.

Muchlinski P, 'The Changing Face of Transnational Business Governance: Private Corporate Law Liability and Accountability of Transnational Groups in a Post-Financial Crisis World' (2011) 18(2) *Indiana Journal of Global Legal Studies* 665.

Palmer V, 'Why Privity Entered Tort – An Historical Reexamination of Winterbottom v. Wright' (1983) 27(1) *American Journal of Legal History* 85.

Phillips J & Lim S-K, 'Their Brother's Keeper: Global Buyers and The Legal Duty to Protect Supplier's Employees' (2009) 61(2) *Rutgers Law Review* 333.

Powell W W, 'Neither Market nor Hierarchy: Network Forms of Organization' (1990) 12 *Research in Organizational Behavior* 295.

Prahalad C K & Hamel G, 'The Core Competence of the Corporation' (1990) 68 *Harvard Business Review* 79.

Pratt L A, 'Decreasing Dirty Dumping? A Reevaluation of Toxic Waste Colonialism and the Global Management of Transboundary Hazardous Waste' (2011) 35(2) *William and Mary Environmental Law and Policy Review* 581.

Prosser W L, 'The Assault upon the Citadel (Strict Liability to the Consumer)' (1960) 69 *Yale Law Journal* 1099.

Prosser W L, 'The Fall of the Citadel (Strict Liability to the Consumer)' (1966) 50 *Minnesota Law Review* 791.

Quentin D, 'Corporate Tax Reform and "Value Creation": Towards Unfettered Diagonal Re-allocation across the Global Inequality Chain' (2016) 7(1) *Accounting, Economics, and Law* 1.
Regier C C, 'The Struggle for Federal Food and Drugs Legislation' (1933) 1(1) *Law and Contemporary Problems* 3.
Rott P & Ulfbeck V, 'Supply Chain Liability of Multinational Corporations?' (2015) 23(3) *European Review of Private Law* 415.
Salminen J, 'Contract-Boundary-Spanning Governance Mechanisms: Conceptualizing Fragmented and Globalized Production as Collectively Governed Entities' (2016) 23(2) *Indiana Journal of Global Legal Studies* 709.
Salminen J, 'The Accord on Fire and Building Safety in Bangladesh: A New Paradigm for Limiting Buyers' Liability in Global Supply Chains?' (2018) 66(2) *American Journal of Comparative Law* 411–451, <https://doi.org/10.1093/ajcl/avy030> September 10, 2018.
Salminen J, 'Sustainability and the Move from Corporate Governance to Governance through Contract' in SjåfjellB & BrunnerC (eds), *Cambridge Handbook on Corporate Governance, Regulation, and Sustainability* (Cambridge University Press, forthcoming 2019).
Sarfaty G, 'Regulating Through Numbers: A Case Study of Corporate Sustainability Reporting' (2013) 53 *Virginia Journal of International Law* 575.
Sarfaty G A, 'Shining Light on Global Supply Chains' (2015) 56(2) *Harvard International Law Journal* 419.
Säteilyturvakeskus, 'Investigation of the Procurement and Supply of the Emergency Diesel Generators (EDG) and Related Auxiliary Systems and Equipment for the Olkiluoto 3 Nuclear Power Plant Unit' (Radiation and Nuclear Safety Authority 2011).
Schwarcz S L, 'Private Ordering' (2002) 97(1) *Northwest University Law Review* 319.
Seuring S & Müller M, 'From a Literature Review to a Conceptual Framework for Sustainable Supply Chain Management' (2008) 16(15) *Journal of Cleaner Production* 1699.
Stapleton J, 'Duty of Care and Economic Loss: A Wider Agenda' (1991) 107(April) *Law Quarterly Review* 249.
StapletonJ, *Product Liability* (Butterworths1994).
Szabó D and Sørensen K, 'Non-financial Reporting, CSR Frameworks and Groups of Undertakings: Application and Consequences' (2017) 17(1) *Journal of Corporate Law Studies* 137
van Dam C, 'Tort Law and Human Rights: Brothers in Arms on the Role of Tort Law in the Area of Business and Human Rights' (2011) 2 *Journal of European Tort Law* 221.
Wagner G, 'The Development of Product Liability in Germany' in WhittakerS (ed), *The Development of Product Liability* (Cambridge University Press 2010).
Whittaker S (ed), *The Development of Product Liability* (Cambridge University Press2010).
Whittaker S (ed), 'The Development of Product Liability in England' in Whittaker S (ed), *The Development of Product Liability* (Cambridge University Press 2010).
Wielsch D, 'Global Law's Toolbox: Private Regulation by Standards' (2012) 60(4) *American Journal of Comparative Law* 1075.

Index

Page numbers in bold refer to tables. Page numbers followed by 'n' refer to notes.

For Product Safety Concerns and Information please contact our EU
representative GPSR@taylorandfrancis.com
Taylor & Francis Verlag GmbH, Kaufingerstraße 24, 80331 München, Germany

www.ingramcontent.com/pod-product-compliance
Ingram Content Group UK Ltd.
Pitfield, Milton Keynes, MK11 3LW, UK
UKHW022125190926
475702UK00013B/1658

* 9 7 8 1 0 3 2 2 4 1 5 5 5 *